THE CLAIMS OF CULTURE

THE CLAIMS OF CULTURE

EQUALITY AND DIVERSITY IN THE GLOBAL ERA

❏ ❏ ❏ ❏

Seyla Benhabib

PRINCETON UNIVERSITY PRESS
PRINCETON AND OXFORD

Copyright © 2002 by Princeton University Press
Published by Princeton University Press, 41 William Street,
Princeton, New Jersey 08540
In the United Kingdom: Princeton University Press,
3 Market Place, Woodstock, Oxfordshire OX20 1SY
All Rights Reserved

Library of Congress Cataloging-in-Publication Data

Benhabib, Seyla.
The claims of culture : equality and diversity in the global era / Seyla Benhabib
p. cm.
Includes bibliographical references and index.
ISBN 0-691-04862-2 (alk. paper)—ISBN 0-691-04863-0 (pbk. : alk. paper)
1. Culture—Social aspects. 2. Politics and culture. 3. Political science. I. Title.
HM631 .B45 2002
306—dc21   20001058083

British Library Cataloging-in-Publication Data is available

This book has been composed in Palatino, Furtura Condensed, Zapf Dingbats

Printed on acid-free paper.∞

www.pup.princeton.edu

Printed in the United States of America

10 9 8 7 6 5 4 3

CONTENTS

❏   ❏   ❏   ❏

PREFACE

❏　❏　❏　❏

  In June 1995, Václav Havel, the president of the Czech Republic, addressed graduating Harvard seniors on the theme of the new global civilization spreading around the world. "This civilization," said Havel, "is immensely fresh, young, new and fragile. . . . In essence, this new, single epidermis of world civilization merely covers or conceals the immense variety of cultures, of peoples, of religious worlds, of historical traditions and historically formed attitudes, all of which in a sense lie 'beneath' it." He noted the irony that the spread of globalization was accompanied by new forms of resistance and struggle and demands for "the right to worship . . . ancient Gods and obey ancient divine injunctions." A world civilization would not be worthy of its name, he declared, if it could not do justice to the "individuality of different spheres of culture and civilization." The new global civilization had to understand itself "as a multicultural and multipolar one" (Havel 1995).

  Indeed, as Havel has reminded us, our contemporary condition is marked by the emergence of new forms of identity politics all around the globe. These new forms complicate and increase centuries-old tensions between the universalistic principles ushered in by the American and French Revolutions and the particularities of nationality, ethnicity, religion, gender, "race," and language. Such identity-driven struggles are taking place not only at the thresholds and borders of new nation-states, which are emerging out of the disintegration of regional regimes like Soviet-style communism in

East Central Europe and Central Asia, or in continents like Africa, where the nation-state, a fragile institution with roots barely half a century old, is crumbling in Rwanda, Uganda, and the Congo, among others. But similar struggles are also occurring within the boundaries of older liberal democracies. Since the late 1970s demands for the recognition of identities based on gender, race, language, ethnic background, and sexual orientation have been challenging the legitimacy of established constitutional democracies.

Reflecting a social dynamic we have hardly begun to comprehend, global integration is proceeding alongside sociocultural disintegration, the resurgence of various separatisms, and international terrorism. Of course, this is not the first time in human history that economic, cultural, and social homogenization have met resistance and subversion, protest and resignification by those concerned to guard the autonomy of their ways of life and value systems. We need only remind ourselves of the resistance of working and peasant classes to the advent of early industrial capitalism in Western Europe. Yet wether we call the current movements "struggles for recognition"(Charles Taylor, Nancy Fraser, and Axel Honneth), "identity/difference movements," (Iris Young, William Connolly), or "movements for cultural rights and multicultural citizenship" (Will Kymlicka), they signal a new political imaginary that propels cultural identity issues in the broadest sense to the forefront of political discourse.

In this book I address the challenges posed to the theory and practice of liberal democracies by the coexistence of these various movements in the same temporal and political space—the "strange multiplicity" of our times, as James Tully has called it (1995). Defending a view that cultures are constituted through contested practices, I argue that the response to this "strange multiplicity" has been a premature normativism in much contemporary political theory, that is, an all-too-quick reification of given group identities, a failure to interrogate the meaning of cultural identity, and a turning away from the sociological and historical literature on these topics, which are dominated by methodological "constructivism." This premature normativism has resulted in hasty policy recommendations that run the risk of freezing existing group differences.

In contrast I propose a deliberative democratic model that permits maximum cultural contestation within the public sphere, in and through the institutions and associations of civil society. While defending constitutional and legal universalism at the level of the polity, I also argue that certain kinds of legal pluralism and institutional power-sharing through regional and local parliaments are perfectly compatible with deliberative democratic approaches.

I distinguish the vocation of the *democratic theorist* from that of the *multiculturalist theorist*, without disputing that most multiculturalists fully support democratic practices and institutions. The emphasis as well as the ordering of our principles are different. Most democratic theorists welcome and support struggles for recognition and identity/difference movements to the degree to which they are movements for democratic inclusion, greater social and political justice, and cultural fluidity. But movements for maintaining the purity or distinctiveness of cultures seem to me irreconcilable with both democratic and more basic epistemological considerations. Philosophically, I do not believe in the purity of cultures, or even in the possibility of identifying them as meaningfully discrete wholes. I think of cultures as complex human practices of signification and representation, of organization and attribution, which are internally riven by conflicting narratives. Cultures are formed through complex dialogues with other cultures. In most cultures that have attained some degree of internal differentiation, the dialogue with the other(s) is internal rather than extrinsic to the culture itself.

If we accept the internal complexity and essential contestability of cultures, then struggles for recognition that expand democratic dialogue by denouncing the exclusivity and hierarchy of existing cultural arrangements deserve our support. Culturalist movements can be critical and subversive to the degree that they are motivated by other than conservationist impulses. It matters a great deal whether we defend culturalist demands because we want to *preserve* minority cultures within the liberal-democratic state or because we want to *expand* the circle of democratic inclusion. Unlike the multiculturalist, the democratic theorist accepts that the political incorporation of new groups into established societies will result most likely in the hybridization of cultural legacies on both sides. Modern individuals may choose to continue or subvert their cultural traditions; equally, immigrants may be incorporated into the majority culture through processes of *boundary crossing, boundary blurring,* or *boundary shifting* between dominant and minority cultures (see Zolberg and Long 1999). In short, democratic inclusion and the continuity and conservation of cultures need not be mutually exclusive. If one must choose, I value the expansion of democratic inclusion and equality over the preservation of cultural distinctiveness, but often one can attain both in some measure. Democratic equality and deliberative practices are quite compatible with cultural experimentation and with new legal and institutional designs that accommodate cultural pluralism.

I bring a comparative cultural, linguistic, and political perspective to this discussion, drawing from cultural politics in Spain as well as the Netherlands, Canada as well as Turkey. A comparative perspective sensitizes us to how movements and demands of the same kind in one country may bear quite different meanings and yield different results in another. Multicultural justice emerges at the interstices of such conflicts and paradoxes; there are no easy ways to reconcile either in theory or in practice rights of individual liberty with rights of collective cultural self-expression. Taking my cue from contemporary cultural conflicts concerning women's and children's rights, I suggest how a vibrant deliberative democratic society may succeed in realizing opportunities for maximum cultural self-ascription and collective intergroup justice.

Throughout this discussion, empirical and normative considerations are woven together to show that, within a deliberative democratic model, sensitivity to the politics of culture and a strong universalist position are not incompatible. Against attempts by other theorists to sacrifice either cultural politics or normative universalism, I argue that a modernist view of cultures as contested

creations of meaning and a universalist view of deliberative democracy complement one another.

On a more personal note: Since writing *Situating the Self:
Gender, Community, and Postmodernism in Contemporary Ethics* (1992),
I have argued that moral and political universalism, properly interpreted, are not irreconciliable with the recognition of, respect for,
and democratic negotiation of certain forms of difference. In the
past, I have tried to make this case by showing how universalism
could be rendered sensitive and receptive to gender differences. In
this book, I address forms of difference originating mainly through
shared life-forms and cultural practices: Not *gender* but *culture* is in
the forefront of my considerations, although, as I argue, there is a
profound and unavoidable connection between cultural diversity
and gender-related differences (see chap. 4 below).

◦   ◦   ◦   ◦

This book begins in a philosophical vein. The introduction and
chapter 2 develop the philosophical aspects of my concepts of culture, narrative, and human identities, as well as outlining the perspective of complex cultural dialogues. I try to show that my vision
of cultures as essentially contested and internally riven narratives
is compatible with a commitment to discourse ethics. Since there is
a great deal of skepticism that normative universalism and a pluralist and contestatory view of cultures can be reconciled at all, chapter 2 asks the question, Is univeralism ethocentric? After answering
in the negative, I take issue with philosophies of strong incommensurability for their incoherence at best and self-contradictions at
worst. Having clarified some of the metaphilosophical issues that
have plagued debates about cultural relativism, I turn in chapters
3 and 4 to the politics of identity/difference in a global context.
Chapter 3 focuses on the much-noted paradigm change in contemporary politics from redistribution to recognition, and considers
three theories of cultural recognition, namely, those of Charles Taylor, Will Kymlicka, and Nancy Fraser. While I consider cultural
preservationist premises that govern some of Taylor's and Kym-

licka's stands on these questions unacceptable, I agree with Fraser that recognition of cultural identities can be seen as matters of universal justice. However, conflicts around the rights of women and children who are members of minority cultural nations or immigrant groups within liberal democracies enable us to see most clearly the moral and political choices involved in advocating the preservation of traditional cultural identities over and above individual rights. Chapter 4, "Multiculturalism and Gendered Citizenship," discusses these dilemmas in the context of three case studies: cultural defense cases in U.S. criminal law; the impact of the personal family code upon the lives of Muslim women in India; and the "scarf affair" in contemporary France.

Chapter 5 expands the model of a dual-track conception of deliberative democracy, which stresses the task of official legislative, political, and adjudicative institutions in civil societies as well as the role of unofficial citizens' associations, public interest groups, and social movements in the public sphere. I defend this model against other attempts in contemporary thought, like John Rawls's "overlapping consensus," Brian Barry's "liberal egalitarianism," and the "multicultural jurisdictions" perspective defended by Ayelet Shachar. I argue that a dual-track approach to multicultural issues and conflicts is a more viable route than ones proposed by these alternative theories, which tend to focus on the official public sphere to the exclusion of a more civil society–based model of cultural learning through cultural conflict. I also maintain that federative institutions as well as certain forms of multicultural jurisdiction that do not undermine the principles of individual and public autonomy are perfectly compatible with deliberative democracy.

Chapter 6 centers around the transformations of the institution of citizenship in contemporary Europe. Europe today is caught between the unifying and centralizing forces of the European Union on the one hand and the forces of multiculturalism, immigration, and cultural separatisms on the other. By focusing on the condition of Europe's Third Country Nationals, who are residents within the European Union countries but not citizens, I analyze the problematic interdependence of nationality and citizenship in the development of the modern nation-state. I argue that what we are witnessing at the level of European institutions is a "disaggregation effect," through which the various components of citizenship, like collective identity, political rights, and the entitlement to social benefits, are being pulled apart. Contemporary multiculturalist movements are players in this larger transformation away from the institutions of unitary citizenship and sovereignty toward "flexible citizenship" and "dispersed sovereignty." I conclude with some observations about the consequences of these transformations on the potential for democratic citizenship in a global civilization.

◻   ◻   ◻   ◻

Although this book was finished in the summer of 2001, prior to the events of September 11, many of the issues discussed have, if anything, gained more salience since the attacks on the World Trade Center and the Pentagon. The condition of Muslim men, women, and children in contemporary European liberal democracies, as well as the situation of the Muslim women in India and Israel, which practice multicultural jurisdictional models, are central to my considerations. By paying attention to the dilemmas and perplexities created by the attempts of these groups to retain their cultural integrity within the institutional boundaries of secular, liberal-democratic states, we can gain some appreciation for the root causes of the discontent harvested by international terrorist networks for their own ends. Neither the normative nor the institutional answers as to how to reconcile the wishes of religious and ethnic Muslim communities to continue their traditional ways of life while living in a culture of liberal-democratic universalism are easily available. Some have drawn the conclusion that coexistence is neither possible nor desirable; but the great majority of Muslim people all over the world, as well as others in whose midst they live, are caught in a democratic learning experiment. In this democratic experiment, the claims of cultures to retain their variety, and to "worship . . . ancient Gods and obey ancient divine injunctions," as Václav Havel reminds us, meet and intermingle within the con-

text of a new global civilization. We are caught in nets of bewilder-
ing and puzzling interdependencies. The claims of cultures to retain their individuality in the face of such interdependencies can be
realized only through risky dialogues with other cultures that can
lead to estrangement and contestation as well as comprehension
and mutual learning.

ACKNOWLEDGMENTS

❑   ❑   ❑   ❑

In the Spring of 1998 I had the honor of delivering three lectures at the invitation of the Gauss Seminars at Princeton University. These had been preceded in 1997 by the Max Horkheimer Lectures, which I gave at Johann Wolfgang-Goethe Universitaet in Frankfurt, under the joint sponsorship of Fischer Publishing House and the Department of Philosophy. The Max Horkheimer lectures have appeared in German in 1999 as *Kulturelle Vielfalt und demokratische Gleichheit: Politische Partizipation im Zeitalter der Globalisierung* (Cultural diversity and democratic equality: Political participation in the era of globalization). This book includes some of that material but has been thoroughly revised and expanded for the English publication. The introduction, chapters 4 and 5, and the conclusion are new; all chapters have been substantially revised.

My thinking on these matters has evolved in the last five years in conversations with a number of individuals. First and foremost, my students Patchen Markell, Sankhar Muthu, Edwina Barvosa, Michaele Ferguson, and Daniel Suleiman have enriched my sense of the significance of culture for politics through their own doctoral dissertations, and in the case of Daniel, his senior thesis. My colleagues in the Committee for the Degree in Social Studies at Harvard—April Flakne, Pratap Mehta, Glyn Morgan, and Sayres Rudy—have lent a sympathetic, even if at times skeptical, ear as I have worked through various stages of these arguments. I am particularly grateful to Carolin Emcke, Rainer Forst, Nancy Fraser,

Bonnie Honig, Morris Kaplan, Lorenzo Simpson, Leslie McCall, and, most of all, to Amelie Rorty and Doris Sommer for reading and commenting on various portions of this manuscript. Annie Stilz has been a meticulous research assistant, proofreader, and discussant of ideas. Without her hard work, this book could not have assumed final form. Thanks also to Raluca Munteanu and Willem Mees from Yale University, whose help in the final stages of this book proved indispensable.

Several conferences and institutional affiliations have aided me in developing these ideas by providing me with opportunities to share them with others. I thank Steven Lukes and Christian Joppke for organizing the terrific conference "Multiculturalism, Minorities, and Citizenship" at the European University Institute in Florence in April 1996. Chapter 2 is based on the publication from the proceedings of that conference (see Benhabib 1999a). I was a Visiting Canada Blanc Foundation professor at the University of Valencia during the spring of 1997, and a Baruch de Spinoza Distinguished Professor at the University of Amsterdam in the summer of 2000. These sojourns sharpened my eye for the multiplicity, variety, and contextual contingency of linguistic and ethnic arrangements in contemporary Europe. I thank Professor Neus Campillo of Valencia and Professors Hent de Vries, Veit Bader, and Karin Vintges of Amsterdam for their insights and comments. Special thanks go as well to members of the University of Toronto Political Theory Group—Ronald Beiner, Joe Carens, and Jennifer Nedelsky—who heard and commented on various portions of chapters 3 and 5 at various stages of their composition.

My hosts during the Gauss Lectures delivered at Princeton University were sympathetic as well as resistant to the claims advanced in these lectures. I have appreciated the comments and criticisms of Amy Gutmann, George Kateb, Jacob Levy, Michèle Lamont, and Michael Walzer.

The Russell Sage Foundation provided a wonderful and supportive institutional environment during the winter of 2001, in which I could complete the final preparation of this manuscript. I also would like to acknowledge a Tozier-Clarke research grant from Harvard University, which supported this work.

Laura and Jim, my family, have shared the trials and tribulations of a difficult couple of years with me. I am grateful to them for their love, wit, humor, and patience and for being there for me.

This book is dedicated to my sisters—Lizet Shamash and Doli Ben-Haviv—who have shown me how to negotiate cultures, languages, territories, and citizenship, while retaining solidarity and dignity.

THE CLAIMS OF CULTURE

ONE

❑   ❑   ❑   ❑

INTRODUCTION

On the Use and Abuse of Culture

CULTURE AND ITS PERMUTATIONS

The emergence of culture as an arena of intense political controversy is one of the most puzzling aspects of our current condition.
From Supreme Court decisions concerning the right of performance
artists to smear themselves with excrement-like substances to a Canadian court's admission of the oral stories of First Nations as legitimate evidence; from disputes over how to preserve historical
memory through public artworks, whose meaning for different cultural groups varies widely, to debates about the teaching of history
in multicultural curriculums, we are daily confronted with culture
"skirmishes," if not wars.

      The claims of diverse groups engaged in the name of this
or that aspect of their cultural identity have become contestants in
the public sphere of capitalist democracies and are embroiled in
characteristic struggles for redistribution and recognition. *Culture*
has become a ubiquitous synonym for *identity*, an identity marker
and differentiator. Of course, culture has always been
the mark of social distinction. What is novel is that groups now
forming around such identity markers demand legal recognition
and resource allocations from the state and its agencies to preserve and protect their cultural specificities. Identity politics draws
the state into culture wars. Accordingly, the very concept of culture
has changed.

Culture derives from the Latin root *colare*, and is associated with activities of preservation, of tending to and caring for. Romans viewed agriculture as the "cultural" activity par excellence. But the emergence of Western modernity, a capitalist commodity economy, the rationalized scientific worldview, and bureaucratic administrative control have radically altered this root meaning of culture. Reflecting the challenge posed by a commodity capitalism, poised to yoke science and industry for ever more rapid expansion, culture in the Romantic period was contrasted with *civilization* whose distinguishing mark was precisely that it did *not* encourage mindful "tending to." In the discourse of German Romantics such as Johann Gottlieb Herder, *Kultur* represents the shared values, meanings, linguistic signs, and symbols of a people, itself considered a unified and homogeneous entity (cf. Parens 1994). *Kultur* refers to forms of expression through which the "spirit" of one people, as distinct from others, is voiced. In this view, an individual's acquisition of culture involves a soul's immersion and shaping through education in the values of the collective. In viewing culture as a process of intellectual-spiritual formation—as *Bildung* (a forming and shaping of the soul)—Herder's definition retains some aspects of the original connotations of a formative activity associated with culture. *Civilization*, by contrast, refers to material values and practices that are shared with other peoples and that do not reflect individuality. It roughly designates the bourgeois capitalist world. This contrast between civilization and culture is associated with other binaries like exteriority versus interiority, superficiality versus depth, linear progress versus organic growth, and individualism versus collectivism.[1]

With the emergence of mass totalitarian movements in Europe in the 1920s and 1930s came anxiety about the very possibility of culture. Could there be "mass" culture? Were the masses capable of culture? This discussion, which had already begun in the Weimar Republic in the 1920s, was transported across the Atlantic during World War II with intellectual refugees such as Hannah Arendt and the Frankfurt School members, who applied it to the experience of mass consumer democracies. Mass culture carried all the negative attributes once associated with the concept of *Zivilisation*—namely, superficiality, homogeneity, reproducibility, lack of durability, and lack of originality. Mass culture is not educative or transformative; it does not shape the soul or express the spirit or collective genius of a people. It is mere entertainment, and in Theodor Adorno's memorable phrase, "entertainment is betrayal" ([1947] 1969, 128–58), promising happiness to those consuming masses who displace onto the screen and figures of Hollywood the *promesse du bonheur* that advanced capitalism always holds before them, but never quite delivers.

Reviewing discussions of culture today within and beyond the academy, one is struck by the obsolescence of the old, value-laden contrast between *Kultur* and *Zivilisation*. What dominates now is an egalitarian understanding of culture drawn from the social anthropology of Bronislaw Malinowski, Evans Pritchard, Margaret Mead, and Claude Levi-Strauss, who were critical of Eurocentric cultural presumptions. They viewed culture as the totality of social systems and practices of signification, representation, and symbolism that have an autonomous logic of their own, a logic separated from and not reducible to the intentions of those through whose actions and doings it emerges and is reproduced. The old contrast between culture and civilization and the anxiety over mass culture it occasioned resurfaces at times in these discussions, but, more often, the ubiquitous notion of an autonomous culture is coupled with the notion of identity. British social anthropology and French structuralism democratize the concept of culture in that they eliminate the binary that made it a term of critique in opposition to the concept of civilization. Yet although Herder's contrast between culture and civilization seems hardly relevant to these approaches, his identification of a people's genius with expressions of its cultural identity persists.

In this sense, much contemporary cultural politics today is an odd mixture of the anthropological view of the democratic equality of all cultural forms of expression and the Romantic, Herderian emphasis on each form's irreducible uniqueness (cf. Joppke and Lukes 1999, 5). Whether in politics or in policy, in courts or in the media, one assumes that each human group "has" some kind of "culture" and that the boundaries between these groups and the contours of their cultures are specifiable and relatively easy to depict. Above all, we are told, it is good to preserve and propagate such cultures and cultural differences. Conservatives argue that cultures should be preserved in order to keep groups separate, because cultural hybridity generates conflict and instability: they hope to avoid the "clash of civilizations" by reinforcing political alliances that closely follow cultural-identity rifts (Huntington 1996), lest attempts to bridge these rifts produce hybridity and confusion.[2] Progressives, by contrast, claim that cultures should be preserved in order to rectify patterns of domination and symbolic injury involving the misrecognition and oppression of some cultures by others.

Whether conservative or progressive, such attempts share faulty epistemic premises: (1) that cultures are clearly delineable wholes; (2) that cultures are congruent with population groups and that a noncontroversial description of the culture of a human group is possible; and (3) that even if cultures and groups do not stand in one-to-one correspondence, even if there is more than one culture within a human group and more than one group that may possess the same cultural traits, this poses no important problems for politics or policy. These assumptions form what I will call the "reductionist sociology of culture." In the words of Terence Turner, such a view "risks essentializing the idea of culture as the property of an ethnic group or race; it risks reifying cultures as separate entities by overemphasizing their boundedness and distinctness; it risks overemphasizing the internal homogeneity of cultures in terms that potentially legitimize repressive demands for communal conformity; and by treating cultures as badges of group identity, it tends to fetishize them in ways that put them beyond the reach of critical analysis" (1993, 412). A central thesis of this book is that much contemporary debate in political and legal philosophy is dominated by this faulty epistemology, which has grave normative political consequences for how we think injustices among groups should be redressed and how we think human diversity and pluralism should be furthered. Our thinking about these questions is hobbled by our adherence to a reductionist sociology of culture.

SOCIAL CONSTRUCTIVISM AND ITS NORMATIVE IMPLICATIONS

Throughout this book I defend social constructivism as a comprehensive explanation of cultural differences and against attempts in normative political theory that reify cultural groups and their struggles for recognition. To be sure, many contemporary writers on multiculturalism reject cultural essentialism as well (see Tully 1995, 7ff.; Parekh 2000, 77–80, 142–58; Carens 2000, 52ff.). But they do not do so for the same reasons, and the epistemic premises that lead them to do so are often unclear. What distinguishes my critique of cultural essentialism from these efforts is the *narrative view of actions and culture* that informs it. In my view, all analyses of cultures, whether empirical or normative, must begin by distinguishing the standpoint of the social observer from that of the social agent. The social observer—whether an eighteenth-century narrator or chronicler; a nineteenth-century general, linguist, or educational reformer; or a twentieth-century anthropologist, secret agent, or development worker—is the one who imposes, together with local elites, unity and coherence on cultures as observed entities. Any view of cultures as clearly delineable wholes is a view from the outside that generates coherence for the purposes of understanding and control. Participants in the culture, by contrast, experience their traditions, stories, rituals and symbols, tools, and material living conditions through shared, albeit contested and contestable, narrative accounts.[3] From within, a culture need not appear as a whole; rather, it forms a horizon that recedes each time one approaches it.

A most spectacular example of the creation of cultural unity through various external discursive interventions is provided by the Hindu practice of sati, according to which a widowed wife immolates herself by ascending the burning funeral pyre of her husband. In her analysis of the politics of tradition formation, Uma

Narayan puzzles over "how and why this particular practice, marginal to many Hindu communities let alone Indian ones, came to be regarded as a central Indian tradition" (1997, 61). Her answer, based on recent historiography of colonial India, is that the meaning and status of sati as a tradition emerged out of negotiations between British colonials and local Indian elites. The colonial administrators, who were driven by their own moral and civilizational revulsion when confronted with this practice, were equally intent that their outlawing of this practice not lead to political unrest. So they investigated the status of sati as a "religious practice," assuming that if it had religious sanction, it would be unwise to abolish it; if it did not, then its abolition could be approved by local elites themselves (62). To determine whether a practice had a religious basis, in turn, meant finding a justification for it in religious scripture. Reasoning analogically that in Hinduism the relationship of scripture to practice was like that in Christianity, British colonial powers trusted accounts of documents produced by Indian *pundits* (religious scholars) as codifying in effect the interpretation of tradition. But since Hinduism, unlike Christianity, does not have a core spiritual text, "the question of where to look for such scriptural evidence was hardly self-evident. The interpretive task was not made any easier by the fact that there seemed to be few, if any, clear and unambiguous textual endorsements of sati" (200). A long historical process of cultural interventions and negotiations ironed out inconsistencies in the accounts of local elites about various myths surrounding the practice of sati. Religious stories in relation to existing practices were codified, and, above all, discrepancies in local Hindu traditions that varied not only from region to region but between the various castes as well were homogenized.

Culture presents itself through narratively contested accounts for two principal reasons. First, human actions and relations are formed through a double hermeneutic: We identify *what* we do through an *account* of what we do; words and deeds are equiprimordial, in the sense that almost all socially significant human action beyond scratching one's nose is identified as a certain *type of doing* through the accounts the agents and others give of that doing.

This is so even when, and especially when, there is disagreement between doer and observer. The second reason why culture presents itself through contested accounts is that not only are human actions and interactions constituted through narratives that together form a "web of narratives" (Arendt [1958] 1973), but they are also constituted through the actors' evaluative stances toward their doings. In other words, there are second-order narratives entailing a certain normative attitude toward accounts of first-order deeds. What we call "culture" is the horizon formed by these evaluative stances, through which the infinite chain of space-time sequences is demarcated into "good" and "bad," "holy" and "profane," "pure" and "impure." Cultures are formed through binaries because human beings live in an evaluative universe.[4]

The demarcations of cultures and of the human groups that are their carriers are extremely contested, fragile as well as delicate. To possess the culture means to be an insider. Not to be acculturated in the appropriate way is to be an outsider. Hence the boundaries of cultures are always securely guarded, their narratives purified, their rituals carefully monitored. These boundaries circumscribe power in that they legitimize its use within the group.

Sociological constructivism does not suggest that cultural differences are shallow or somehow unreal or "fictional." Cultural differences run very deep and are very real. The imagined boundaries between them are not phantoms in deranged minds; imagination can guide human action and behavior as well as any other cause of human action. Yet the student of human affairs should never take groups' and individuals' cultural narratives at face value. Rather, to explain human behavior, the student should seek to understand the totality of circumstances of which culture is an aspect. This is obvious and would not need repeating were constructivism not frequently misidentified with the view that anything goes and that symbols and representations can be shuffled like cards in a deck. In truth, cultural narrative, change, and innovation have their own logics.

Sociological constructivism leads me to the conviction that strong multiculturalism, or what has been called *mosaic multicultur-*

alism, is wrong, empirically as well as normatively, and that intercultural justice between human groups should be defended in the name of justice and freedom and not of an elusive preservation of cultures. By strong or mosaic multiculturalism I mean the view that human groups and cultures are clearly delineated and identifiable entities that coexist, while maintaining firm boundaries, as would pieces of a mosaic. By contrast, it is not a visual but an auditory metaphor that guides my understanding of a complex cultural dialogue. We should view human cultures as constant creations, recreations, and negotiations of imaginary boundaries between "we"' and the "other(s)." The "other" is always also within us and is one of us. A self is a self only because it distinguishes itself from a real, or more often than not imagined, "other." Struggles for recognition among individuals and groups are really efforts to negate the status of "otherness," insofar as otherness is taken to entail disrespect, domination, and inequality. Individuals and groups struggle to attain respect, self-worth, freedom, and equality while also retaining some sense of selfhood. Whether in the psyche of the individual or in the imagined community of a nation, it is very difficult to accept the "other" as deeply different while recognizing his/her fundamental human equality and dignity. I argue that the task of *democratic equality* is to create impartial institutions in the public sphere and civil society where this struggle for the recognition of cultural differences and the contestation for cultural narratives can take place without domination.

Nationalist ideologies and movements reject the constitutive "otherness" at the source of all culture; more often than not, they seek to "purge" the culture of its impure or foreign elements and thus render it whole again. Ironically, nationalisms reverse the participant/observer perspective, in that the adherents and ideologues of nationalist movements attempt to create forced unity out of diversity, coherence out of inconsistencies, and homogeneity out of narrative dissonance.

In his essay "DissemiNation: Time, Narrative, and the Margins of the Modern Nation," Homi K. Bhabha lays bare the narrative strategies and tropes through which nationalist ideologies are constructed. "The 'scraps, patches and rags' of daily life," Bhabha writes, referring to a phrase of Ernst Gellner,

> must be repeatedly turned into the signs of a coherent national culture, while the very act of the narrative performance interpolates a growing circle of national subjects. In the production of *nation as narration,* there is a split between the continuist, accumulative temporality of the pedagogical, and the repetitious, recursive strategy of the performative. It is through this process of splitting that the conceptual ambivalence of modern society becomes the site of *writing the nation.*" (1994, 145–46; the first emphasis mine; second emphasis in the text)

What Bhabha names the "continuist, accumulative temporality of the pedagogical" refers to narrative strategies, to the writing, production, and teaching of histories, myths, and other collective tales, through which the nation as one represents itself as a continuous unit. In such strategies of representation, "the people" is constituted as one. Time is rendered homogeneous, in that the conflicting, irreconcilable, often contradictory and illogical daily narratives and experiences of individuals and collectivities are re-presented as aspects, elements, stages, or in Hegelian language, as "moments," of a unified narrative. The "recursive strategy of the performative," by contrast, is the invention by intellectuals and ideologues, artists and politicians, of narrative and representational strategies through which the "nation's self-generation" is reenacted. What Homi Bhahba names the "pedagogical" and the "performative" aspects of the national narrative have somehow to hang or fit together. It is precisely this fit that the student of human affairs tries to explain.

Let me give an example that would be quite unfamiliar to European and North American students of nationalism. The creation of modern Turkey through the reforms of Kemal Ataturk can be viewed as a paradigmatic example of civic nationalism. In order to forge a new civic identity out of the old Ottoman Empire, which prided itself in being composed of seventy-two *millets* (peoples or nations in the nonterritorial sense of the term), Ataturk had to position the new nation in opposition to the Persian and Arab legacies that dominated the cultural life of the empire. In a radically constructivist gesture, Ataturk abolished the old script, which was written in Arabic letters and was a mélange of Persian, Turkish, and Arabic, in 1923 and created a new official language, using a modified version of the Latin alphabet and the vocabulary of the vernacular Turkish, spoken in the countryside as well as the city, albeit with different accents. In abolishing the old Arabic alphabet and choosing the Latin script, Ataturk was combining the pedagogical and the performative in a most interesting way.

The new alphabet, this primary instrument of the pedagogy of the nation, reinforced a certain new identity by contributing to the resolution of the identity conflicts that had plagued the Ottoman Empire since the eighteenth century. These had been caused by the fact that the Ottomans, while ruling a Muslim empire, controlled significant parts of Europe in the regions of Greece and the Balkans and thus acted as a bridge between Europe and the Orient, the West and the East. Ataturk simply chose the West, expressing this most dramatically by abolishing the cultural and literary medium in which the Muslim elite of the empire had expressed itself. Here, clearly, "the cultural shreds and patches used by nationalism" (Gellner 1983, 56) were not arbitrary historical inventions. They had to fit together; they had to tell a story and perform a narrative that made sense, that was plausible and coherent, and that motivated people to the point that they were willing to sacrifice their lives for it. It is also the case that such collective narratives can cease to make sense, cohere, motivate, or hold people together. Such appears to be the case in contemporary Turkey, where the dominant ideology of Kemalism has fallen out of grace, and new and competing collective narratives are clamoring to take its place.

□   □   □   □

I want to emphasize that sociological constructivism is a very broad concept in social theory that can cover distinct methodological strategies, ranging from postmodernism to critical social theory, from postcolonial studies to Marxist or non-Marxist functionalism.

Very often, constructivist strategies have failed to *explain* identity-based movements, in that they do not account for the "fit" between the cultural shreds and patches that movements and militants pick up from the culture around them and the more enduring identity dilemmas and options these shreds and patches appear to resolve.[5] Identity/difference politics is afflicted by the paradox of wanting to preserve the purity of the impure, the immutability of the historical, and the fundamentalness of the contingent. Constructivism enlightens us about the processes that transform each of the first terms in these pairs of opposites into the second. A social constructivism that considers the interplay between structural and cultural imperatives is possible as well as desirable: Throughout this book I will try to keep in view the functional/structural imperatives of material systems of action like the economy, bureaucracy, and various social technologies on the one hand, and the symbolic-representative imperatives of systems of cultural signification on the other.

DISCOURSE ETHICS AND MULTICULTURALISM

My reflections on the cultural politics of capitalist societies follow the broad normative principles I developed in *Situating the Self* (1992). Expanding there on the program of a communicative or discourse ethics, I stipulated norms of *universal respect* and *egalitarian reciprocity* as guiding principles of human interaction. With Juergen Habermas, I hold that only those norms and normative institutional arrangements can be deemed valid only if all who would be affected by their consequences can be participants in a practical discourse through which the norms are adopted. Norms of universal respect and egalitarian reciprocity already undergird practices of discursive argumentation: they must be presupposed in some form for practical discourses. This reflects not a vicious circle but a virtuous one: Moral and political dialogues begin with the presumption of respect, equality, and reciprocity between the participants. We engage in discourses with an assumed background, and we understand that these norms apply to all participants. Through discourses, the participants subject these assumed background interpretations to intersubjective validation. Discourses are procedures of *recursive validation* through which abstract norms and principles are concretized and legitimized. We may all claim that we respect one another, but we cannot know what such respect requires or entails in the face of deep cultural conflicts; while some of us may consider certain practices and judgments an affront to human dignity, others may consider our evaluations a species of ethnocentric imperialism. Practical discourses, in the broadest sense, include *moral discourses* about universal norms of justice, *ethical discourses* about forms of the good life, and *political-pragmatic* discourses about the feasible. These are dialogic processes through which we not only concretize and contextualize the meaning of such norms; we also determine what kind of a problem is being debated. Very often, moral dialogue is necessary to identify an issue as one of legislation rather than morality, of aesthetics rather than politics. Participants must not only reach understanding of the norms in question; they also must share a *situational* understanding of these norms' intended applications. Discourses in multicultural societies often require negotiation of such shared, situational understandings. What kind of practice we think a specific cultural practice is—religious or aesthetic, moral or legal—will determine which norms we think should apply to it.

Let me illustrate again with reference to sati. The British colonial administratuion, cooked in the cauldron of the religious wars in Europe that had pitted Protestants against Catholics, Anglicans against both, and sectarian and millenarian movements against all, sought to apply to India the lessons of religious tolerance as practiced in the modern European secular state. As long as a practice was considered central to one's religion, some tolerance was to be shown. But if it was not *religious* but merely *cultural*, in the sense that members of the same religion felt free to engage in it or not, colonial administrators presumed that it should be less protected from colonial intervention, especially if the practice in question could also be considered odious and offensive to human dignity.

Most liberal democracies still operate with some version of this distinction between cultural and religious practices, and between central and subsidiary practices of a religion.[6] My point here is not to challenge this distinction; I want to stress that very often we do not know what *type of practice* is in question, for we do not share a common understanding of the disputed practice itself. Is it religion, culture, or morality? What if it is all, or none? What if its meaning shifts and changes with social and cultural interactions, across time and within shared space? (This is precisely what is taking place now around the practice of "veiling" in different communities of Muslim women, in countries of immigration as well as in their own societies.) In other words, practices themselves are often resignified. Practical discourses are processes through which such resignifications can unfold. Attention to such processes of resignification and narrative retelling will alter the line between the universalizable content of moral discourses and the ethical discourses of the good life without erasing it altogether.

Discourse ethics has one distinctive virtue when compared with other variants of contractarian and universalist models of normative validity: its participants feel free to introduce into the dialogue their life-world moral dilemmas and conflicts without any constraints imposed by counterfactual experiments and idealizations. Discourses do not prescribe the content of moral argument through thought experiments or definitional boundary drawings between the public and the private. Furthermore, individuals' needs as well as principles, life stories as well as moral judgments, can be freely shared with others, but discourse participants may also keep "private" aspects of their personal narratives they prefer not to share. There is no obligation to self-disclosure in the discursive space.

The lack of idealized strictures on discursive content and a greater need for the possibility of individual self-presentations within communicative ethics led me in an earlier work to distinguish *universalist* from *substitutionalist* universalisms (Benhabib 1992). The latter, like those of Immanuel Kant and John Rawls, proceed from a certain definition of human agency and rationality. In them, the subject matter of practical discourses is restricted to what each can will or choose, in conjunction with all, to be a universal law. Or it is restricted to those principles of a just society, to which rational agents, placed behind the epistemic strictures of a "veil of ignorance," would agree. Such theories have the advantage over the discourse model of being able to provide a more *determinate* or *concrete* content of choice and deliberation. Yet this determinacy of content is attained at the cost of restricting the agenda of the conversation as well as of abstracting away from the identity of the individuals involved. Substitionalist moral theories view individuals as generalized, not as concrete, others (1992).

Interactive universalism, by contrast, accepts that all moral beings capable of sentience, speech, and action are potential moral conversation partners.[7] It does not privilege observers and philosophers. The boundaries of moral discourses are set only by the extent of our doings as a consequence of which we affect one another's well-being and freedom. The boundaries of moral discourses are indeterminate; they include all beings, and not just rational humans, whose interests can be affected by the consequences of one's actions. According to interactive universalism, I can learn the *whoness* of the other(s) only through their narratives of self-identification. The norm of universal respect enjoins me to enter the conversation insofar as one is considered a generalized other; but I can become aware of the *otherness of others*, of those aspects of their identity that make them concrete others to me, only through their own narratives. And because cultural narratives (which comprise linguistic, ethnic, religious, as well as territorial and regional accounts) are crucial to the narrative constitution of individual self-identities, such processes of interactive universalism are crucial in multicultural societies. My specific reformulation of discourse ethics through interactive universalism permits me then to extend this model to the dilemmas of multiculturalism, since cultures provide us with narratives as well as practices, sayings as well as doings. We encounter each other and ourselves as others through such processes of doing and saying.

NARRATIVITY AND THE SELF

To be and to become a self is to insert oneself into webs of interlocution; it is to know how to answer when one is addressed and to know how to address others (cf. Benhabib 1999e). Strictly speaking, we never really *insert* ourselves, but rather are *thrown* into these webs of interlocution, in the Heideggerian sense of "thrownness" as *Geworfenheit:* We are born into webs of interlocution or narrative, from familial and gender narratives to linguistic ones and to the macronarratives of collective identity. We become aware of who we are by learning to become conversation partners in these narratives. Although we do not choose the webs in whose nets we are initially caught, or select those with whom we wish to converse, our agency consists in our capacity to weave out of those narratives our individual life stories, which make sense for us as unique selves. Codes of established narratives in various cultures define our capacities to tell our individual stories. There are only so many ways in which a cultural code may be varied; beyond them, one may run the risk of becoming an outcast or a convert, a marginal figure or a deserter of the tribe. But just as it is always possible in a conversation to drop the last remark and let it reverberate on the floor in silence, or to carry on and keep the dialogue alive, or to become whimsical, ironic, and critical and turn the conversation back on itself, so too do we always have options in telling a life story. These options are not ahistorical but culturally and historically specific, inflected by the master narratives of family structure and gender roles into which each individual is thrown. Nonetheless, just as the grammatical rules of a language, once acquired, do not exhaust our capacity to build an infinite number of well-formed sentences in a language, so socialization and acculturation do not determine an individual's life story or his or her capacity to initiate new actions and new sentences in conversation. Donald Spence, a psychoanalyst, formulates the link between the self and narration insightfully:

> It is by means of continuous dialogue with ourselves—in daydreams, partial thoughts, and full-fledged plans—that we search for

ways to interact with our environment and turn happenings into meanings, and we organize these reactions by putting our reactions into words. . . . Language offers a mechanism for putting myself into the world, as Heidegger might phrase it, and for making the world part of me; and language very likely determines the way in which experience will be registered and later recalled." (1987, 134)

My approach to the politics of multiculturalism is defined by these theoretical commitments: the discourse theory of ethics; the dialogic and narrative constitution of the self; and the view of discourses as deliberative practices that center not only on norms of action and interaction, but also on negotiating situationally shared understandings across multicultural divides.

Strong or mosaic multiculturalism is very often mired in futile attempts to single out one master narrative as more significant than others in the constitution of personal identities. Proceeding from an overly socialized vision of the self, strong multiculturalists have to face the embarassing fact that most individual identities are defined through many collective affinities and through many narratives. The multiculturalist resistance to seeing cultures as internally riven and contested carries over to visions of selves, who are then construed as equally unified and harmonious beings with a unique cultural center. By contrast, I view individuality as the unique and fragile achievement of selves in weaving together conflicting narratives and allegiances into a unique life history. Practical autonomy, in the moral and political sphere, is defined as the capacity to exercise choice and agency over the conditions of one's narrative identifications. Such capabilities necessarily include some disposition of material resources, such as income and access to education and professional development as well as to public institutions and spaces. Using this dialogic and narrative model of identity constitution, I propose to define group identities much more dynamically and to argue that in reflecting upon politics of identity/difference, our focus should be less on what the group *is* but more on what the political leaders of such groups *demand* in the public sphere.

A DYNAMIC MODEL OF IDENTITY GROUPS

Contemporary discussion of these issues is often mired in two short-comings: (*a*) Processes of group formation are not treated dynamically enough and too much effort is spent on identifying what a group is, in terms of structural indicators of economic oppression or cultural indicators of discrimination, marginalization, and the like (Young 2000, 97–98); (*b*) this literature, which rehashes the Marxian dichotomies of base versus superstructure in light of the new categories of economic versus cultural processes of group formation, ignores processes through which existing social and cultural cleavages are transformed into political mobilization (Kymlicka 1995, 1997; and cf. chap. 3 below). Thus, the likelihood that ethnic and language politics in a given case reflects class politics is often considered; but the reverse, namely that class politics may channel itself into ethnic lobbying, is not. To give two examples: It can be plausibly argued that part of what motivates the Québecois and the Catalonian separatist movements is the emergence of local elites, sufficiently independent of Ottawa in the case of Quebec, and Madrid in the case of Barcelona, to carry on their own economic and cultural transactions. The new global economy permits the growth of regional networks over and beyond the boundaries of nation-states, making it plausible for them to short-circuit traditional centralized decision making in banking, finance, communications, and transportation. These political and economic facts are manifesting themselves in linguistic nationalism and separatism, precisely because the lingua franca of the global economy is not based on the old national linguistic idioms. Even Québecois nationalism, which wants to retain French as the only and official language of the province of Quebec, is made possible by the interconnectedness of Quebec to networks of global capitalism by virtue of its being a part of the Canadian federation (see Ignatieff 1995).

In another case, the majority of the Oriental Jews in Israel, whose families came from Morocco, Yemen, Tunisia, Iraq, Iran, and Turkey, tend to vote for religious right-wing parties like Shas (less so in the case of the Jews from Iraq, Iran, and Turkey). Oriental Jews come generally from the working class; they have not made sufficient inroads into the military, scientific, political, and media elite of the country. Their vote for religious parties who actually have more regressive economic and social policies vis-à-vis their constituencies than do social democrats in Israel—the Marah—may be seen as reflecting their ethnic group identity; but it may be better understood through the failure of Eurocentric Israeli elites to build a common idiom and political culture through which to integrate these groups into the democratic public sphere. As the case of David Levy, who represented this constituency, demonstrates very well, they can shift allegiances from the right-wing religious Shas to the Marah around social and economic policy issues. One cannot understand their politics through an analysis of ethnic or cultural identity alone. One needs to pay more attention to the mobilization of social and cultural cleavages in political movements and to focus on the public political demands of such actors[8] (see Offe 1998).

Here we reach the most important difference between the approaches of democratic and multicultural theorists. The democratic theorist is concerned with the public manifestation of cultural identities in civic spaces; the multiculturalist is interested in classifying and naming groups and then in developing a normative theory on the basis of classificatory taxonomies. History as well as social study shows us that any minority group in human society may adopt any of a number of political positions; political attitudes cannot be derived from group identities. In the contemporary United States, for example, there are gay males who are Republican; there are conservative libertarian lesbians; there are black Muslims, just as there are postmodernist black cultural activists. Likewise, regionalism in Europe can extend from the right-wing politics of the Lega Nord in Italy to the ecological demands of left-leaning French groups of Provence. Demands for cultural autonomy may reflect the aspirations of the new global elites or the agony and frustrations of a people like the Kurds, who have been denied their own language, customs, and schools through the cumulative oppression by the Turkish, Iraqi, and Iranian governments (see Randal 1997).

Democratic theorists should support movements for equality and justice and for increasing the space of narrative self-determination in cultural terms. Yet there is increasing skepticism toward the model of universalism that I defend. As globalization and the cultural pluralization of societies proceed apace, arguments are advanced for a legal pluralism that would countenance a coexistence of jurisdictional systems for different cultural and religious traditions and accept varieties of institutional design for societies with strong ethnic, cultural, and linguistic cleavages. Focusing on the dilemmas of multiculturalism and women's issues in countries with pluralist traditions, I will argue that as long as these pluralist structures do not violate three normative conditions, they can be quite compatible with a universalist deliberative democracy model. I call these the conditions of *egalitarian reciprocity, voluntary self-ascription,* and *freedom of exit and association* (see chapters 4 and 5 below for a fuller justification of these principles):

1. *egalitarian reciprocity.* Members of cultural, religious, linguistic and other minorities must not, in virtue of their membership status, be entitled to lesser degrees of civil, political, economic, and cultural rights than the majority.

2. *voluntary self-ascription.* In consociationalist or federative multicultural societies, An individual must not be automatically assigned to a cultural, religious, or linguistic group by virtue of his or her birth. An individual's group membership must permit the most extensive forms of self-ascription and self-identification possible. There will be many cases when such self-identifications may be contested, but the state should not simply grant the right to define and control membership to the group at the expense of the individual; it is desirable that at some point in their adult lives individuals be asked whether they accept their continuing membership in their communities of origin.

3. *freedom of exit and association.* The freedom of the individual to exit the ascriptive group must be unrestricted, although exit may be accompanied by the loss of certain kinds of formal and informal privileges. However, the wish of individuals to remain group members,

even while outmarrying, must not be rejected; accommodations must be found for intergroup marriages and the children of such marriages.

Whether cultural groups can survive as distinct entities under these conditions is an open question,[9] but I believe these conditions are necessary if legal pluralism in liberal-democratic states is to achieve the goals of cultural diversity as well as democratic equality, without compromising the rights of women and children of minority cultures.

Whether multiculturalist aspirations and liberal-democratic universalism are or can be made compatible is a contested issue. In chapter 5, I consider a variety of contemporary positions, such as the model of overlapping liberal consensus (John Rawls); the model of liberal egalitarianism (Brian Barry); the model of pluralist interlocking power hierarchies (Ayelet Shachar); and the deliberative democracy approach (James Bohman, Jorge Valadez and Melissa Williams). Rawls's political liberalism introduces several crucial distinctions into the debate that, in my view, are foundational for any future discourse on liberal democracy. These include the distinction between constitutional essentials, on the one hand, and specific institutional and policy arrangements, on the other, which show great variation across actually existing democratic systems. Rawls also argues that from the standpoint of the major institutions of society, persons are to be considered as capable of forming their own senses of the good, and of cooperating with others around principles of justice. This is the public view of the person as an autonomous being. I accept the Rawlsian insight that political liberalism must respect the public autonomy of individuals and constitutional essentials.

Yet Rawls's attempt to restrict public reason to discourses concerning constitutional essentials alone is unconvincing on philosophical and sociological grounds. I argue that the domain of public reason must not be restricted to constitutional essentials, and that "the background culture," which surrounds and infuses the task of reason with particular content, must be considered essential to consensus formation in liberal democracies. Following Habermas, I defend a *dual-track approach* to multiculturalism: In deliberative democracy, as distinguished from political liberalism, the *official* public sphere of representative institutions, which includes the legislature, executive and public bureaucracies, the judiciary, and political parties, is not the only site of political contestation and of opinion and will formation. Deliberative democracy focuses on social movements, and on the civil, cultural, religious, artistic, and political associations of the *unofficial* public sphere, as well. The public sphere is composed of the anonymous and interlocking conversation and contestation resulting from the activities of these various groups. It is in this domain that multicultural conflicts and politics have their place. Rawls's approach, but Brian Barry's as well (which is quite critical of Rawls's), neglects this dimension and instead attempts to solve multicultural conflicts through a juridical calculus of liberal rights. While I argue that certain normative constraints—like the norms of egalitarian reciprocity, voluntary self-ascription, freedom of exit and association—must be respected by multicultural groups, I also accept that certain forms of legal and political pluralism, including multiple jurisdictional systems and regional parliaments, may be compatible with deliberative democratic universalism.

One of the central contentions among deliberative democrats working on multiculturalism is whether our normative model denies strong incommensurability among worldviews, belief systems, and the like, and privileges a unitary polity. I will argue in chapters 2 and 5 that strong incommensurability is an incoherent philosophical position, but that intractable political and epistemological conflicts can sometimes be resolved through moral compromises. From a political perspective, I do not see that separatist movements offer a magical solution to the dilemmas of coexistence among different ethnic and cultural groups. While separatism is often inevitable and sometimes desirable, all modern separatist movements that aspire to state formation face the tension and indeed outright contradiction between their democratic sovereignty claims and respect for universal human rights. In chapter 6, I focus on transformations of citizenship and the status of immigrants and aliens in contemporary Europe in order to illustrate how and why conflicts between universal rights and sovereign self-determination are intrinsic to democratic state-forms. Postnational democracies must engage in self-reflexive questioning of their own practices of inclusion and exclusion.

COMPLEX CULTURAL DIALOGUES

To make more vivid the relationships between interactive universalism, the narrative constitution of self, and complex cultural dialogue, I would like to conclude this introduction with a personal memory. In the late 1980s I was lecturing at the Inter-University Center of the city of Dubrovnik, currently part of the Republic of Croatia, but at the time part of the Federal Republic of Yugoslavia. I cited a passage from John Locke's *Second Treatise of Civil Government* on the "state of nature," which reminds us that this figure of speech, while a metaphor, may have some factual basis as well. Locke recounts by way of illustration "the two men on the desert island, mentioned by Garcilaso de la Vega, in his history of *Peru;* or between a Swiss and an *Indian,* in the woods of America" ([1690] 1980, 13). After the lecture I was approached by a colleague of Peruvian descent. He asked me for the reference to the full citation because he was astonished that John Locke knew of Garcilaso de la Vega. I was in turn astonished that this detail would interest him that much, for my lecture had been a feminist critique of the concept of individuality implicit in early liberal political theory as articulated by the metaphor of the state of nature. Who *was* Garcilaso de la Vega? Why should he matter to my feminist critique?

Garcilaso de la Vega, also known as "El Inca," is hailed by Arnold Toynbee as "an early representative of a class which has been important throughout the history of the encounters between modern Western civilization and all the other surviving civilizations and precivilizational cultures on the face of our planet, and which is supremely important today" (1966, xii). Thanks to his mixed Andean-European descent and to his acculturation in both ancestral traditions—a double education that was the privilege, or burden, of his mestizo blood—Garcilaso was able to serve as an interpreter or mediator between two different cultures that had suddenly been brought into contact. Born in the ancient Inca capital of Cuzco in 1539 of a Spanish conqueror of noble lineage and an Indian princess, he was one of the first mestizos. After much family misfortune, the forced separation of his parents, and the annulment of their mixed marriage by the Catholic Church, he left his native Peru, never to return, and it was in the seclusion of a small Andalusian town that he wrote his great work, *Royal Commentaries of the Incas and General History of Peru*. It is divided into two parts, which were published separately, one in Lisbon in 1609 and the other in Cordoba, posthumously, in 1616–17.

Had John Locke actually read Garcilaso when he published his *Two Treatises of Civil Government*? Was his construction of the "state of nature" based on Garcilaso's *Royal Commentaries* or on his *Florida* (de la Vega [1616–17] 1980), in which Garcilaso tells the tale of an expedition to explore and occupy territories inhabited by half-savage Indians, many of them cannibals? What is revealing in this anecdote is how my interests as a feminist scholar led me to focus on some of the marginalia in the text of the *Second Treatise*, and how the interests of another scholar showed me the way to an encounter with another culture implicit in the subtext of John Locke's famous work. Depending indeed upon how Locke read or misread, presented or misrepresented Garcilaso, we gain fascinating insights into the process of the construction of "others" in the texts of Western political thought. I concur with Homi Bhabha that "the borderline work of culture demands an encounter with 'newness' that is not part of a continuum of past and present. It creates a sense of the new as an insurgent act of cultural translation"(1994, 70.) I attempt in the following chapters to spell out the political consequences of treating the "new" as an insurgent act of cultural translation.

T W O

□   □   □   □

"NOUS" ET LES "AUTRES"
(WE AND THE OTHERS)

Is Universalism Ethnocentric?

The question Is universalism ethnocentric? betrays an anxiety that has haunted the West since the conquest of the Americas. It grows from beliefs that Western ways of life and systems of value are radically different from those of other civilizations. This widespread anxiety rests on false generalizations about the West itself, about the homogeneity of its identity, the uniformity of its developmental processes, and the cohesion of its value systems. The suggestion that universalism is ethnocentric often also presupposes a homogenizing view of other cultures and civilizations, neglecting elements in them that may be perfectly compatible with, and may even lie at the root of, the West's own discovery of universalism.

Consider an episode in the rise of Renaissance culture: After the division of the Roman Empire in A.D. 395 and the fall of its western part in A.D. 476, Greek philosophy, in particular the thought of Plato and Aristotle, was forgotten in the West. It is well known that Arab and Jewish philosophers of the Middle Ages, Ibn Sina (Avicenna), Ibn Rushd (Averroes), Moshe ben Maimon (Maimonides), and Ibn Gabirol (Avicebron) kept the classical tradition alive.[1] In the thirteenth century in Anatolia the poet Yunus Emre developed a form of mystical Neoplatonism that anticipated not only elements of Renaissance humanism but also pantheistic philosophies of the nineteenth century. Emre advocated the view that the human person is at the center of a divine chain of being of ascending complexity, beauty, and perfection; we reach the height of our spiritual capacities insofar as we partake through our minds of the divine order of these forms. Emre, one of the great mystical poets of Islam, blended Plato's teaching of the forms with an Aristotelian ontology. Galileo's claim, several centuries later, that "the book of nature was written in mathematics"[2] has much in common with Yunus Emre's belief that the universe is an intelligible, ordered hierarchy of forms.

When we pose the question "Is universalism ethnocentric?" do we take account of this complex global dialogue across cultures and civilizations? Or do we rest satisfied with the gesture of self-criticism emerging out of the radical doubt that European culture, in particular, experienced about itself at the end of the eighteenth century and increasingly in the nineteenth century? The question "Is universalism ethnocentric?" presupposes that we know who the "West and its others," or in Tzvetan Todorov's famous words — "Nous et les autres"— are (1993). But who are we? Who are the so-called others? Are they really our others?

More often than not, the answer in recent debates on cognitive and moral relativism has turned on a holistic view of cultures and societies as internally coherent, seamless wholes. This view has prevented us from seeing the complexity of global civilizational dialogues and encounters, which are increasingly our lot, and it has encouraged the binaries of "we" and "the other(s)." Fortunately, current concerns about multiculturalism and multicultural citizenship are bringing to an end this preoccupation with the supposed tension between relativism and universalism, discussions that had been dominated by strong theses of "incommensurability" and "untranslatability." Nevertheless, and despite the waning of epistemological relativisms (see Krausz 1989), false assumptions about cultures, their coherence and purity, still influence the work of various contemporary multicultural theorists. This chapter pleads for a recognition of the radical hybridity and polyvocality of all cultures; cultures themselves, as well as societies, are not holistic but polyvocal, multilayered, decentered, and fractured systems of action and signification. Politically, the right to cultural self-expression needs to be grounded upon, rather than considered an alternative to, universally recognized citizenship rights.

UNIVERSALISM IN CONTEMPORARY
PHILOSOPHICAL DEBATES

The term *universalism* can stand for several clusters of views.

1. It may signify the philosophical belief that there is a fundamental human nature or human essence that defines who we are as humans. Some may say, as did most philosophers of the eighteenth century, that human nature consists of stable and predictable passions and dispositions, instincts and emotions, all of which can be studied. Thomas Hobbes, David Hume, and Adam Smith, but also Claude-Adrien Helvétius and Baron Paul-Henri Diterich d'Holbach come to mind here. Others may argue that there is no fixed human nature (Rousseau), or that even if there were, it would be irrelevant to determining what is most essential about us as humans (Kant): namely, our capacity to formulate and to live by universalizable moral principles. Still others, like Jean-Paul Sartre, may repudiate empirical psychology, philosophical anthropology, and rationalist ethics, and maintain that what is universal about the human condition is that we are doomed to choose for ourselves and create meaning and value through our actions in a universe that would otherwise be devoid of both. Although most philosophical universalists are essentialists, the example of Sartre shows that they need not be. They can be existentialists, instead.

2. Universalism in contemporary philosophical debates has come to mean, most prominently, a justification strategy. Questioning whether there can be an "impartial," "objective," and "neutral" philosophical reason, hermeneuticists like Hans-Georg Gadamer, strong contextualists like Richard Rorty, postmodern skeptics like Jean-François Lyotard, and power/knowledge theorists like Michel Foucault maintain that all justificatory strategies, all pretenses to philosophical objectivity, are trapped within historical horizons and in

cultural, social, and psychological currents. In Thomas McCarthy's words, these philosophers advocate a "critique of impure reason" (1991, 43–76).

Opposed to them are universalists like Karl Otto-Apel, Hilary Putnam, Juergen Habermas, Ronald Dworkin, Thomas Nagel, Thomas Scanlon, and John Rawls (at least in his *Theory of Justice*). These justificatory universalists may not be essentialists: some may entertain very few rock-bottom beliefs about human nature and psychology. But they all share strong beliefs in the normative content of human reason—that is, in the validity of procedures of inquiry, evidence, and questioning that have been considered the cognitive legacy of Western philosophy since the Enlightenment. Impartiality, objectivity, intersubjective verification of results, arguments and data, consistency of belief, and self-reflexivity minimally define this normative content.

3. Universalism is not only a term in cognitive inquiry; equally significantly, it has a moral meaning. I would associate it with the principle that all human beings, regardless of race, gender, sexual preference, ethnic, cultural, linguistic, and religious background, are to be considered moral equals and are therefore to be treated as equally entitled to moral respect. The hard question in philosophical ethics today is whether one can defend this moral universalism without supporting strong cognitive universalism in the senses of either 1 or 2.

4. Finally, universalism may have a legal meaning. Many who are skeptical of human nature or rationality, or of philosophical justifications, may nonetheless urge that the following norms and principles be accorded universal respect by all legal systems: all human beings are entitled to certain basic rights, including, minimally, the rights to life, liberty, security, due process before the law, and freedom of speech and association, including freedom of religion and conscience. Some would add socioeconomic rights, such as the right to work and to health care, disability, and old-age benefits; others would insist on participatory democratic, as well as cultural, rights.

Richard Rorty's defence of "postmodernist bourgeois liberalism," for example, fits this model (Rorty 1983). John Rawls's position in

The Law of Peoples (1999) is quite consistent with it, as are Jacques Derrida's many interventions against apartheid and on behalf of minorities and civil rights (see Derrida 1992). Rorty, Rawls, and Derrida all attempt to disassociate legal universalism from essentialism. They attempt to show that universalism, like justice, can be political without being metaphysical.[3] Although I believe that universalism without metaphysics is possible, I question whether moral and legal universalisms can be defended without a strong commitment to the normative content of reason.

□   □   □   □

Let me consider briefly the argument that universalism, however defined, is a form of ethnocentrism. I will call this position "the relativism of frameworks," and I will take some early writings of Jean-François Lyotard and Richard Rorty as exemplifying it. Framework relativists do not defend the indefensible; they do not argue that "anything goes" in morality, in the sphere of law, in epistemology or ethics. They recognize criteria of validity for action, conduct, and inquiry in all of these fields. Yet they argue that judgments of validity are "framework relative," whether these frameworks are defined as language games, epistemological worldviews, or ethnocentric traditions. Furthermore, a preference for one framework over another cannot be established in universal, rational terms, since such terms themselves would be framework relative.

Against these views, I maintain that framework relativism fails because the very process of individuating and identifying frameworks contradicts the claims of framework relativism. Frameworks could be individuated only if there were framework-transcending criteria of evaluation, comparison and individuation. So framework relativists' strong distinction between being "within" and "outside" a framework cannot be maintained. Establishing this point alone is not sufficient to help us decide *which* set of framework-transcending criteria ought to be defended over others. Independent arguments would then be needed to defend such criteria in turn. This chapter develops only some epistemic arguments to further strengthen the model of complex cultural dialogues advocated in the Introduction. My model of complex cultural dialogue and discursive ethics is further developed in chapters 3, 4, and 5.

THE CHALLENGE OF RELATIVISM

Contemporary philosophical arguments about relativism often proceed from insights developed in the philosophy of language. Incommensurability, incompatibility, and untranslatability claims are usually formulated with reference to linguistic systems and address the possibility of communication across them. For Jean-François Lyotard, for example, the "phrase," is the most elementary unit of analysis, which is "constituted according to a set of rules (its regimen)" (Lyotard 1988). Thus a genre of discourse, like teaching, can entail phrase regimens of knowing, interrogating, showing, ordering, and classifying. Phrase regimens and genres of discourse always exist in the plural; furthermore, and this is crucial, genres of discourse are not only plural but also "heterogeneous," that is, irreducible to a common or comprehensive discourse. This is the problem of the *différend*. A différend is a case of a conflict between two parties that cannot be resolved equitably for lack of a common or shared rule of judgment that would be applicable to both cases.

Lyotard's vision is that of a quasi-Nietzschean metaphysic of struggle and the will to power, extending throughout our linguistic, symbolic, cognitive, and political universe. He writes of phrase "regimens," the "civil war of language," the impossibility of "subjecting" heterogeneous phrase regimens to a common law, except by force. His vision is one of contestation, struggle, battle, the ubiquitous presence of power everywhere. "To speak," wrote Lyotard earlier, "is to fight" (1984, 10).

Yet there is also something remarkably brief, impatient, almost staccato in these formulations. The premise of the absolute heterogeneity and incommensurability of regimens and discourses is never argued for; it is simply asserted. It corresponds to what Richard Bernstein has called a "pervasive amorphous mood" (1981,

117). Incommensurability is the central epistemic premise of Lyotard's philosophy of language, and also its weakest. He nowhere distinguishes between incommensurability, heterogeneity, incompatibility, and untranslatability. He assembles under the heading of *le différend* a range of meanings, extending from radical untranslatability in language to the sense of unfairness or injustice that may be experienced when the language of the victor is invoked to describe the wounds of the vanquished.[4]

The thesis of radical untranslatability of genres of discourse and phrase regimens is no more meaningful, however, than the thesis of the radical incommensurability of conceptual frameworks. If frameworks, linguistic or conceptual, are so radically incommensurable, then we would not even be able to know that much; our ability to describe a framework as a framework in the first place rests upon the possibility that we can identify and select certain features of these other frameworks as sufficiently like ours to be characterized as conceptual activities in the first place. Radical incommensurability and radical untranslatability are incoherent notions, for in order to be able to identify a pattern of thought, a language—and, we may add, a culture—as the complex meaningful human systems of action and signification that they are, we must first at least have recognized that concepts, words, rituals, and symbols in these other systems have a meaning and reference that we can select and describe in a manner intelligible to us—as being concepts at all, for example, rather than mere exclamations. If radical untranslatability were true, we could not even recognize the other set of utterances as part of a language, as, that is, a practice that is more or less rule-governed and shared in fairly predictable ways. If cultures were so radically divergent, we would not be able to isolate complex human activities, with their myths, rituals, and symbols, as meaningful and intelligible wholes and describe these as a marriage ceremony, a feast, or a prayer. As Hilary Putnam has noted: "It is a constitutive fact about human experience in a world of different cultures interacting in history while individually undergoing slower or more rapid change that we are, as a matter of universal human experience, able to *do* this; able to interpret one another's beliefs, desires, and utterances so that it all makes some kind of *sense*" (1981, 117, emphasis in original).

If phrase regimens and genres of discourse were so radically heterogeneous, disparate, untranslatable, then indeed it would be impossible to account for one of the most common competencies of language users: that in the course of the same conversation, we can move from teaching to advertising, from informing to seducing, from judging to ironizing. As competent users of a language, we can negotiate these nuances of meaning, shifts of style, suggestions of innuendo, playfulness, or irony. But if ordinary language use and performance suggest that phrase regimens and genres of discourse are not insular and unbridgeable units, what becomes of the thesis of their absolute heterogeneity?

To be sure, there is a conceptual as well as moral danger in insisting too glibly and rapidly upon total commensurability. Experiences of incommensuration can range from total bafflement in the face of another culture's rituals and practices to more mundane and frustrating encounters with others when we simply say, "I just don't get it. What do you really mean?" Such experiences and encounters need to be seen as calls to further conversation and interaction; breakdowns in communication often generate hostility and indifference, or even aggression and violence. But at times the breakdown of communication can also have the salutory effect of extending the horizons of one's comprehension, as we try to understand others better. That is why talk of commensurability and incommensurability always involves an epistemic as well as a moral dimension. Understanding the other is not just a cognitive act; it is a moral and political deed. Theories of strong incommensurability distract us from the many subtle epistemic and moral negotiations that take place across cultures, within cultures, among individuals, and even within individuals themselves in dealing with discrepancy, ambiguity, discordancy, and conflict.

While for Jean-François Lyotard cultural relativism is but one aspect of the larger problem of the incommensurability, Richard Rorty maintains that the very terms of this debate between universalism and relativism are outmoded: "they are remnants of a vocabulary which we should try to replace" (1986, 44). Rorty sees his own commitment to the values of liberalism not in some metaphysical and transcendent terms, but as a simpler preference for a certain self-description. At times he, like Lyotard, argues that narratives of our cultures do what they do without any need for further justification: "we do not need to scratch where it does not itch" (54). At other points, he acknowledges that liberal culture institutionalizes the search for reflexive justification in science, ethics, aesthetics, jurisprudence, and politics, but refuses to attribute to this fact any gain in rationality. For Rorty the attempt to question and to challenge the values and norms of one's own culture, or any other culture, in terms that transcend the self-understanding of this culture is illusory (59).

Yet unlike Lyotard, Rorty rejects radical incommensurability and untranslatability. In "Solidarity or Objectivity" he writes, "The distinction between different cultures does not differ in kind from the distinction between different theories held by members of a single culture. . . . The same Quinean arguments which dispose of the positivists' distinction between analytic and synthetic truth dispose of the anthropologists' distinction between the intercultural and the intracultural" (1985, 9). But the consequences of this argument are much more damaging for Rorty's own position than he acknowledges. If in effect there is no asymmetry between disputations among members of one culture and disputations among members of different cultures; if it is merely a matter of the degree and extent of divergent belief systems, then Rorty's talk about "us" versus "them," about "our ethnocentrism" versus "theirs" is misleading and self-contradictory. The lines between us and them do not necessarily correspond to the lines between members of our culture and those of another. The community with which one solidarizes is not ethnically or ethnocentrically defined; communities of solidarity may or may not be ethnically established. There is no necessary overlap between solidarity and ethnocentrism, only a contingent one.

By Rorty's own philosophical admission, all that the pragmatist should be warranted to say is that "among human beings there are those who can be actual or potential participants with me in a community of conversation and those who are not and may never be."[5] Yet this community of conversation has a shifting identity and no fixed boundaries. It is not coincident with an ethnos, with any homogeneous "we." Membership in this community is defined through the topic of the conversation, the task at hand, or the problem being debated. For a true pragmatist, the formation and definition of identity would follow suit upon identification of a set of shared interests, be they scientific, artistic, cultural, linguistic, economic, or national. We are all participants in different communities of conversation, as constituted by the intersecting axes of our different interests, projects, and life situations. A consistent pragmatist could say only that all inquiry, whether scientific or moral; all justification, whether in aesthetics or jurisprudence; and all demonstrations, whether in banking or in physics, are conversations that can occur only in the presence of others who share enough of our beliefs to enable us to communicate. In his continuing references to "they" versus "us," "their" versus "our" group, Rorty ignores the fact that most of us today are members of more than one community, one linguistic group, one ethnos. Millions of people the world over engage in economic, political, or artistic migrations. More than ever before, "true nations," "pure" linguistic groups, and unsullied ethnic identities are truly "imagined" communities. The latter were created through the imagination of nineteenth-century poets, novelists, historians, and, of course, statesmen and ideologues. Who are we? And what is ours?

THE PARTIAL TRUTH OF CULTURAL RELATIVISM: FROM COMMUNITIES OF CONVERSATION TO COMMUNITIES OF INTERDEPENDENCE

Even if views of radical incommensurability and untranslatability inspired by philosophies of language are untenable, many of us still feel that there is some deep truth in the cultural relativist position. The intuition that some aspects of cultural relativism are true derives from certain features of our modern world, although knowledge of the variability of human cultures is as old as human culture itself.[6] As moderns, we know much more than people of the eighteenth and nineteenth centuries did about the sheer variety and incongruity of human cultures, systems of belief, value hierarchies, and modes of representation. As our knowledge of other cultures and of ourselves increases, so does our sense of relativity. Paradoxically, the more we understand, the more we can forgive: in the study of human culture and society, "Tout comprendre c'est tout pardonner." That is the *hermeneutic truth of cultural relativism.*

All understanding, be it of the past, of a different culture, or of a work of art, must begin with a methodological and moral imperative to reconstruct meaning as it appears to its creators and makers. What is this strange artifact we see there in the corner in an antique store, we ask? Is it a weather vane, the spoke of a wheel, or a kitchen fixture? What was it used for and what did its makers intend? Why does the poet use this metaphor at this point? Why does Paul Celan write of "your ashen hair Shulamith," at this point, evoking at once the blond hair of Aryan women and the name of the murdered Jewish woman? Or is it not hair color but the reference to ashes and cremation that we are asked to recollect? [7] Contemporary discussions about authorial intention, "the death of the author," and the like, do not change the principle that there can be no reconstruction of meaning without interpretation, without placing the object of one's study, be this an artifact or a poem, in some other framework, from the standpoint of which it makes sense. In this process of making sense, the belief system studied meets one's own framework. These systems enter into dialogue; they challenge and dislodge each other. Hans-Georg Gadamer has used the phrase *Horizontverschmelzung,* "a melting or merging or blending into one another of horizons," to describe this process ([1960] 1975). In this sense, "all understanding is interpretation." To be sure, sometimes the hermeneutic conversation is far from civil, egalitarian, and mutually enriching: Wars, conquests, and plunders bring cultures and civilizations together as much as do *le doux commerce* and other peaceful human transactions. Some conversations are confrontations; and confrontations can be more or less violent. They may not permit a *Verschmelzung*, a melting together and into one another. They may present us with tragic alternatives in which there are winners and losers, in which opting for one language and pattern of interpretation may require excluding the other. But they may also force us to revise our visions and paradigms. The most successful hermeneutic conversations are uncomfortable precisely because they set in motion processes of mutual challenging, questioning, and learning.[8]

This conclusion still does not permit us to answer the question: Even if every act of understanding and interpretation implies a *Horizontverschmelzung*, do we know *which* set of presuppositions, which horizon, is the most reasonable and correct? Some of the most difficult issues facing us today arise primarily from real confrontations between cultural horizons. The distinction between periphery and center has been superseded; the periphery is at the center. The condition of global interdependence has practically transformed all cross-cultural communication and exchange into a real confrontation: Bernard Williams's insight that the notion of "real confrontation" is to some extent a sociological notion is crucial.[9] The worldwide development of means of transportation and communication along with the growth of international markets in labor, capital, and finance are multiplying and increasing the effects of local activities on a global scale. Take the case of ecological damage. The real confrontation between different cultures is producing not only a community of conversation, but also a community of interdependence. Not only what we say and think but also what we eat, burn, produce, and waste has consequences for others about whom we may know nothing, but whose lives are affected by our actions. I am not suggesting that our sociological condition provides an answer to the philosophical query of how to choose among varieties of framework-transcending criteria, which may be epistemological or evaluative, constitutional or aesthetic. All I have suggested so far is that theses of radical incommensurability are wrong. The burdens of choice and judgment between different institutions as well as traditions remain. In fact, judgments about "exclusivity" and "coexistence" have a philosophical as well as a social dimension (see chaps. 4 and 5 below).

In this context, the articulation of a pluralistically enlightened ethical universalism on a global scale emerges as a possibility and as a necessity.

1. The interpretation of cultures as hermetic, sealed, internally self-consistent wholes is untenable and reflects the reductionist sociology of knowledge.

2. This view of cultures as self-consistent wholes is also refuted by philosophical arguments concerning the impossibility of radical incommensurability and untranslatability.

3. If all understanding and interpretation of the other(s) must also make sense to us from where we stand today, then the boundaries of the community of conversation extend as far as our never-ending attempts to understand, interpret, and communicate with the other(s). We have become moral contemporaries, even if not moral partners,[10] caught in a net of interdependence, and our contemporaneous actions will also have uncontemporaneous consequences. This global situation creates a new "community of interdependence."

4. If in effect the contemporary global situation is creating real confrontations between cultures, languages, and nations, and if the unintended results of such real confrontations is to impinge upon the lives of others, then we have a *pragmatic imperative* to understand each other and to enter into a cross-cultural dialogue.

5. Such a pragmatic imperative bears moral consequences. A community of interdependence becomes a moral community only if it resolves to settle those issues of common concern to all via dialogical procedures in which all are participants. This "all" refers to all of humanity, not because one has to invoke some philosophically essentialist theory of human nature, but because the condition of planetary interdependence has created a situation of worldwide reciprocal exchange, influence, and interaction.

6. All dialogue, in order to be distinguished from cajoling, propaganda, brainwashing, and strategic bargaining, presupposes normative rules. Minimally formulated, these entail that we recognize the

right to equal participation between conversation partners, whom I define provisionally as "all whose interests are actually or potentially affected by the courses of action and decisions which may ensue from such conversations." Furthermore, all participants have an equal right to suggest topics of conversation, to introduce new points of view, questions, and criticism into the conversation, and to challenge the rules of the conversation insofar as these seem to exclude the voice of some and privilege that of others. These norms can be summed up as "universal respect" and "egalitarian reciprocity" (see chap. 5).

7. In the context of cross-cultural, international, and global exchanges, but not only in such cases, these norms of universal respect and egalitarian reciprocity are counterfactual guides to action. The limits of universal respect are always tested by differences among us; egalitarian reciprocity will probably never be realized in a world community where states and peoples are at different levels of technological, economic, and military development and are subject to different social, historical, and cultural structures and constraints. What these norms of universal respect and egalitarian reciprocity articulate are guideposts for our intuitions; they are normative principles to guide our judgments and deliberations in complex human situations.

In *Situating the Self* (1992), I explained that to justify the norms of universal respect and egalitarian reciprocity involves strategies derived from different traditions of philosophical reflection on human conduct and inquiry. I agree with Karl Otto-Apel and Juergen Habermas that these norms are in a minimal sense necessary for us to distinguish a consensus, rationally and freely attained among participants, from other forms of agreement that may be based on power and violence, tradition and custom, ruses of egoistic self-interest as well as moral indifference. The minimal norms of universal respect for each other as conversation partners, and the fairness and equality of procedures for reaching agreements—the sum total of which can be summarized as egalitarian reciprocity—are bound up with the pragmatics as well as semantics of what we understand by free and rational agreement. Clearly, the ideal of a rationally motivated consensus is central to democratic theory and practice. An analysis that showed these norms' interdependence with practices of rational agreement would produce a kind of "transcendental argument" in the weak sense. This would not be a strong transcendental argument proving the necessity and singularity of certain conditions without which some aspect of our world, conduct, and consciousness *could* not be what it is. A weak transcendental argument would demonstrate more modestly that certain conditions need to be fulfilled for us to judge those practices to be of a certain sort rather than of a different kind. For example, without showing equal respect for one's conversation partners, without an equal distribution of the rights to speak, interrogate, and propose alternatives, we would find it hard to call the agreement reached at the end of a conversation fair, rational, or free. This does not mean that these conditions do not themselves permit interpretation, disagreement, or contention, or that they are rooted in the deep structure of human consciousness. I call them "weak transcendental conditions" in the sense that they are *necessary* and *constitutive* for the moral, political, and social practices of reaching reasoned agreement. Unless such conditions are met, one cannot claim that such practices have been fulfilled.

However, the justification of these norms through a recourse to the internal logic of argumentation situations alone will not get us very far. Such recourse is important but clearly insufficient. The norm of universal respect presupposes a generalized moral attitude of equality toward other human beings. The boundaries of the community of moral discourse are open-ended; "all those whose interests are affected" are part of the moral conversation. But in the case of most human communities and cultures, we can take for granted neither that this generalized moral attitude toward human equality will be shared nor that all other human beings will be considered worthy conversation partners in settling social, moral, and political matters. I believe that a generalized attitude of moral equality spreads in human history through conversations as well as confrontations across cultures, and through commerce as well as wars; international agreements as well as international threats contribute to its emergence. This is a sociological and historical observation. I believe in moral learning through moral transformation, and I assume that it is not the deep structure of the mind or psyche that makes us believe in universalism, but rather such historical and moral experiences. Therefore, in addition to weak transcendentalism, I would defend a historically enlightened universalism.

What happens, however, when we situate moral discourses within the horizons of specific cultures? I have assumed that a distinction between moral and cultural discourses is possible and viable. I have assumed further that moral discourses concern *all* as equal participants in a dialogue, insofar as their interests are affected. But since moral discourses are situated in cultural lifeworlds, is it plausible to want to separate them? Can they be separated? What if the model of complex cultural dialogue cannot prove that other cultural traditions and life-worlds are receptive to these universalist norms? Is this an empirical question about cultural history or a philosophical question about human morality? Clearly, I do not want to conflate the two. Questions about the philosophical justification of an ethics of conversation—its range, its internal coherence—remain within the domain of normative philosophy. I am arguing that my view of a complex cultural dialogue is a better, empirically more defensible, and more correct understanding of the development of human culture and history. Philosophical theses of strong incommensurability, I want to suggest, also produce bad historiography.

There is an influential position in contemporary moral and political theory that I shall call *strong contextualism*. Displaying some affinities to Richard Rorty, Michael Walzer has advanced the strongest case for this position in his *Spheres of Justice* (1983). Walzer is not a relativist, though at times it is hard to see how he can avoid relativism. Proceeding from the central hermeneutic insight that all meaning must first be interpreted and understood from the standpoint of its producers, Walzer writes: "One characteristic above all is central to my arguments. We are (all of us) culture producing creatures; we make and inhabit meaningful worlds. Since there is no way to rank and order these worlds with respect to their understanding of social goods, we do justice to men and women by respecting their particular creations" (314). Walzer thus takes cultural context seriously, but he collapses the distinction between moral and cultural discourses and does not seem to believe that such a distinction is viable. By contrast, I believe that cultures permit varying degrees of differentiation between *the moral*, which concerns what is right or just for all insofar as we are considered simply as human beings; *the ethical*, which concerns what is appropriate for us insofar as we are members of a specific collectivity, with its unique history and tradition; and *the evaluative*, which concerns what we individually or collectively hold to be valuable, worth striving for, and essential to human happiness. Admittedly, such differentiations are most characteristic of cultural life-worlds and worldviews under conditions of modernity. Increasingly though, the globalized world we are inhabiting compels cultural traditions that may not have generated these differentiations in the course of their own development to internalize them or to learn to coexist in a political and legal world with other cultures that operate with some form of these differentiations. Many traditional cultures, for example, still consider women's and children's rights as an aspect of their ethical life-world, of the way things are done in that particular culture. However, the international discourse on women's rights, the activism of international development and aid organizations, migration, and television programs are transforming these assumptions. The rights of women and children are now being considered in the light of a universalist moral language, which is context independent, in that it is argued that women have a right to work and support themselves, for example, or that regardless of which religion or culture these women and children belong to, child labor and prostitution are wrong (see chap. 4).

The social goods Walzer discusses, which range from attitudes toward health care to attitudes toward the family and noncitizens, are composites bundled together through strands of moral, ethical, and evaluative stances and argumentations. It does not follow that if we respect human beings as culture-creating beings that we must either "rank or order" their worlds as a *whole* or disrespect them by dismissing their life-worlds altogether. We may disagree with *some* aspect of their moral, ethical, or evaluative practices without dismissing or holding in disrespect their life-worlds *altogether.* Most human encounters, with the exception of attempts by murderous regimes to annihilate the world of the other, occur in this in-between space of partial evaluations, translations, and contestations. It would be just as foolish to deny the existence of regimes of annihilation both in premodern and modern times—the Spanish Inquisition and the destruction of the Inca and Maya at the cusp of modernity; the Nazi regime and ethnic cleansing in the twentieth century—as to forget that they are the exception and not the rule in human history. Most human history unfolds in this in-between space of commerce and confrontation, battle and association.

Michael Walzer's claims are too holistic; they do not permit us to make the fine-grained differentiations we need for cross-cultural judgment and evaluation. For example, one can condemn the ancient Chinese tradition of foot binding of women while admiring Chinese calligraphy, pottery, and dedication to the value of honest work. Likewise, one can condemn the controversial rite of sati (widow burning) while praising Indian erotic traditions, Indian pluralism, and the everyday sense of the aesthetic. In others words, we need not approach cultural traditions and worlds as wholes. The method of complex cultural dialogue suggests that we focus on the interpenetration of traditions and discourses and disclose the interdependence of images of the self and the other. As Walzer argues, it indeed makes no sense "to rank and order these worlds," for the category of "these worlds" is itself a conceptual shorthand we use to distill coherence out of the multiplicity of conflicting narratives and practices, symbolizations and rituals that constitute life-worlds. The lived universe of cultures always appears in the plural. We need to be attentive to the positioning and repositioning of the other and the self, of "us" and "them," in this complex dialogue. Walzer's strong contextualism does not permit us to make the necessary analytical distinctions in evaluating cultural universes. As soon as we produce rich, contextually informed accounts of "these worlds," we see that their understandings of social goods permit multiple and conflicting evaluations and that this hermeneutic complexity permits us to enter into some kind of dialogue with the inhabitants of these "other worlds." It is not just "us" versus "them"; there are those with whom we agree, who inhabit other cultures and worlds, but whose evaluations we find plausible and comprehensible, and still others whose ways of life as well as systems of belief will be abhorrent to us. But who are "we"? Isn't the "we" attempting this evaluation just as much a subject of cultural multiplicity, diversity, and rifts as the others whom the "we" is studying? Where exactly is the moral asymmetry here, if there is one? I think such purported moral asymmetries between insider and outsider positions are usually the consequences of bad cultural narratives following upon the heels of wrong philosophical assumptions.

JOHN LOCKE AND THE LIMITS OF COMPLEX CULTURAL DIALOGUE

I want to conclude this chapter by returning to John Locke and his *Second Treatise on Civil Government* (1690), which I discussed in chapter 1. I focus once more on the metaphor of the "state of nature" in order to unveil the discourse of the *Second Treatise* as an argument in moral philosophy and a complex intervention in the justification of a newly emergent colonizing property regime. Locke's parable about what was wrong and right about Western modernity and universalism is situated at the critical juncture between the restoration of constitutional government in England; the consolidation of the bourgeois liberal regime of representative government based upon respect for the rights of life, liberty, and property; the colonization of the Americas; and the beginnings of the African slave trade.

As is well known, Locke begins by positing that all men in the state of nature are equal and "naturally endowed" by their Maker with life, liberty, and property. The "state of nature" is a metaphor that compounds the historical with the psychological, the analytic with the cultural, in a most resonant way. It refers to the condition men would be in were they not governed by common laws. In that sense, it is an analytical abstraction that answers the hypothetical question of what the human condition would be like outside the boundaries of civil government. But Locke's metaphor also contains oblique references to a distant historical past. Although it is unlikely that human beings ever existed without some form of government, Locke assures us, we have some vague historical sense of primitive forms of human organization in times past that would almost amount to a lack of civil government altogether. Locke adds an anthropological reference to "the two men on the desert island, mentioned by Garcilaso de la Vega, in his history of *Peru;* or between a Swiss and an *Indian*, in the woods of America" ([1690] 1980, 13). These peoples on faraway islands and woods, even if they are our historical contemporaries, now become part of our historical past; their culture and forms of government are thus reordered within a uniform chronological sequence. The otherness of their way of life now loses its otherness and becomes familiar, because it is seen as being like our past, the past of the Europeans.

Psychologically, the state of nature metaphor is an affirmation of individualism, autonomy, independence, and self-reliance. The male is seen as one who owes nothing to others for the rights to which he is entitled; it is not his historical community of birth and entitlement which endows him with these rights; rather, it is his "Maker" and the law of nature, which all men of sound reason and goodwill can consult in order to discover this radical message of equality and autonomy. This gesture of reasoning about the limits of legitimate government through a radical abstraction is breathtaking, yet it is not new with Locke. It was used by Stoic moral philosophers and was revived in more vivid terms by Thomas Hobbes in his *Leviathan* in 1651. Nonetheless, whereas Stoic moral philosophers used this metaphor to reason about moral dilemmas under conditions where no civil law could guide individuals, modern political philosophers revived it to project onto the beginning of human history and of human government an image of individual autonomy, equality and self-reliance. Gone were the motley ties, hierarchies, and encumbrances of the feudal order under which an individual was in fact defined by the social rank and the estate into which he was born. The modern bourgeois individual faces his Maker alone, and it is this presumptive radical independence and autonomy of creatures "promiscuously born to the same God" that he must transform into civil dependence upon laws of legitimate civil government.

Locke's universalist portrait of bourgeois freedom has serious limitations. It will turn out that, after all, we are not all similarly equal, rational, and deserving in the eyes of God. "In the beginning all the World was America," writes Locke in section 49 ([1690] 1980, 29). What does he mean? "America" for Locke becomes a placeholder for "the state of nature." Thus does a logical abstraction get superimposed upon an existing place and on the inhabitants of the Americas, "the Amerindians" who now come to represent "men in the state of nature." In Locke's view, the state of nature involves first and foremost the exercise of individual judgment in the "execution of the Law of Nature," since there is no common authority to whom all have consented; it also involves exclusive individual rights over one's labor and its products: Every man has property "in the labor of his body and the work of his hands"; to this no one but himself is entitled.

In a brilliant and provocative reading of these passages, James Tully shows that Locke's seemingly innocent incorporation of the Amerindians into an evolutionary account of the history of European civil society, where they represent the stage of the state of nature, accomplishes two ends.

First, Locke defines political society in such a way that Amerindian government does not qualify as a legitimate form of political society. Rather, it is construed as a historically less developed form of European political organization located in the later stages of the "state of nature" and thus not on a par with modern European political formations. Second, Locke defines property in such a way that Amerindian customary land use is not a legitimate type of property. Rather, it is construed as individual labor-based possession and assimilated to an earlier stage of European development in the state of nature, and thus not an equal footing with European property. (1993, 139)

The consequences of these rhetorical moves on Locke's part, who may genuinely have believed that Amerindian forms of organization and land use were simply another version of the European,[11] are far-reaching. The uniqueness of Amerindian political organization is disregarded, and Amerindian forms of property ownership are denied and eventually replaced by a system of "primitive accumulation" based upon individual labor. The result is an elaborate philosophical justification of the colonization of the Americas (151).

Locke accomplishes this first and foremost through his argument on property, which for him is coeval to the development of civil society. If God gave the earth to men in common, and every man has property in the labor of his body and the work of his hands, how does an "individual" system of property, with clearly defined boundaries, emerge? At first, the extent of appropriation is set by need—every man has a right to accumulate and take of the earth's common possession as much as he can use without it spoiling or going to waste ([1690] 1980, 28). But this spoilage condition is soon upset by two factors: some are more industrious and far-sighted and frugal than others, and can thus accumulate and put to prudent use more than others who do not possess these qualities. Yet at first even this condition of "differential rationality" does not negate the stipulation that the limits of property are set by need, for Locke assumes that there will still be "enough and as good to go around for others." It is the second factor—namely, the introduction of money—that destroys this delicate balance of need and appropriation by giving individuals an item that does not spoil. In fact, money is unnatural in that it disrupts the physical link between appropriation, property, and need by introducing an abstraction named "value" into the equation. The value of money has few consequences for the satisfaction of needs; the value of money is its exchange value in procuring through buying and selling other useful objects, desired for the satisfaction of concrete human needs.

With the introduction of money, the link between the means of appropriation, which are supplied by the human body, and the title to the property appropriated completely dissolves. It is money that supplies the title to property and, in particular, to land. And since Locke mysteriously assumes that there is a morally justifiable connection between the amount of money one possesses and the virtues of rationality and thrift that create distinctions between individuals in the state of nature, the claim to the land by those who can purchase it and then augment its value by laboring upon it is also morally justified. The dispossession of the Amerindians is not only a historical fact; in Locke's hands it also becomes sanctified as a moral act.

What consequences should we draw from this reading of Locke's *Second Treatise*? One of the seminal texts of Western political thought turns out to be engaged in a complex cultural dialogue that positions and repositions the "we" and the "others" in complex, multiple, and unpredictable ways. The Amerindians become just like the Europeans; their otherness is buried in the early stages of our own past. But because we are like them, or rather *were* like them, the order of government and property that we bring upon them is not alien to them, but simply a better and higher version of what they lack. Thus colonization becomes an act of speeding up a developmental process toward consensual government and a regime of private property.

It is impossible to take seriously Locke's fantastical and oft illogical derivation of the origins of human property. In fact, the Amerindian view, which would consider property—and particularly property of the land—an entitlement insofar as one is a member of a human community, is the more correct view anthropologically, since most human cultures practiced some form of communal property in the land until the emergence of early capitalism. Furthermore, in most precapitalist economic formations, individuals were considered entitled to own property in virtue of their membership in some human community (cf. Polanyi 1971). Karl Marx appropriately called Lockean theories "the Robinsonnades" of early bourgeois thought ([1857–58] 1973, 83). Yet what about

Locke's claim that civil government rests upon the consent of those considered equals in their entitlement to a set of equal rights? Can we dispense with that principle? I think not. We can criticize Locke's derivation of property rights; we can take apart the contradictions in his understanding of the law of nature; we can show the outrageous exclusions of women, propertyless servants, and other races from the ark of equality; but at the end of the day the ideal of government based upon the consensual agreement of equals prevails as a foundation for all democratic theory and practice. Thus the perspective of complex cultural dialogues enables us to evaluate the discourses of "we" and the "others" more fully, without leading to the reductionist conclusion that all philosophical validity is context specific. Locke's argument about what may be called *the appropriation theory of property* is wrong, not only because it excludes and delegitimizes the Amerindian land holding traditions, but because it posits a human person and a set of human relationships that are simply historically inaccurate. As Marx noted a long time ago, Locke projects onto the beginnings of human history a degree of individuation and individualism in social bonds, which is itself only the product of history (Marx [1857–58] 1973). But these fanciful reconstructions of the hypothetical beginnings of human history need to be untangled from Locke's philosophical argument concerning consent and political legitimacy. The validity of the latter does not stand or fall with the validity of the former. This conflation of validity and genesis is a mistake that strong contextualists as well postmodernists frequently make.

My goal so far has been to clear up the philosophical underbrush, that is, those epistemological and methodological assumptions that have dominated philosophical debates about universalism/relativism. Contemporary debates about "multiculturalism and the politics of recognition," to use Charles Taylor's felicitous phrase (1995, 25–75), begin from the epistemological vantage point that cross-cultural dialogue and coexistence are real, unavoidable, and necessary. The confrontation between various currents of Islamic thought and the varieties of the Western tradition, to name but one case, is no longer merely a "notional confrontation," in Bernard Williams's sense. It is carried out every day in a variety of forms in a myriad of countries: from debates about Koran schools in postunification Germany; to struggles about the rights of young Muslim women in the Pakistani community of Bradford, England, to refuse arranged marriages; to the desire of girls of Islamic faith to wear the scarf (*foulard*) in French public schools and to not be required to participate in coeducational physical education classes. The clash of cultures, and since September 11, 2001, the violent confrontation in the name of different civilizations, is right here in our cities, parliaments, marketplaces, and public spheres. "Complex cultural dialogue" is not only a sociological reality, but also an epistemological vantage point with methodological implications for social science and moral inquiry. What consequences does such a viewpoint have for current multiculturalism debates?

The following three chapters refocus the analysis away from epistemology and toward the politics of multiculturalism, while continuing to explore the links between them. I begin with an analysis of the much noted paradigm change in contemporary political theory from *redistribution* to *recognition*, and consider three contemporary theories of cultural recognition, namely, those of Charles Taylor, Will Kymlicka, and Nancy Fraser. After probing the persistence of certain problematic assumptions concerning culture in Taylor's and Kymlicka's contributions, I turn to an analysis of the interdependence of recognition and redistribution, as such policies create and reproduce *corporate group identities*.

THREE

❏ ❏ ❏ ❏

FROM REDISTRIBUTION TO RECOGNITION?
The Paradigm Change of Contemporary Politics

The phrases the "struggles for recognition" and from "redistribution to recognition" are widely used in contemporary debates to mark the novelty and distinctiveness of the new politics of identity/difference (Fraser 1997b). In her book *Justice Interruptus: Critical Reflections on the "Postsocialist" Condition*, Nancy Fraser articulates the purpose behind this phraseology very well.

> The "postsocialist" condition concerns a shift in the grammar of political claims-making. Claims for the recognition of group difference have become increasingly salient in the recent period, at times eclipsing claims for social equality. This phenomenon can be observed at two levels. Empirically, of course, we have seen the rise of "identity politics," the decentering of class, and, until very recently, the corresponding decline of social democracy. More deeply, however, we are witnessing an apparent shift in the political imaginary, especially in the way in which justice is imagined. . . The result is a decoupling of cultural politics from social politics and the relative eclipse of the latter by the former. (Fraser 1997b, 2)

The phrase "the politics of recognition" was first introduced into the debate by Charles Taylor in his famous essay "Multiculturalism and the Politics of Recognition" (1992; see also 1994). Reflecting on the array of contemporary movements, Taylor argued that they aimed at the recognition of specific identity claims: "Our identity is partly shaped by recognition or its absence, often by the misrecognition of others, and so a person or a group of people can suffer real damage, real distortion, if the people or the society around them mirror back to them a confining or demeaning or contemptible picture of themselves" (1992, 25). Extracting the term *recognition* from the famous episode of the struggle between two self-consciousnesses, as presented in Hegel's *Phenomenology of Spirit* ([1807] 1977, chap. 4), Taylor gave the term an unusual currency. The concept of 'recognition,' first used in the philosophy of German Idealism to reflect upon the intersubjective formation of individual identities through confrontation and interaction with the other(s) (see Honneth 1996), now became the master concept for reflection upon what appeared at first sight to be a disparate array of sociocultural movements and struggles. These ranged from contemporary women's movements to movements for linguistic autonomy, from "subaltern" cultural struggles to full-scale nationalist contestations.

As is often the case with felicitous synthetic terms (*postmodernism* is another example), initial usefulness in illuminating a confusing landscape is soon accompanied by obscurities caused by imprecise differentiations. The more these terms cover, the less they seem to clarify. So it is with the term *recognition*. Do all these social and political movements really aim at *recognition*? By whom or how is recognition to be granted, indicated, or distributed? Are the "politics of recognition" adequate to capture the "postsocialist condition"? What is the relationship between multiculturalism and the politics of recognition?

This chapter begins with an examination of Charles Taylor's intervention. I argue that there is a risky conflation in his well-known essay between ontology and advocacy. I then examine Will Kymlicka's theory of multicultural rights and conclude with observations on the interdependence of recognition and redistribution claims in contemporary politics.

TAYLOR AND THE AMBIGUITIES OF
THE POLITICS OF RECOGNITION

Charles Taylor's influential essay "The Politics of Recognition" weaves together themes central to his philosophy: the development of an intersubjective conception of identity based on a dialogical model of "webs of interlocution," and his reconstruction of the philosophy of modern subjectivity in the light of demands for equal dignity and authenticity.

The thesis that social practices of recognition are crucial to the formation or malformation of the self is shared by a number of contemporary authors, most notably Axel Honneth (1996) and Jessica Benjamin (1988). Along with Taylor, Honneth and Benjamin have contributed to our understanding of moral and psychological processes through which one's sense of self-confidence, self-respect and self-worth develop. I certainly subscribe to this thesis of the intersubjective constitution of the self through dialogic moral practices. What is less clear to me is its implications for politics, and in particular the implications that assumptions at the level of ontology or moral psychology may or may not have for contemporary politics of identity/difference.

From one perspective, there is a clear analogy between distorted processes of recognition, which inflict wounds on the development of the self, and processes of collective oppression or marginalization, which damage a group's sense of collective worth. The lack of recognition by significant others can damage all three aspects of moral and psychological well-being singled out by Honneth: namely, self-confidence, self-respect, and self-esteem (see 1996). Collective practices can result in individual injuries: Through the denigration of one's collective identity in the public sphere, individuals in a group may lose self-confidence and internalize hateful images of themselves. Known forms of collective *self-hatred*, particularly among members of outcast and "feared" minorities, like homosexuals, Jews at one time in history, and Gypsies still today, come to mind here.

The withholding of equal rights of participation and self-governance from minority groups may also destroy their sense of *self-respect*, and, through the marginalization and silencing of certain experiences, a group's sense of *self-esteem* may be shattered. While the experience of African Americans prior to the Civil Rights movement is a clear example of self-respect damaged by practices of racist discrimination and exclusion, the experience of many immigrant groups—take the case of Muslim minorities in contemporary Europe—can be seen as a poignant example of shattered self-esteem that results from others' hostile reactions. Despite this plausible analogy between the individual and collective significations of *recognition*, however, the term permits an all too easy slide between different levels of analysis and evaluation. Just as oppressed minorities may have the individual and collective resources to bear with pride and fortitude the wounds and the indignities inflicted upon them, individual claims to authentic self-expression need not run in tandem with collective aspirations to cultural recognition. They may even contradict one another. Taylor's theses rest on the ambiguities of recognition, as this term slides between individual and collective spheres (see Markell 1999).

According to Taylor's reconstruction of the development of modern European subjectivity, the rise of modernity brings first a shift from the aristocratic code of *honor* to the bourgeois notion of *dignity*. The politics of universalism and of equal dignity emerge with this shift. Taylor further claims that "the second change, the development of the modern notion of identity," gives rise to a politics of difference (1992, 38–39). He characterizes this second shift as follows: "The politics of difference grows organically out of the politics of dignity through one of those shifts with which we are long familiar, where a new understanding of the human social condition imparts a radically new meaning to an old principle" (39).

What exactly is the link between the politics of collective difference and the recognition of one's individual, unique identity? Why should an individual's search for authenticity, for the expression of one's unique identity, take the form of a search for collective self-expression?[1] Think of the competing claims that different collectivities, clamoring for the recognition of their group identities, can make upon the individual. For example, the goals of nationalist movements very often conflict with the goals of women's movements. From the antiwar activities of many women during World War I to the conflict between feminists and nationalists during many wars of liberation, to name but two cases, tensions have existed and will continue to exist between various collectivities. Why should the individual's search for an authentic selfhood be subordinated to the struggles of any of these collectivities, unless we have some ontological or hierarchical ordering of the groups to which the individual belongs, so that one group, more than other groups, can be said to portray a more authentic expression of one's individuality? Surely this is an extremely illiberal conclusion that would subordinate the individual's search for authentic identity to the self-assertion of particular groups. It is not a conclusion that Taylor would endorse, yet can he avoid it?

It is both theoretically wrong and politically dangerous to conflate the individual's search for the expression of his/her unique identity with politics of identity/difference. The theoretical mistake comes from the homology drawn between individual and collective claims, a homology facilitated by the ambiguities of the term *recognition*. Politically such a move is dangerous because it subordinates moral autonomy to movements of collective identity; I would argue that the right of the modern self to authentic self-expression derives from the moral right of the modern self to the autonomous pursuit of the good life, and not vice versa (cf Cooke 1997).

Surely Taylor believes that autonomy and authenticity are not competing but complementary normative principles; he holds that "everyone should be recognized for his or her unique identity." The right to equal dignity—autonomy—undergirds the right to authenticity. But if so, Taylor must also admit the possibility that collective movements for the assertion of group rights may conflict with individual claims to autonomy, necessitating a certain ordering of one's principles. Let me give an illustration from the Canadian experience: In recent debates about the rights of First Nations in Canada, a problem vexing to many women's groups has been that while some First Nations recognize the right of the males of the tribe to outmarry and to transfer citizenship rights to their spouses, the same does not hold for the women who outmarry. These practices were established by the Indian Act of 1876. "Indian ethnic belongingness could only be legally established through the male line of descendance. As a result, Indian women suffered from discrimination on the basis of their sex and marital status. Indian women, in contrast to men, could lose their legal status as Indians upon marriage to a non-Indian man, including their offspring. Status Indians, who were automatically band members, enjoyed certain exclusive rights such as the right to live on a reserve, to participate in band politics, and to receive free education and health care assistance" (Krosenbrink-Gelissen 1993, 220).

This asymmetry in the inheritance of citizenship rights contradicts the Canadian Charter of Rights and Freedoms of 1982, which grants women equal civil and political status with men. Section 15 of the Charter states: "Every individual is equal before and under the law and has the right to the equal protection and equal benefit of the law without discrimination and, in particular, without discrimination based on race, national or ethnic origin, colour, religion, sex, age or mental or physical disability."[2] Faced with the claims of First Nations, and in particular of their male leaders, to preserve their authentic customs, and the demands by women of First Nations for full equal civil and political rights, what would be Charles Taylor's position? [3]

"A society with strong collective goals can be liberal, on this view," writes Taylor, "provided it is also capable of respecting diversity, especially when dealing with those who do not share its common goals; and provided it can offer adequate safeguards for fundamental rights" (1992, 59). Historically, the pursuit of strong "collective goals," commonly referred to as nationalism, has usually come at great cost to sexual, cultural, or ethnic minorities. Taylor subscribes to the fundamentals of political liberalism in that he takes "an invariant defense of certain rights" like habeas corpus as a basis (61). However, he also suggests that "there is a broad range of immunities and presumptions of uniform treatment" that can be weighed against the importance of cultural survival, and one will sometimes opt in favor of the latter as opposed to the former. To distinguish constitutional essentials from other midrange immunities that would accrue to individuals insofar as they are members of certain groups strikes me as a plausible solution to some of the dilemmas of contemporary politics of recognition. This does not free us from having to order our principles in such a way that in situations of conflict, the principles and the facts can be brought into some kind of "moral reflective equilibrium." For this to be accomplished, a clearer differentiation between the claims of autonomy and those of authenticity is needed.

In the introduction to this work I discussed the influence of the Herderian ideal of culture upon contemporary understandings of this term. In particular, I called attention to Herder's view of culture as the unique expression of a people's individuality. Language, for Herder as well as for Charles Taylor, is the paradigmatic cultural achievement of humanity (see Taylor 1985, 230–34). Through language a world is constituted; languages are the primary filter through which we experience the world as "our" world. All natural languages are thus informed by a unique worldview; it is through language that a people expresses its "genius," its historical memory and sense of future identity. "Language," writes Taylor, "does not only serve to *depict* ourselves and the world, it also helps *constitute* our lives" (1985, 10).

Taylor has been one of the principal exponents of this Herderian vision of language in Anglo-American philosophy (see 1985 and 1995). His positive appreciation of the contemporary politics of recognition is based upon an understanding of culture in analogy with language. He views culture, like language, as a world-constituting set of discursive practices through immersion in which the self becomes who it is. Insofar as these discursive practices are essential to our sense of selfhood, claims Taylor, movements that seek their preservation and enhancement are worthy of our support.

In *Sources of the Self*, which is the most comprehensive philosophical work through which Taylor develops his theory of modern subjectivity, he uses the concept of a "web of interlocution" to describe this relationship between self and language. "I am a self only in relation to certain interlocutors: in one way in relation to those conversation partners which are essential to my achieving self-definition; in another in relation to those who are now crucial to my continuing grasp of languages of self-understanding—and, of course, these classes may overlap. A self exists only within what I call 'webs of interlocution'" (1989, 36).

Suppose one agrees with Taylor, as I do, that human identities can be formed only through webs of interlocution, that we become who we are not solely but in a crucial sense through our immersion in various communities of language and socialization. What follows from this claim about the linguistic constitution of human identity—which is ultimately a claim at the level of ontology—for the politics of difference? From the general principle that all human identities are linguistically constituted, no arguments can be derived about *which* webs of interlocution should be normatively privileged, and under *which* circumstances and *by whom*. All we can say is that every human person is dependent for his or her successful and intact socialization upon certain communities of discourse, and certain "webs of interlocution." The task of the state would be to preserve in general those social practices and institutions that aid in the most equitable and integral development of the human person. From this most general principle of the state's obligation to its citizens, and without the addition of further normative assumptions, nothing follows about *which* collective life-forms should be privileged over others. In other words, the individual can be seen to have a "right"—that is, a morally justifiable claim of some sort—to the recognition by others of structures of interlocution within which he or she articulates her identity, only if it is also accepted that each individual is equally worthy of equal treatment and respect. The claim to the recognition of individuality must be undergirded by the moral premise that such individuality is equally worthy of respect in the pursuit of its own self-realization; otherwise, the aspiration on the part of the self toward self-realization and the pursuit of authenticity cannot generate reciprocal moral claims upon others to respect such aspirations.

At this point, we see the true idealism of this picture. This world is without conflict and contention; self-actualization claims seem to presuppose a seamless web of interlocution through which individuals are held together. In a world without conflict, questions of justice, which are always also about the allocation of certain goods and entitlements to certain individuals, are held at bay. What if the search for recognition on the part of some creates conflict with others who claim that some individuals are neither worthy of recognition nor that such recognition should entitle them to certain resources? How does the *politics of authenticity* allow us to arbitrate or adjudicate between such conflicts? Whose recognition and redistribution struggles are more worthy of our support, and on what grounds?

The *politics of equal dignity* resurfaces in struggles for recognition; in fact, it is only the presumption of each individual's *equal claim* to develop the conditions of his or her selfhood within certain webs of interlocution that gives the politics of the recognition its normative bite. Claims to authenticity presuppose claims to justice; or the pursuit of collective difference presupposes a framework sustained by the premises of individual equality. Yet if this is so, then conflicts between individuals and movements searching for recognition are inevitable, and in dealing with such conflicts a certain ordering of our principles becomes necessary.

Taylor is careful on this score: just as each individual's claim to the recognition of his or her individuality cannot provide us with a normative obligation to respect this claim without also assuming (on the basis of some other moral principle or good) that individuals are *equally worthy of such moral respect*, so too there is no prima facie injunction to respect all cultures. Therefore, cultures have only a "presumption" of equality (1992, 66). But then some cultures can be "inferior" to others in the degree of respect for equal dignity as well as individuality they can grant their members; thus intercultural as well intracultural evaluations and hard choices are inevitable.

Let me note that I am altogether uncomfortable with the language of the "superiority" and "inferiority" of cultures, for I do not think that it is coherent to judge cultures as wholes. Precisely because I see the idea of a "culture as a whole" as an analytical error—what was American culture in the sixties? what was the culture of the Renaissance?—it makes no sense to pass such value judgments on the totality of a culture. At any one point in time, we can certainly observe, analyze, and isolate certain practices as central to a certain culture, and these we can certainly judge to be just or unjust, hierarchical or egalitarian, solidaristic or selfish. We can isolate and analyze certain forms of viewing and evaluating the world, and these too we can judge to be rational or irrational, reflexive or dogmatic, tolerant or closed. But it is an analytical error— the logical mistake of the *pars pro toto*, "substituting the part for the whole"—to want to judge cultures as wholes. We are then back to the question of how to delineate carefully and sift through cultural practices and systems of belief. Because "cultures have propositional content" (Barry 2001, 270)—and because propositions express beliefs with truth as well as validity claims about certain aspects of the external, the intersubjective, and the subjective world—the "presumption of equality of cultures" can only be established after examining such cultural beliefs and practices with respect to the propositional content of their truth and validity claims. Intercultural dialogue, understanding, and disagreement concern evaluations of such specific assertions and practices.[4] Holistic statements about the presumptive equality of cultures as wholes are no less misguided than statements about their worthlessness. Defenders as well detractors of cultural recognition claims still commit this holistic fallacy.

All movements that struggle for recognition exhibit complex cultural patterns; the fact that such struggles may be just as fundamental to the development of modern selfhood as struggles for equal dignity are and have been provides us with no criteria of judgment and evaluation in the event of conflict and contestation between these goals and struggles. We still face the burdens of judgment and cultural evaluation.

To sharpen the contrasts between the politics of equal dignity and the politics of authenticity, let me turn to Will Kymlicka's influential theory of what he has referred to as "cultural rights" (1995), "group-differentiated citizens' rights" (1996), or "minority rights" (1997). Kymlicka's endorsement of the politics of recognition is not Hegelian; he has one of the most compelling cases for group-differentiated citizenship rights, articulated within the framework of a liberal moral and political theory (1995, 1996, and 1997). In considering Kymlicka's position, I will restrict myself to his understanding of culture. As in my discussion of Taylor, I am both questioning the philosophical assumptions about culture in Kymlicka's work and prodding the ordering of justice and cultural recognition claims.

KYMLICKA AND THE RIGHT TO CULTURE

In a number of influential publications, Kymlicka has argued that the basic principles of liberalism are those of individual freedom, and that "liberals can only endorse minority rights in so far as they are consistent with respect for the freedom and autonomy of individuals" (1995, 75; 2001). He attempts to soften clashes that may occur between liberal principles of freedom and cultural groups' practices by distinguishing between "internal restrictions" and "external protections" (35). While internal restrictions refer to the claims of a group against its own members, external protections are those directed by members of a group against the larger society. Kymlicka plausibly concludes that "liberals can and should endorse certain external protections, where they promote fairness between groups, but should reject internal restrictions which limit the right of group members to question and revise traditional authorities and practices " (37). Thus, the kinship and marriage regulations of Canadian First Nations, which differentiate along gender lines, would be unacceptable from Kymlicka's standpoint. I agree with this conclusion, and above all I agree with his premise that the maximum freedom and autonomy of the individual, compatible with the like freedom for others, is the premise of political liberalism.

Nonetheless, I think that Kymlicka's understanding of culture, as well as his privileging of certain forms of collective identity over other possible identity markers—let us say gender or sexual preference—force him into an illegitimate reification of "national" and "ethno-cultural" identities over other forms. His concept of culture and his liberal defense of external freedoms over internal restrictions are in much deeper conflict than he acknowledges.

Kymlicka proposes to focus on what he calls a "societal culture." This is a culture "which provides its members with meaningful ways of life across the full range of human activities, including social, educational, religious, recreational, and economic life, encompassing both public and private spheres. These cultures tend to be territorially concentrated, and based on a shared language" (76). But there are no such "societal cultures." Kymlicka has conflated institutionalized forms of collective public identities with the concept of culture. There are British, French, and Algerian nations and societies that are organized as states; but there are no British, French, or Algerian "societal cultures" in Kymlicka's sense. Any complex human society, at any point in time, is composed of multiple material and symbolic practices with a history. This history is the sedimented repository of struggles for power, symbolization, and signification—in short, for cultural and political hegemony carried out among groups, classes, and genders. There is never a single culture, one coherent system of beliefs, significations, symbolizations, and practices, that would extend "across the full range of human activities." I am arguing that there cannot be such a single principle of societal culture, and also that at any point in time there are competing collective narratives and significations that range across institutions and form the dialogue of cultures.

Kymlicka's assumption that there can be a single principle "encompassing both public and private spheres" is also false. Social institutions are not only culturally but structurally and organizationally determined. Societal culture, whether in Hong Kong, Tokyo, New York, or London, does not define the working of the international stock market or of the NYSE average. The private practices of individual stockbrokers in informal and everyday social interactions are all culturally determined; but as stock traders they follow the same logic of instrumental-purposive action. I seek a stronger differentiation than Kymlicka allows between social action systems, cultures, and personality structures. His definition of societal cultures is holistic, monochronic, and idealistic in that it confuses social structure with social signification. What are the consequences of this definition of culture for his normative position?

Kymlicka cannot maintain the strong distinction he wishes to draw between national minority rights and the rights of immigrant groups. He wants us "to aim at ensuring that all national groups have the opportunity to maintain themselves as a distinct culture, if they so choose." Immigrants' claims to equal access to a societal culture can be met by enabling them to integrate into the "mainstream cultures." He wants to achieve this "by providing language training and fighting patterns of discrimination and prejudice" (114). Except for special Sabbath and Sunday closing laws and certain dress codes for immigrants, polyethnic cultural rights are to be subordinated to assimilation to mainstream national cultures.

Yet cultures are not homogeneous wholes; they are constituted through the narratives and symbolizations of their members, who articulate these in the course of partaking of complex social and significative practices. Cultural practices rarely reach the level of coherence and clarity that a theorist, as opposed to a practitioner, can tease out of first-level articulations and engagements. Any collective experience, sustained over time, may constitute a culture. Why privilege institutionalized cultures over ones that may be more informal and amorphous, less recognized in public, and perhaps even of origin that is more recent? Kymlicka falls into the trap of culturalist essentialism when he argues, "Given the enormous significance of social institutions in our lives, and in determining our options, *any culture which is not a societal culture will be reduced to ever-increasing marginalization.* The capacity and motivation to form and maintain such a distinct culture is characteristic of 'nations' or 'peoples' (i.e., culturally distinct, geographically concentrated, and institutionally complex societies.) Societal cultures, then, tend to be national cultures" (80, emphasis mine).

Kymlicka makes a distinction between national minorities and ethnic groups. National minorities are defined as "previously self-governing, territorially concentrated cultures" (10). They have been incorporated into a larger state either through conquest or federation. Ethnic groups, by contrast, are "loose associations" of voluntary immigrants. These "immigrant groups are not 'nations', and do not occupy homelands. Their distinctiveness is primarily manifested in their family lives and in voluntary associations, and is not inconsistent with institutional integration" (14). Thus Native Hawaiians and Eskimos, as well as Native Americans, would be national minorities, whereas the Irish, the Italian, the Jews, and so forth, who have come to North America since the nineteenth century would be classified as immigrants. This distinction is at first reading a descriptive and not a normative one. Even at the descriptive level, however, the assumption that ethnic groups form only through immigration, while national minorities are self-governing and territorially concentrated, is hard to sustain. Ethnic groups may be united through a common language. Take the case of the large German-speaking minority in East European, Baltic, and Russian territories. Likewise, a "national minority" may become more and more like an ethnic group through historical developments. Arguably, this is the case for Puerto Ricans in the United States today. Puerto Rico was forcibly incorporated into the United States and retains commonwealth status within it; but through frequent immigration to major cities like New York, Boston, Chicago, and Los Angeles; through intermarriage with Central American and Spanish-speaking communities; through the seasonal migrations induced by the labor market, Puerto Ricans have become one of the largest ethnic and immigrant groups in the United States, and not a "territorially bounded national minority." This condition may explain why votes for an independent Puerto Rico, despite all the efforts of the *independentistas*, produce quite divided and unclear results. In other words, even the distinction between national minorities and ethnic groups is not as easy to sustain as it might first appear, and certainly without a clarification of the *normative principles* involved, it hardly suffices to justify a theory of differential rights (see Carens 2000 for a similar critique).

Kymlicka concedes that many groups fit neither model very well. Guestworkers, refugees, African American slaves, and descendants of colonizing and conquering powers are given as examples. Nevertheless, and despite the fact that the normative justification for it is unclear, this distinction between multinations and ethnocultural groups plays a crucial role in his argument. Is Kymlicka claiming that "voluntary" as opposed to "forced" integration and conquest generate distinct rights for minority and majority cultures? Ethnic groups, particularly immigrants, seem to have fewer claims to cultural rights precisely because, supposedly, they have voluntarily accepted migration and integration into a larger society. National minorities have more substantive entitlements to certain "group-differentiated rights" because they have been "forcibly incorporated" through conquest, war, and even the purchase of territories. This argument is certainly plausible, since the basis of all political legitimacy must be some form of consent of the governed. However, it is no longer the distinctiveness of societal cultures and the differences between their cultures that permit us to make such claims, but rather it is claims about justice, about democratic inclusion and exclusion that justify our disparate treatment of groups. Yet here too caution is necessary. Often the history of annexation, conquest, and incorporation may lie very far back, and such conquered groups may assimilate successfully into the larger society. They may then come to resemble ethnic minorities more than they do separate nations. To insist upon the historical genealogy of their incorporation, particularly if their own historical memory and life conditions do not actively keep this alive, may be tantamount to cultural essentialism. At the other end of the spectrum, successfully integrated minorities at some point may *rediscover* their separate and unique histories, and retrieve a separate path out of what seemed a common journey. Arguably the Québecois in Canada, the Catalan minority in Spain, and the Scots in the United Kingdom may now have embarked on this path. Whereas at one time they were regarded, and most likely regarded themselves, as ethnic groups, now they aspire to the status of distinct nations. The distinction then between multinations and ethnocultural groups is not static but dynamic, and it alone cannot suffice for us to differentiate between the recognition claims and aspirations of distinct human groupings.

There is an additional difficulty with the sharp distinction Kymlicka wishes to draw between national minorities and ethnic groups. Very little attention is paid in Kymlicka's theory to *dynamic constructions of identity*. He tends to use *objectivist* criteria like territorial concentration, the viability of a societal culture, or a shared language in distinguishing national minorities from ethnic groups. His procedure cannot capture fluid transitions that may occur in the status of groups as these shift from one category to another; more significantly, he ignores the fact that the kind of group one views oneself to be a member of may itself emerge and change through the process of political struggle. For example, in contemporary Spain, Catalonia is an independent province enjoying considerable cultural and administrative autonomy in the running of its own affairs. Yet partially through the provocative policies of its Prime Minister Jordi Pujol, who takes Quebec as his model, and partly through the enormous economic significance of Barcelona in the newly developing economies of the European Union, Catalan identity is undergoing a significant political transformation from an ethnic to a quasi-national identity. Catalonia meets Kymlicka's criteria of "territorial concentration, shared language" and provides its members "meaningful ways of life." But these criteria are not very helpful in understanding the dilemmas of contemporary Catalan identity: some want independence up to the point of territorial sovereignty; others want to emulate Québec and attain more rights from the central government; still others want to be members of a united Europe, and thus attain greater regional and linguistic autonomy.

I suppose what Kymlicka's distinction between national minorities and ethnic groups would lead us to say is that if and when a movement for independence from the central Spanish government and for some form of increased autonomy develops in Catalonia, then liberal theorists of multicultural rights ought to support it. I would say, Study their demands and their platform first! How extensive are the rights they guarantee to all residents of their territories, not only to Catalan nationals, but to other Spaniards like Andalusians as well as Valencianos and Basques? Will this new regime be committed to democratic institutions and the fair and equal treatment of all, including minorities or other ethnic groups? What about the immigration and naturalization policies of such a new regime? How will the regime treat its guestworkers? Its women? What will be the foreign policy goals of this new regime? In other words, the distinction between national minority and ethnic group status does very little to determine whether an identity/ difference–driven movement is democratic, liberal, inclusive, and universalist. We have to examine what the political actors are saying about their own goals and, more importantly, how they are acting to realize them before we can lend them our support. This at least should be the position of progressive democratic egalitarians.[5] Kymlicka's own arguments for reconciling liberalism with cultural rights, however, are based on culturalist premises rather than political evaluations of movements and their goals. It is these assumptions that I am criticizing.

I suggested above that I saw a parallelism between some of Kymlicka's arguments and Taylor's illicit move from the right of the individual to pursue an authentic form of life to the claim that groups pursuing politics of identity/difference would accommodate the realization of such individual authenticity. Kymlicka's holism about cultures, like Taylor's concept of groups, is far too unitary and flattens out the contradictions and antagonisms that surround group experiences as well as interpretations of culture.[6] Another, stronger parallelism in their arguments comes from the slide, in Kymlicka's case as well, from ontology to advocacy.

Remember Kymlicka's thesis that reconciles political liberalism with the right of national and ethnonational cultures to maintain themselves? Liberalism rests on the value of individual autonomy, on allowing individuals to make free and informed choices about their lives; "but what enables this sort of autonomy," according to Kymlicka, is the fact that our "societal culture makes various options available to us. Freedom, in the first instance, is the ability to explore and revise the ways of life which are made available by our societal culture" (1997, 75). To ensure freedom and equality among citizens, public institutions and policies should give everyone "equal membership in, and access to, the opportunities made available by the societal culture" (75).

If culture is valuable from the standpoint of political liberalism because it enables a meaningful range of choices in the conduct of our lives and because it forms the parameters within which we form a life plan in the first place, then, objectively, there is no basis for the theorist to privilege national cultures over immigrant ones, or the cultures of religious groups over those of social movements.[7] Suppose we grant that the value of culture for political liberalism is in its being *an enabling condition for individual choice*. To proceed from this premise to the conclusion that only in societal cultures can such a value be realized for the individual is to reify ontology. More precisely, it is transforming a general philosophical argument about the conditions of individual choice and freedom too rapidly into institutional and policy-advocating recommendations. If the right to culture derives from the right of autonomous individuals to have access to a meaningful range of choices in their lives, then no differentiations can be allowed between different cultures' value or worth *except as expressed* through the activities of individuals. It is individuals and groups who determine, through their activities, the value of such cultural allegiances.[8] So the goal of any public policy for the preservation of cultures must be the empowerment of the members of cultural groups to appropriate, enrich, and even subvert the terms of their own cultures as they may decide. Therefore, the right to cultural membership entails the right to say no to the various cultural offers made to one by one's upbringing, one's nation, one's religious or familial community. Members of cultural groups cannot be autonomous if they are unable to participate in cultural reproduction and cultural struggle, including the transformation of some cultural traditions. Against this standard, Kymlicka's understanding of culture is remarkably static and preservationist.

Recent anthropological research discloses the mistaken assumptions underlying Kymlicka's model in which culture, space, and place are fundamentally linked. Akhil Gupta and James Ferguson write, in their introduction to a special issue of *Cultural Anthropology* on space, identity, and the politics of difference (1992), that

> representations of space in the social sciences are remarkably dependent on images of break, rupture, and disjunction. The distinctiveness of societies, nations, and cultures is based upon a seemingly unproblematic division of space, on the fact that they occupy "naturally" discontinuous spaces. . . . It is so taken for granted that each country embodies its own distinctive culture and society that the terms "society" and "culture" are routinely simply appended to the names of nation-states, as when a tourist visits India to understand "Indian culture" and "Indian society." (6–7)

Analytically, space becomes a kind of neutral container for cultural difference, societal practices, and conflicting historical memories. "It is in this way," the authors conclude, "that space functions as a central organizing principle in the social sciences at the same time that it disappears from analytic purview" (7). Despite its many merits, not the least of which is to have brought the whole problem of multicultural rights to the attention of contemporary political theory, Kymlicka's concept of societal culture and his distinction between immigrant groups and national minorities is most guilty of the analytical "disappearance" of the problematic isomorphism of space, place, and culture.

❑ ❑ ❑ ❑

So far I have argued against Charles Taylor's unacknowledged move from the *individual right* to pursue an authentic life to the normative justification of groups searching for *collective self-expression*; against Kymlicka, I have maintained that his concept of culture is sociologically naïve and leads him to introduce certain normative differentiations among cultural groups that, on closer scrutiny, cannot be sustained. Let me clarify here that the argument based on culture is not the only or, from my point of view obviously, the most perspicacious, one that Taylor and Kymlicka use in their reflections on these issues. When reflecting on Canadian politics, Taylor has introduced the concept of "shared" and "divergent" values to analyze some of the dilemmas of Québecois aspirations (1993, 155ff.). Kymlicka's argument includes a "justice" strand concerning democratic equality and inclusion, as well as arguments based on "public culture and historical memory." Nevertheless, particularly in their early interventions in these debates, which unfolded during the early to mid-1990s, the argument from culture had a certain centrality. And this culture-based argument yields illiberal consequences that neither author would like to support: (1) the drawing of too rigid and firm boundaries around cultural identities; (2) the acceptance of the need to "police" these boundaries to regulate internal membership and "authentic" life-forms; (3) the privileging of the continuity and preservation of cultures over time as opposed to their reinvention, reappropriation, and even subversion; and (4) the legitimation of culture-controlling elites through a lack of open confrontation with their cultures' inegalitarian and exclusionary practices.[9]

But is such a culture preservationist policy a necessary component of a politics of recognition? Can there be a politics of recognition that accepts the fluidity, porousness, and essential contestability of all cultures? The case that a politics of recognition need not lead to cultural essentialism or enclavism or both has been made most convincingly by Nancy Fraser.

REDISTRIBUTION AND RECOGNITION: FRASER'S POSITION

In several recent contributions (1997a, 1977c, 2001) and most notably in *Justice Interruptus: Critical Reflections on the "Postsocialist" Condition* (1997b), Nancy Fraser has argued that redistribution and recognition claims and the contemporary struggles driven by them constitute two mutually interconnected but distinct and irreducible *paradigms of justice* (2001, 5). The redistribution paradigm focuses on injustices defined as socioeconomic, such as "exploitation (having the fruits of one's labor appropriated for the benefit of others); economic marginalization (being confined to undesirable or poorly paid work or being denied access to income-generating labor altogether); and deprivation (being denied an adequate material standard of living). The recognition paradigm, in contrast, targets injustices it understands as cultural, which it presumes to be rooted in social patterns of representation, interpretation, and communication" (6). Fraser's aim is to use these two paradigms to explain the dynamics of social struggles in contemporary societies, and in doing so, to accommodate defensible claims for social equality and economic justice as well as for the recognition of difference. Onto this twofold paradigm, Fraser maps four types of collective identity formation: class, gender, "race," and "despised" sexualities. Her argument is that race and gender are bivalent collectivities that cut across the redistribution and recognition spectrum. Thus, being a woman and a member of an oppressed "race" will have consequences for one's standing both in the redistributive scheme and in the recognition scheme. To eliminate gender discrimination as well as racism will require not only a restructuring at the level of socioeconomic relations, but a transformation of schemata of recognition as well. Fraser assumes that class identities will be transformed primarily, though not exclusively, through redistributive struggles, while the status of despised sexualities can be transformed only through cultural or symbolic change.[10]

Fraser's contributions have the merit of giving the concept of *recognition* an empirical as well as analytical content, which had been missing in rather vague references to acknowledgment of the other, self-realization, self-affirmation, and the like. Struggles for recognition can be addressed by changing our cultural patterns of interpretation, communication, and representation. Such changes have distributive consequences, in that the transformation of the cultural status of misrecognized groups can result in the improvement of their lot socioeconomically, in the extension to them of unemployment, retirement, medical, and schooling benefits, and in their inclusion in the democratic public sphere. For Fraser, *recognition politics* cannot be equated with *identity politics*, because recognition claims need not involve only affirmation of a group's cultural or other form of specificity. This leads her to the conclusion that remedies for misrecognition "could involve upwardly revaluing disrespected identities and cultural products of maligned groups; or transforming wholesale social patterns of representation, interpretation, and communication in ways that would change everyone's social identity" (2001, 7).

The analytical distinction between the politics of recognition and identity politics of group affirmation is extremely important. It suggests that we can and should do justice to certain claims for recognition without accepting that the only way to do so is by affirming a group's right to define the content as well as the boundaries of its own identity. Indeed, this may be one form of the politics of recognition, but as I have suggested throughout this chapter, it is an extremely problematical form. Social patterns of representation, interpretation and communication, which oppressed minorities and excluded groups justly criticize, can also be transformed through an acknowledgment of the fluidity of group boundaries, through the telling of stories of the interdependence of the self and the other, of "we" and "them." The politics of recognition, instead of leading to cultural separatism or balkanization, can initiate critical dialogue and reflection in public life about the very identity of the collectivity itself. Through such dialogue and reflection, the inevitable and problematical interdependence of images and conceptions of self and other are brought to light. Narratives of self and other are now rewoven together to take account of new contestations, retellings, and repositionings. The politics of complex cultural dialogue indeed involves the reconstitution of the boundaries of the polity through the recognition of the claims of groups that have been wronged historically and whose very suffering and exclusion has, in some deep sense, been constitutive of the seemingly unitary identity of the "we" who constitutes the polity. [11] Such processes may be named the *reflexive reconstitution of collective identities*, and, in my opinion, they offer a clear alternative to the politics of cultural enclavism, in that they allow democratic dissent, debate, contestation, and challenge to be at the center of practices through which cultures are appropriated. I want to illustrate such processes of identity constitution by focusing briefly on the interdependence of welfare-state policies and the emergence of identity politics. In doing so, I will expand Fraser's framework in a more historical and institutional direction.

INSTITUTIONAL DYNAMICS AND
CORPORATE GROUP IDENTITIES

Analyzing the interdependence of recognition and redistribution claims is clearly one of the crucial issues facing the political sociology and political philosophy of the welfare state. To distribute X (goods, services, entitlements) to Y (persons) always implies recognizing Y to be a certain kind of Gm (group member) in virtue of which Y is entitled to X. In any society, we are entitled to health benefits *by virtue* of being wage earners, senior citizens, welfare mothers, and so forth. As members of one kind of social group, we have an entitlement to certain rights claims and not to others. As citizens, whether through birth, descent, or naturalization, we are entitled to vote; as foreigners and residents, we are not. Redistribution and recognition are analytically distinguishable but in practice these kinds of claims are deeply implicated in each other.

Daniel Bell noted in *The Cultural Contradictions of Capitalism* ([1978]; 1999) that the welfare state, which sought to redress social and economic inequalities among groups by rectifying their differential forms of disadvantage in society, would give rise to a proliferation of group identities by encouraging a revolution of entitlements. An ever-growing number of social groups would be able to show that they were placed in unequal and unfair positions vis-à-vis the job market, education, housing, health care, or employment in professional and scientific institutions. By extending the net of social equality beyond mere income distribution to encompass equality of opportunity in the major sectors of a society like health, education, and housing, the welfare state created a form of public political culture that encouraged the formation of corporate group identities.

I will use the term *corporate identities* to refer to group identities that are officially recognized by the state and its institutions. This usage departs from legal parlance, for in the eyes of the law not only groups, but also artificial entities like cities, towns, and financial or industrial corporations have a "corporate identity" (cf. Frug 1980). For my purposes, what is important is the relationship between group identities based on their individual members' experience of language, gender, race, ethnicity, religion, and culture, on the one hand, and forms of group identity recognized by the state and its institutions as legal or quasi-legal collective entities, by virtue of which their members are the granted certain rights and privileges, on the other. It is important to make this distinction because recognition politics very often argues that differences of language, gender, culture, ethnicity, or religion are essential, and that states and their institutions should give these essential differences public recognition by allocating to them public resources and by deeming them officially established corporate identity forms.

In order to analyze the interdependence of redistribution and recognition struggles in the case of social movements it is crucial, therefore, to look at the historical and institutional legacies of different capitalist welfare-state democracies. The American welfare state, unlike its European counterparts, is unique in that it has both typical redistributionist policies in the areas of social security, unemployment compensation, retirement, medical, and housing benefits, and policies dedicated to completing the Civil Rights movement's agenda of racial, gender, and ethnic equality. In the United States, social security benefits and unemployment compensation are rights and entitlements that are *universalistic*, in that they accrue to individuals irrespective of their gender, racial, ethnic, and cultural characteristics, and in virtue of their status as wage earners alone. Other rights like housing and educational subsidies of various kinds are usually more particularistic in their scope, in that they recognize certain forms of difference either to constitute a *legitimate basis for entitlement* to these benefits, or in that they select certain identity markers and privilege them in the *administrative distribution* of these entitlements. Nathan Glazer has noted that in the process of implementing the Civil Rights Act of 1964, big administrative units like hospitals and governmental agencies created certain "protected groups" to check their compliance with it. The Act itself, however, had left the category of "protected" groups, except for African Americans, unspecified; the category of Hispanics was introduced by various public and private bureaucracies for the purposes of self-monitoring (1997, 125ff.).

In *Postethnic America*, David Hollinger discusses the pentagon of multiethnic groups that were officially recognized by the American census until the 2000 count. Originally these groups were (1) African Americans, (2) Americans of Asian origin and from the Pacific Islands, (3) Native Americans, (4) Eskimos and residents of Alaska, and (5) all others. What was the basis for the separation of the population into such distinct groupings? Historically, the U.S. census was principally interested in the black/white divide, to the point that, following the "one drop of blood" rule, individuals of African American descent were carefully typed as "quadroon," "mulatto," and the like (Edmonston 1996, 5). The rest of the population, commonly referred to as "those of white stock," were then sorted into Scots, Germans, Irishmen, Italians, Englishmen, Jews, Poles, etc. Clearly, the black/white divide has always been carefully tracked and monitored in the United States. The "one drop of blood" rule, which dictated that a person who had even one black ancestor among eight would be carefully classified as being "other than white," reflects this deep legacy of racism. The reduction of individuals' identities to their genetic makeup and genealogical ancestry flatly contradicts the self-defining and presumably self-owning Lockean individual who is also at the root of much American self-understanding.

The tragic conflict between the ideals of self-definition, on the one hand, and the reduction of individuals to their genealogical stock for the purposes of government classification and administrative management, on the other, is at the heart of the dilemmas of the political culture of the United States. As Hollinger astutely observes: "*What is the authority by which claims about an individual's identity are warranted?* To what extent does this authority reside in the will of the individual? If individual will is not a sufficiently authoritative basis for identity, who has the authority to ascribe identity to an individual, and what is the theoretical foundation for that authority? And on the basis of what considerations do these "ascribers" select, even to their own satisfaction, one identity rather than another to assign to a given individual?" (1999, 122, emphasis in original). Hollinger's answer is that most parties to this debate cling to the doctrine that "identity is singular, that color and culture go together, and that one can't really choose one's culture because, after all, one's culture is indissolubly bound up with one's color" (122).

Debates ranging over the classification of census groups in the contemporary United States not only exemplify this tension between the ideals of self-definition versus ascribed identities among the population, but they also illustrate the political and social processes of corporate group formation. The number of children from mixed-race families grew from 500,000 in 1970 to 2 million in 1990 and to 6.8 million, or 2.4 percent of the population, according to the results of the 2000 census.[12] Individuals from a mixed-race background want a census category that registers these mixtures—be it among African Americans, Asian Americans, Hispanic Americans, or whites. Opponents of this classification and, primarily among them, major civil rights organizations like the NAACP (National Association for the Advancement of Colored People) argue that the introduction of this new category into the census will have the effect of only reducing the numbers of African Americans, and effectively result in the diminution of entitlements specific to this group, ranging from affirmative action advantages to the reduction in number of black congressional districts. Surely, given the dual legacy of the American welfare state, which was built around an end to racial segregation and discrimination, *and* the extension of the benefits of the Great Society to African Americans via specific education, housing, and employment programs, these concerns should not be underestimated. But neither can one neglect the irony that just as many Americans want to depart from the "one-drop rule," advocates of group solidarity are asking their members to force themselves into the procrustean categories developed by the Census Bureau.

The politics of cultural affirmation, as advocated by Taylor and Kymlicka, would suggest that the claims of major African American organizations be given priority in this context. They represent the voices of those whose claims to recognition have been tragically denied for hundreds of years.

By contrast, the politics of complex cultural dialogue that I am advocating and the politics of recognition that Nancy Fraser is defending would hold that the categories of self- and other-identification in public life should be as complex and as richly textured as social reality itself. Bureaucratic shorthand and administrative reductions of complexity for the sake of retaining group privileges are not acceptable; the census should be based increasingly upon procedures of self-identification, and more so than it is now.[13] At the present time, individuals are indeed asked to identify themselves, but the categories of identification into which they are asked to place themselves are generated by various boards and committees; public feedback is minimal, as is open and free public political debate about these issues. Facing the inevitable arbitrariness of many of these ascribed identity categories, and yet recognizing what a crucial role they play in our public life, may force us to deal more honestly with the fundamental paradoxes at the heart of American identity.[14]

In summarizing the conclusions of a workshop convened by the Committee on National Statistics in February 1994 on the current federal standards for ethnic and racial classification (embodied in Directive 15 of the U.S. Office of Management and Budget), Barry Edmonston and his colleagues note that Directive 15 does not confer legal status on "protected groups," in that "being defined as a separate category is not the same as being recognized as a protected class for civil rights compliance or being an officially designated ethnic group for other than federal statistical and administrative reporting purposes" (1996, 8) Yet they acknowledge that "there is a symbiotic relationship between categories for the tabulation of data and the processes of group consciousness and social recognition, which in turn can be reflected in specific legislation and social policy" (9). What I am pleading for is greater public political reflection and deliberation about these categories that permeate our social lives, and greater transparency on the part of the welfare state and its agencies about how and why they select the corporate group categories that they do.[15]

I would indeed agree with defenders of strong group identities that to redress entrenched social inequalities redistributive programs need to be in place, and that the democratic dialogue about collective identity should not result in the neglect of the needs of the weak, the needy, the downtrodden, and the victims of discrimination. Here again a more universalistic perspective suggests itself: In the allocation of distributive benefits, why not find programs and procedures that foster group solidarity across color, culture, ethnic, and racial lines? Why not universalize the entitlement to certain benefits to all groups in a society? Raising the level of the guaranteed minimum wage would be one such measure: it would undoubtedly affect workers who are members of minority cultural groups—like blacks, Hispanics, and Asian immigrants—perhaps more disproportionately than it would white workers; but since everyone who looks for a job or who becomes unemployed can potentially face a minimum-wage job one day, there would be greater societal solidarity for such a measure than for job programs targeted at specific minority groups only (see McCall 2001). Similar institutional remedies in health care as well as education at all levels can be formulated and discussed. The public conversation would then be about redistribution as well as recognition. Yet the goal would be to redress socioeconomic inequalities among the population at large via measures and policies that reflect intergroup solidarity and cultural hybridity (see Guinier 1998, 1999).

Consider two examples of the politics of corporate identity formation from contemporary Europe in order to appreciate the variations in policy as well as institutional patterns that can exist in dealing with multiculturalist group claims. In *Limits of Citizenship:*

Migrants and Postnational Membership in Europe, Yasemin Soysal introduced the concept of an "incorporation regime" (1994). Every host country possesses certain legal, economic, and policy regulations that define the status of "foreigner." Often, however, the collective status and identity of such groups are simply considered the consequence of cultural traditions and histories these groups are said to have brought with them from their country of origin. The interaction between the home and the host cultures and traditions is thereby ignored.

The incorporation policy of the former Federal Republic of Germany was to integrate guestworkers into the juridical system, not by virtue of their membership in a particular ethnic group, but rather, in the first place, by their status as individual persons and, in the second place, qua workers and employees. Civil and social rights accrued to these individuals in their capacity as workers (*Arbeitnehmer*) and as human persons (the German Constitution entitles all individuals to certain rights insofar as they are simply *Menschen* (human beings). It is this corporate status identity which entitled these individuals to specific sets of rights and benefits. (For further discussions of the German case, see chapter 6 below.)

In the Netherlands, by contrast, the regime of incorporation of foreigners has proceeded quite differently. The National Advisory Council of Ethnic Minorities, which was founded by the Dutch government in 1982, designated Turks, Moroccans, Tunisians, Surinamese, populations of the Netherlands Antilles, Moluccans, as well as Greeks, Spanish, Portugese, and Gypsies as "official minorities" (Van Amersfoort 1982). When an ethnic group attains the status of an official minority, then the claims of such groups to housing, education, employment, and other forms of social support are granted. Such official minority groups then acquire the rights to establish cultural, religious, and educational organizations, and to carry out second-language instruction in their own languages. The Dutch practice a model of "cultural enclavism" and "cultural preservationism" that is very close to the one advocated by Kymlicka.

The readiness of Dutch society to accept such clear group delineations, as much as the resistance of the German one against introducing any collective identity categories into public life at all, are partially, but only partially, explainable in the light of the historical culture of these societies. The Dutch frequently refer to their traditions of tolerance and "pillarization" in explaining their multiculturalist politics. Pillarization, however, refers to the division of society into two faith groups—the Protestants and the Catholics—a third socialist pillar, and a secular liberal pillar. The problematic transposition of a category based on religious and confessional differences onto the sphere of cultural groups and cultural difference is left unchallenged. Is culture like religion? If Dutch society treats cultural groups as confessional unities, what does this imply about its policies vis-á-vis the internal affairs of these groups, especially in those instances when human rights violations may be involved? The model of the separation of church and state would suggest that the state should not interfere in the internal organization or the disciplinary and membership practices of faith-based groups. Suppose, however, that a Moroccan, a Chinese, or a Moluccan father argues that how he disciplines his children, and what kinds of schooling, professional pursuits, and choice of partner he permits to them, is his business. What happens then? How far should the analogy between religion and culture be pushed? Just as there is considerable resistance in German culture, after the experience of National Socialism, to the reintroduction of strong concepts of cultural group identities into public policy and debate, for fear that race and culture may be mixed once more in German history, so too, there is a tendency in Dutch culture to resist acknowledging the heterogeneity of culture and religion, and to want to reduce cultural differences to faith-based ones.

The challenge of the politics of complex cultural dialogue I am advocating would be the following: In a country like Germany, the status of foreign guestworkers and of their children should be considered in light of the separation as well as the interdependence of democratic institutions with cultural traditions, and ethnic identities. Is it possible to conceive of a postnational, reflexively constituted new German identity, which would draw its strength in the new Berlin Republic from a certain kind of civic culture of "constitutional patriotism," which, no matter how problematically, itself has resonances in German culture and history? (Habermas 1996b and 1998).

In the Netherlands, a public debate about these issues was initiated in the spring of 2000 by the journalist Paul Scheffer, who asked whether in fact the Dutch model of multicultural integration was as successful as it was believed to be.[16] A number of indicators, ranging from increasing unemployment among immigrant youth to poor learning conditions in what are significantly referred to as "black school districts," were suggesting that this may not have been the case. Furthermore, under conditions of European unification and the passage of the Schengen and Dublin agreements, the Netherlands found itself having to depart from its liberal and tolerant attitudes toward refugees and asylum seekers (see chap. 6 below). The consequence has been a wide-ranging but inconclusive debate about the changing character of Dutch society and democracy, and, more felicitously, the initiation of two policies that indicate a reconsideration of the strong multicultural enclavist policy course hitherto pursued.

In 1999 the city council of Amsterdam passed a decree encouraging "inter-" as opposed to "intracultural" centers, policies, and groups. Proposals and initiatives involving two or more minority cultural groups would be preferred to those which sought support for one cultural or faith group only. Additionally, the city of Amsterdam now grants city citizenship to all foreign residents and third-country nationals after a period of five years residency. Citizens of Amsterdam can vote as well as stand for and hold office, in citywide elections. Both measures, in my opinion, have the advantage of revising in subtle ways the strong mosaic multiculturalism that had hitherto been Dutch government policy. These new policies encourage the integration of foreigners into Dutch society through more fluid, egalitarian, and democratic means, all the while acknowledging the complexity of the constitution of collective identities in a small country in which close to 5 percent of the population is foreign born. In the city of Amsterdam itself this number approaches over 50 percent.

I have focused on these three examples in order to illustrate the relationship between redistributionist measures and polices adopted by welfare-state democracies, on the one hand, and processes of cultural corporate group formation, on the other. Of course, the public political recognition of certain group titles for the purposes of classification is by no means enough to understand how these categories impact the subjective lives of individuals. There is indeed a symbiotic relationship between objective identity ascriptions by others and one's own understanding of who one is, but never a one-to-one correlation. Objective ascriptions can be adopted or rejected, resisted or celebrated by those to whom they are supposed to apply. Nevertheless, what these examples suggest is that the constitution of collective identities is now subject to bureaucratic and administrative control, direction, and manipulation. It could indeed be argued that it has been so since the beginnings of political modernity, and that the modern state "creates," rather than "finds" the nation of which it is the state. The politics of democratic welfare states, however, both reveal and conceal such processes of identity creation. Whereas a preservationist politics of cultural recognition accepts these categories of collective classification as benchmarks of objective and subjective indicators of identities, I am suggesting that the democratization of collective identities would require us to challenge the hidden logic of many of these categories. The goal would be to move a democratic society toward a model of public life in which narratives of self-identification would be more determinant of one's status in public life than would designators and indices imposed upon one by others. Call this a postnational, egalitarian democratic vision of modernist cultural vistas.

The following chapter will focus on the conflict between multiculturalist claims and the rights of women and children in minority communities. The status of women and children is a litmus test for multiculturalist aspirations and their theoretical defenders, because the tension between a universalizing human-rights perspective and the defense of culturally specific practices, which may deny such a rights perspective, comes to a head around these issues. In the next chapter, I will also develop the outlines of the deliberative democratic approach to multicultural conflicts. The deliberative democratic model views individuals as beings capable of cultural narration and resignification, who through their actions reappropriate and transform their cultural legacies. As opposed to the one-sided effort of much contemporary liberal theory to find a juridical answer to multicultural dilemmas, I emphasize processes of cultural communication, contestation, and resignification occurring within civil society. Legal measures and guidelines surely have a crucial role in framing the limits within which our actions ought to unfold; however, cross-cultural understanding is furthered primarily by processes of understanding and communication within civil society.

FOUR

◻︎   ◻︎   ◻︎   ◻︎

MULTICULTURALISM AND GENDERED CITIZENSHIP

For as long as human societies and cultures have interacted and compared themselves with another, the status of women and children and the rituals of sex, marriage, and death have occupied a special place in intercultural understandings. Plato's discussion of the status of women and children in *The Republic* is one such memorable episode, situated at the very beginnings of the Western philosophical tradition. Socrates in bk. 5 of *The Republic*, exercising his characteristically cagey shyness, introduces the idea that the guardian classes will have their wives and children in common and will be asked to mate according to principles of eugenic selection (Plato 1968, 138). Aware of how deeply he was affronting prevailing views of the Greek household—the *oikos*—among his fellow citizens through his proposals, Socrates, in order to compensate for the loss of special feelings of attachment and loyalty between parents and their offspring that his proposals would generate, then avails himself of the myth that the earth is the mother of all.

Returning to this episode, Aristotle in his *Politics* voiced some of the common sentiments of Athenian citizens with respect to Plato's and Socrates' radical social experimentation. Aristotle objected that Plato had a faulty idea of the kind of unity appropriate to each sphere of human life. Plato, in Aristotle's view, tried to create a family-like unity in the *polis*, while dissolving familial unity for the sake of the impersonal solidarity of those "born from the earth" at the end of a specific mating cycle (Aristotle 1941, 1261a,

10–25). For Aristotle, the fact that the Greeks did not treat their citizen-wives as slaves but distinguished carefully between their status and that of female slaves and concubines, who were usually non-Greek and non-Athenian, was a *point d'honneur.* The limited freedom of the Athenian citizen wife is for Aristotle clearly superior to the condition of female slavery he assumes to be prevalent among the Persians.

This philosophical exchange between Socrates, Plato, and Aristotle is one of the earliest instances of complex multicultural dialogue concerning the status of women and children. Not only such intercultural comparisons but also the "traffic in women"— or the exchange of women through barter and marriage, war and conquest among the males of the human species—have been firm features of most known human societies everywhere. It should thus come as no surprise that the status of the private sphere,[1] broadly conceived to include women and children and the regulation of sex, birth, and death, leads to some of the most bitter and deeply divisive cultural struggles in our own days as well. When distinct cultural groups interact, the rifts of intercultural difference are most deeply felt along the boundaries demarcating the public from the private sphere.

In his comprehensive treatment of the puzzles of multicultural coexistence, Bhikhu Parekh lists twelve practices that most frequently lead to clashes of intercultural evaluation: female circumcision; polygamy; Muslim and Jewish methods of animal slaughter; arranged marriages; marriages within prohibited degrees of relationships; scarring children's cheeks or other parts of the body; Muslim withdrawal of girls from coeducational practices such as sports and swimming lessons; Muslim insistence that girls wear the *hijab,* or headscarf; Sikh insistence on wearing or taking off the traditional turbans; Gypsy and Amish refusal to send their children to public schools either altogether or after a certain age; Hindu requests to be allowed to cremate their deceased; the subordinate status of women and all that entails (2000, 264–65). Of the twelve practices listed by Parekh, seven concern the status of women in distinct cultural communities; two bear on dress codes pertaining to both sexes (the wearing of the turban and the *hijab*); two are about the lines separating private from public jurisdictional authority in the education of children; and one each concerns dietary codes and funeral rites. How can we account for the preponderance of cultural practices concerning the status of women, girls, marriage, and sexuality that lead to intercultural conflict?

The sphere of sexual and reproductive lives is a central focus of most human cultures (Okin 1999, 12–13). The regulation of these functions forms the dividing line between nature and culture: all animal species need to mate and reproduce in order to survive, but the regulation of mating, sexuality, and reproduction in accordance with "kinship patterns" is, as Claude Levi-Strauss argued in *The Elementary Structures of Kinship* (1969), the line that separates *fusis* from *nomos*. Nature does not dictate who should mate with whom; but all known human societies regulate mating for reproductive or nonreproductive purposes and create a symbolic universe of significations in accordance with which kinship patterns are formed and sexual taboos established. Women and their bodies are the symbolic-cultural site upon which human societies inscript their moral order. In virtue of their capacity for sexual reproduction, women mediate between nature and culture, between the animal species to which we all belong and the symbolic order that makes us into cultural beings.

Since Simone de Beauvoir's *Second Sex* (1949), feminist theory has dissected why this function of women as mediators between nature and culture also makes them the object of longing and fear, desire and flight.[2] The passages in and out of human life are usually marked by the presence of the female: always and inevitably in the case of birth; usually, but not necessarily, in the case of death, since male magicians, priests, and shamans can also play a significant role in the death ceremony. The female of the species, who presides over these functions, controls moments of the greatest vulnerability in human life: when we enter life we are helpless as infants, and when we leave it we are all equally helpless in the face of death. Such vulnerability generates emotions of intense ambivalence toward females, who are seen to be gatekeepers of these human passages. Ontogenetically—that is, in the life of the human individual—the private sphere is encountered the earliest, and thus leaves the deepest marks of ambivalence upon the psyche. Because processes in this sphere mark the human psyche during its earliest, formative stages, they also cut closest to core identity issues. Intercultural conflicts, which challenge the symbolic order of these spheres because they delve into the earliest and deepest recesses of the psyche, are likely to generate the most intense emotional response. Thus the loss of one's culture, cultural uprooting, and the mixture of cultures are often presented in sexualized terms: one's culture has been "raped," say primordialists, by the new and foreign customs and habits imposed upon it; cultural intermixture is very often described as mongrelization, or *mestizaje*. The use of these metaphors is not accidental: fundamentalist movements know very well the deep recesses of psychic vulnerability they tap when doing so (Kakar 1990).

These interconnections between psychic identity, the practices of the private sphere, and cultural difference assume a new configuration in modern liberal democracies. These societies demarcate the private from the public along the following lines: the political sphere, together with the economy and certain domains of civil society, is considered "public" in multiple senses: accessible to all; shared by all; and in the interests of all. The household is considered private, in the sense that it strictly regulates access through kinship and marriage, and does not concern itself with the interest of all. In liberal societies, institutional patterns of regulating the private and the public spheres are undergirded by other assumptions as well. Liberalism is based on the conviction that privacy extends to those most deeply held beliefs pertaining to religion, culture, aesthetics, and lifestyle. Liberalism not only respects "the privacy" of the familial-domestic sphere; it also requires that the state not regulate matters of religious, cultural, and aesthetic belief. As Thomas Hobbes put it succinctly many centuries ago, "the liberty of the subjects is the silence of the laws" ([1651] 1996). Of course, matters are never that simple, and the line between the public and the private is always contested. From the standpoint of the liberal state, the family is a public institution in which practices governing marriage and divorce are defined and regulated by political as well as legal norms. The state confers fiscal and economic status upon the family in that it defines the tax status of those who are considered family members; in not recognizing same-sex unions as marriages, the state also upholds a specific conception of the family. Viewed as an institution within the modern state, then, the family has nothing "private" about it. Likewise, the lines separating religion from the state, aesthetics from politics, are always hotly contested.

In this chapter I focus on a number of highly publicized multicultural disputes regarding criminal as well as family law, in the course of which traditional distinctions between the public and the private were contested and resignified. I then revisit the debate in feminist theory initiated by Susan Moller Okin's provocative question, "Is multiculturalism bad for women?" (1999). I argue that this manner of posing the question has led to an unnecessary impasse and polarization, because both opponents and proponents of multiculturalism, despite disclaimers to the contrary, continue to defend a faulty understanding of cultures as unified, holistic, and self-consistent wholes. Therefore cultural processes of resignification and reinterpretation, which women in minority ethnic communities engaged in, are ignored. A deliberative democratic multicultural politics does not confine women and children to their communities of origin against their will, but encourages them to develop their autonomous agency vis-à-vis their ascribed identities.

In chapter 5 I elucidate several political and philosophical approaches toward multiculturalist dilemmas, all of which are attentive to the potential conflict between claims to cultural difference and universalist human-rights norms. I develop the philosophical argument supporting deliberative democracy in this context.

MULTICULTURAL DEFENSE AND CRIMINAL LAW

In June 1996, Doriane Lambelet Coleman, from the Howard University School of Law, published an article in the *Columbia Law Review* called "Individualizing Justice through Multiculturalism: The Liberals' Dilemma" (1996). She drew attention to a series of legal cases involving immigrant defendants in which "the defense presented, and the prosecutor or court accepted, cultural evidence as an excuse for the otherwise criminal conduct of immigrant defendants" (1994). The prevailing assumption in these cases was that the moral culpability of an immigrant defendant should be judged according to his or her own cultural standards.[3] Although no individual state recognizes legally the use of cultural evidence as exonerating, Coleman pointed out that some commentators and judges have called this the strategy of "cultural defense" (1994).

What were some cases in which the "cultural defense" was used as a strategy? In California, a Japanese American mother drowns her two young children and then attempts to kill herself; rescuers save her before she drowns. She later explains that in Japan, her actions would be understood as the time-honored custom of parent-child suicide (oya-ko-shinzu), prompted in this case by the unfaithfulness of her husband. She spends only the year that she is on trial in jail—in other words, she is acquitted.

In New York, a Chinese American woman is bludgeoned to death by her husband. He explains that his actions accord with the Chinese custom of removing the shame brought upon him by an unfaithful wife. He is acquitted of murder charges.

In California, a young Laotian American woman is abducted from her work at Fresno State University and is forced to have intercourse against her will. Her assailant, a Hmong immigrant (one of the boat people who fled Cambodia and Laos in the final stages of the Vietnam War), explains that among his tribe this behavior is accepted as the customary way to choose a bride. He is sentenced to 120 days in jail, and his victim receives $900 in reparations.

The use of the cultural defense strategy in these cases—or what Bonnie Honig playfully calls "My culture made me do it" (1999, 35–41)—subverts some of the basic elements of the antidiscrimination clause of U.S. law in two ways[4]: first, to the extent that the cultural defense strategy is used to excuse some perpetrators from criminal prosecution or to commute others' sentences it results in the disparate treatment of individuals from foreign cultures; second, the acceptance by the courts of different cultural norms, some of which are inherently discriminatory in that they devalue women and children and condone their treatment as morally and politically less valued beings, undermines aspects of the multiculturalist agenda itself. The purpose of introducing the cultural defense into criminal cases is to do justice to the defendant through contextualizing his or her actions in the light of his or her cultural background. Yet in doing justice to the defendant, injustice is done to the victims of this very same culture. The defense assumes that "someone raised in a foreign culture should not be held fully accountable for conduct that violates United States law ... [if that conduct] would be acceptable in his or her native culture" (Spatz 1991 in Coleman 1996, 1101). In support of this assumption, it is argued either that this individual may not have had an opportunity to learn about U.S. customs and laws; or that even if she has, her own customs, values, and laws should be respected. The second claim, of course, opens the floodgates of cultural relativism and, particularly in criminal cases, can lead to the total undermining of the equal protection and antidiscrimination clauses of the U.S. Constitution.

Coleman calls the conundrums generated by the increasing use of the cultural defense in U.S. courts "the liberals' dilemma" (1996). She could just as well have named them "the liberals' nightmare." The attempt on the part of liberal courts to do justice to cultural pluralism and to the varieties of immigrants' cultural experiences has led to the increased vulnerability of the weakest members of these groups—namely, women and children. Children in all cases and women in most cases are denied the full protection of the U.S. laws because their legal identity is defined first and foremost in light of their membership in their communities of origin. In the case of the Laotian American woman from Fresno State University, who was an American citizen, the court disregarded her U.S. citizenship and judged her, according to a cruel primordialist logic, through her membership in the Hmong community, although she had gained U.S. citizenship through birthright or her refugee status. The Hmong community, itself an embattled minority, was mobilized to write "friend of the court" briefs to explain their customs and traditions to an uncomprehending American legal system and media.

Yet what if the young woman who was raped was a symbolic victim in a series of subtle intercultural negotiations? Perhaps the judge who ruled to reduce her assailant's sentence was also thereby acknowledging the wrong that the United States had perpetrated during the Vietnam War upon the people of Laos and Cambodia. Could it be that like Iphegenia—Agammemnon's daughter, who had to be sacrificed to appease the angry gods so they would send winds to the Athenian fleet—the courts, in accepting the custom of "marriage by rape" among the Hmong immigrants, recognized belatedly the integrity of a culture that, only five decades earlier, the U.S. government had sought to destroy? Would it be an exaggeration to see in all these cases an instance of that "traffic in women" through which the males of the dominant and minority cultures signal to each other their recognition and respect for the customs of the other? Where is the space in these situations—the cultural, legal, political, and moral space—for challenging the assumption that all individuals socialized in a culture must act in similar ways and must be intensely motivated by similar values and concerns? Do all Chinese men who have been cuckolded by their wives murder them as the immigrant from New York did? Do all Japanese women who have been jilted by their husbands attempt to murder their children and themselves? The cultural defense strategy imprisons the individual in a cage of univocal cultural interpretations and psychological motivations; individuals' intentions are reduced to cultural stereotypes; moral agency is reduced to cultural puppetry.

Likewise, encounters between diverse cultural practices take the form in these cases of totalizations that eliminate the space for renegotiation, resignification, and cultural boundary shifting. White liberal guilt is pitted against the "crimes of passion" committed by Third World individuals. In all these cases, the judges could have upheld stricter sentencing of the defendant, thus protecting the equal rights of women and children under the Constitution. This would have signaled to the rest of the communities involved that they were confronted with cultural negotiations through which they would need to learn to maintain their cultural integrity without engaging in discrimination against and subordination of their women and children. In upholding the defendants' cultural defenses, the judges confirmed the view of these other cultures as monolithic wholes, impervious to internal change and transformation. It is as if there were no conceivable alternatives to the arrogance of the dominant culture, on the one hand, or a given community's right to retain the most regressive elements of their cultures, on the other. As Coleman concludes, "Indeed, permitting cultural evidence to be dispositive in criminal cases violated both the fundamental principle that society has a right to government protection against crime, and the equal protection doctrine that holds that whatever protections are provided by government must be provided to all equally, without regard to race, gender, or national origin" (1996, 1136).

The increasing influence of the cultural defense argument in U.S. courts is different in one crucial respect from many other legal practices through which multiculturalism is usually institutionalized. In many countries, including India, Israel, Australia, and increasingly in Canada and the United Kingdom (see Shachar 2000), legal pluralism (that is, the acceptance that jurisdiction over certain aspects of human actions and interactions may rest with cultural communities different from and smaller than the national state) takes the form of a *code of personal and family law*, administered by these cultural communities, their courts and judges. Usually, these subordinate cultural communities defer to a common *criminal and civil code*—including the laws governing the economy—and claim jurisdictional autonomy only over marriage and divorce, alimony, child custody, and in some cases, inheritance.[5] The U.S. legal practice of cultural defense concerns *criminal law*, which in most other cases is left to national jurisdiction. However, these other cases over the status of women and children reveal as well the tenuous balance that has been struck between the male elites of the dominant and subordinate cultures, as well as illustrating how issues of gender justice upset the fragile multicultural peace. The much-discussed Shah Bano case is a spectacular illustration of both points (see Das 1994; Nussbaum 1999).

MULTICULTURALISM AND PERSONAL AND FAMILY LAW

A divorced Muslim woman, Shah Bano Begum, filed an application for maintenance under section 125 of the Indian Code of Criminal Procedure against her husband, the advocate Mohammad Ahmad Khan (Das 1994, 27ff.). Married to Ahmad Khan in 1932, Shah Bano was driven out of the matrimonial home in 1975. In April 1978, she filed an application against her husband in the court of the judicial magisrate, Indore, asking for maintenance at the rate of 500 rupees. On November 6, 1978 the apellant (Khan) divorced the respondent (Shah Bano) by an irrevocable *talaq* (divorce), permitted under Muslim personal law. Mohammad Ahmad Khan filed a criminal appeal against Shah Bano Begum and others in the Supreme Court of India in 1985. His claim was that Shah Bano had ceased to be his wife after his second marriage, and that in accordance with Muslim law, he had paid a maintenance allowance for two years prior to the date at which Shah Bano filed her claim, as well as depositing 3,000 rupees by way of a dower (Das 1994, 27). The principal legal dispute centered on whether section 125 of the Code of Criminal Procedure was applicable to Muslims in India.

The judgment of the Indian Supreme Court, which decided that the Code of Criminal Procedure was indeed applicable to Muslims, ordered the appellant to raise his maintenance to Shah Bano from 70 to 130 rupees. But the court's decision went much further than this. Chief Justice Chandrachud commented on the injustice done to women of all religions, on the desirability of evolving a common civil code as envisaged by paragraph 44 of the Indian Federal Constitution, and on the provisions in the Shariat (Muslim religious law) regarding the obligation of a husband to his divorced wife. According to most interpreters, the Supreme Court of India thus opened the floodgates to a series of debates between the Muslim and Indian communities, and within the Muslim community itself—between "progressives" and "fundamentalists," between women's groups and Muslim leaders, and so forth. The political debates, pressures, and counterpressures led to the passage of the Muslim Women (Protection of Rights and Divorce) Bill of 1986. Clearly, the Shah Bano controversy raised issues that went far beyond the case at hand, into the very heart of the practice of legal pluralism, of religious coexistence and tolerance, and of the meaning of Indian national unity and identity. As Upendra Baxi observes:

> The real meaning of the Shah Bano litigation was an attempt to se-
> cure a reversal of two earlier decisions of the Court allowing mainte-
> nance to divorced Muslim wives under section 125 of the Criminal
> Procedure Code. The litigation was devised to reinstate the Shariat.
> And it succeeded in the first round when Justice Fazal Ali explicitly
> referred to a five-judge bench the question whether the earlier deci-
> sions were in consonance with the Shariat Act, 1937, which laid
> down that in all matters of family, including divorce and mainte-
> nance, courts will decide the questions in the light of the Shariat.[6]

The motives of the leaders of the Muslim community who sided with Mohammed Ahmad Khanwere were counterbalanced by those of the Indian Supreme Court justices, who saw this case as an opportunity to reflect upon the unfinished task of the nation in its evolution toward a common civil code, thus ending the auton-omy of the Muslim community in determining personal and family law. Ironically, the codification of the Shariat for the purposes of administering personal law was created through the colonial Brit-ish courts in 1937. The subsumption of Shah Bano's request for in-creased alimony maintenance under the Code of Criminal Pro-cedure followed colonial legacy as well, in that section 125 of the Criminal Code was intended to prevent "vagrancy or at least prevent its consequences," according to the intentions of Sir James Fitzjames Stephen, the architect of the code (Das 1994, 128).

The Muslim community was forced to rework distinctions and modalities of coexistence in view of growing demands for the recognition of women's equality on the one hand and changing family lives and economic patterns on the other. A movement for the passing of the Muslim Women's Bill developed. As passed in 1986, this bill stipulated that a divorced woman was to be supported by relatives, such as brothers and sons, who were in the category of heirs, and when such relatives were unable to support the woman, then it was the responsibility of the community to support her through its *waqf* (obligatory charitable organizations) boards. Clearly, the purpose of even this supposed reform bill was to anchor the dependency of women upon a male-dominated, hierarchical structure, either the natal family or the community board. The possibility of assuring the divorced woman's independence through integrating her into a larger civil society and making her to some extent financially autonomous was totally blocked. As in the case of the young Hmong woman from Fresno State University, here too the dominant legal institutions worked out compromises that imprisoned women in their families and communities of birth. Under pressure from the Muslim community, Shah Bano eventually withdrew her claim and accepted the earlier alimony settlement. Multiculturalist juggling, in this case as well, produced the defeat of women.

In her excellent account of this case, Veena Das raises the crucial question, "How would one resolve conflicts which arise between the desire to preserve culture by a filiative community such as an ethnic or religious minority, and a similar but affiliate community, such as the community of women, which wishes to reinterpret that culture according to a different set of principles?" (1994, 137) Particularly at a time of increased global mobility and integration, when women's issues are being discussed worldwide by many diverse movements, governments, and nongovernmental organizations, legal pluralist institutions that block women's economic, educational, and civil opportunities for the sake of policing community boundaries must be met with skepticism.

The existence of personal laws, administered by each religious group and its courts, is itself a legacy of colonial India. It was Warren Hastings, governor-general of India, who required in his 1772 plan that in regard to the topics of "inheritance, marriage, caste, and other religious usages, or institutions, the laws of the

Koran with respect to the Mahometans, and those of the Shaster with respect to the Gentoos, shall be invariably adhered to" (cited in Mansfield 1993, 145). This commitment was subsequently extended to other groups. But the logic of subsuming practices such as "inheritance, marriage, and caste" under religious usages was itself not challenged. In many cases, religious practice and scripture itself suggested contradictory messages with respect to these issues; in other cases, it failed to regulate them at all. The Shah Bano case could have also occasioned a much deeper discussion about the identification of culture with religion, and of the view that religious traditions sanctified the boundaries to be drawn around the private sphere. Although laws prohibiting discrimination based on the caste system have been altered and brought under the federal jurisdiction of Indian courts, the status of religiously based family law governing the private sphere has been retained. It is this political and religious compromise at the heart of secular, democratic, and multicultural India, which the Shah Bano case exposed to light in all its contradictions.

MULTICULTURALISM, LAICITÉ, AND THE SCARF AFFAIR IN FRANCE

Consider now what has been referred to as *l'affaire foulard*—the scarf affair—in France. Whereas in the cases of "cultural defense" and Shah Bano, we have encountered the liberal-democratic state and its institutions reinscribing women's identities within their natal communities of faith and culture, in the foulard affair we encounter public officials and institutions that supposedly champion women's emancipation from these communities by suppressing the practice of veiling. The state here acts as the champion of women's emancipation from their communities of birth. Yet, as we shall see, some women resisted the state not to affirm their religious and sexual subordination as much as to assert a quasi-personal identity independent of the dominant French culture.

The practice of veiling among Muslim women is a complex institution that exhibits great variety across many Muslim countries. The terms *chador, hijab, niqab,* and *foulard* refer to distinct items of clothing worn by women from different Muslim communities: for example, the chador is essentially Iranian and refers to the long black robe and head scarf worn in a rectangular manner around the face; the niqab is a veil that covers the eyes and the mouth and leaves only the nose exposed; it may or may not be worn in conjunction with the chador. Most Muslim women from Turkey are likely to wear either long overcoats and a foulard (a head scarf) or a *carsaf* (a black garment that most resembles the chador). These items of clothing have a symbolic function within the Muslim community itself: women from different countries signal to one another their ethnic and national origins through their clothing, as well as their distance or proximity to tradition. The brighter the colors of their overcoats and scarves—bright blue, green, beige, lilac, as opposed to brown, gray, navy, and, of course, black—and the more fashionable their cuts and material by Western standards, the more we can assume the distance from Islamic orthodoxy of the women who wear them. Seen from the outside, however, this complex semiotic of dress codes is reduced to one or two items of clothing that then assume the function of crucial symbols of complex negotiations between Muslim religious and cultural identities and Western cultures.

L'affaire foulard refers to a long and drawn-out set of public confrontations that began in France in 1989 with the explusions from their school in Creil (Oise) of three scarf-wearing Muslim girls and continued to the mass exclusion of twenty-three Muslim girls from their schools in November 1996 upon the decision of the Conseil d'Etat.[7] The affair, referred to as a "national drama" (Gaspard and Krosrokhavar 1995, 11) or even a "national trauma" (Brun-Rovet 2000, 2), occurred in the wake of France's celebration of the second centennial of the French Revolution and seemed to question the foundations of the French educational system and its philosophical principle, *laicité*. This concept is difficult to translate in terms like the "separation of Church and State" or even secularization: at its best, it can be understood as the public and manifest neutrality of the state toward all kinds of religious practices, institutionalized through a vigilant removal of sectarian religious symbols, signs, icons, and items of clothing from official public spheres. Yet within the French Republic the balance between respecting the individual's right to freedom of conscience and religion, on the one hand, and maintaining a public sphere devoid of all religious symbolisms, on the other, was so fragile that it took only the actions of a handful of teenagers to expose this fragility. The ensuing debate went far beyond the original dispute and touched upon the self-understanding of French republicanism for the left as well as the right, on the meaning of social and sexual equality, and liberalism versus republicanism versus multiculturalism in French life.

The affair began when on October 19, 1989, Ernest Chenière, headmaster of the college Gabriel-Havez of Creil, forbade three girls—Fatima, Leila, and Samira—to attend classes with their heads covered. Each had appeared in class that morning wearing her scarf, despite a compromise reached between their headmasters and their parents encouraging them to go unscarfed. The three girls had apparently decided to wear the scarf once more upon the advice of Daniel Youssouf Leclerq, the head of an organization called Integrité and the former president of the National Federation of Muslims in France (FNMF). Although hardly noted in the press, the fact that the girls had been in touch with Leclerq indicates that wearing the scarf was a conscious political gesture on their part, a complex act of identification and defiance. In doing so, Fatima, Leila, and Samira on the one hand claimed to exercise their freedom of religion as French citizens; on the other hand they exhibited their Muslim and North African origins in a context that sought to envelop them, as students of the nation, within an egalitarian, secularist ideal of republican citizenship. In the years to come, their followers and supporters forced what the French state wanted to view as a private symbol—an individual item of clothing—into the shared public sphere, thus challenging the boundaries between the public and the private. Ironically, they used the freedom given to them by French society and French political traditions, not the least of which is the availability of free and compulsory public education for all children on French soil, to juxtapose an aspect of their private identity onto the public sphere. In doing so, they problematized the school as well as the home: they no longer treated the school as a neutral space of French acculturation, but openly manifested their cultural and religious differences. They used the symbol of the home in the public sphere, retaining the modesty required of them by Islam in covering their heads; yet at the same time, they left the home to become public actors in a civil public space, in which they defied the state. Those who saw in the girls' actions simply an indication of their oppression were just as blind to the symbolic meaning of their deeds as were those who defended their rights simply on the basis of freedom of religion. Like Antigone in Sophocles' tragedy, who uses obligations to her home and religion to bury and thereby honor her brother Polyneices, who had defied the polis, these young girls used the symbols of the private realm to challenge the ordinances of the public sphere.

The French sociologists Gaspard and Khosrokhavar capture these complex symbolic negotiations as follows:

> [The veil] mirrors in the eyes of the parents and the grandparents the illusions of continuity whereas it is a factor of discontinuity; it makes possible the transition to otherness (modernity), under the pretext of identity (tradition); it creates the sentiment of identity with the society of origin whereas its meaning is inscribed within the dynamic of relations with the receiving society. . . . it is the vehicle of the passage to modernity within a promiscuity which confounds traditional distinctions, of an access to the public sphere which was forbidden to traditional women as a space of action and the constitution of individual autonomy. (1995, 44–45, my translation)

The complexity of the social and cultural negotiations hidden behind the simple act of veiling elicited an equally ambigious and complex decision by the French Conseil d'Etat. On November 4, 1989, the French minister of education, Lionel Jospin, took the matter to the Conseil d'Etat (the French Supreme Court). The Conseil rendered a notoriously ambiguous decision. The minister of education asked three questions, two of which were related to the administrative handling of the answer, which would result from an answer to the first question: "If, in view of the principles of the Constitution and the laws of the Republic and with respect to the totality of rules pertaining to the organization and functioning of the public school, the wearing of signs of belonging to a religious community is or is not compatible with the principle of laïcité" (cited in Brun-Rovet 2000, 28). The court responded by citing France's adherence to constitutional and legislative texts and to international conventions, and invoked from the outset the necessity of doing justice to two principles: that the laïcité and neutrality of the state be retained in the rendering of public services and that the liberty of conscience of the students be respected. All discrimination based upon the religious convictions or beliefs of the students would be inadmissable. The court then concluded that

> the wearing by students, in the schools, of signs whereby they believe to be manifesting their adherence to one religion is itself not incompatible with the principle of laïcité, since it constitutes the exercise of their liberty of expression and manifestation of their religious beliefs; but this liberty does not permit students to exhibit [d'arborer] signs of religious belonging which, by their nature, by the conditions under which they are worn individually or collectively, or by their ostentatious or combative [revendicatif] character, would constitute an act of pressure, provocation, proselytizing or propaganda, threatening to the dignity or liberty of the student or to the other members of the educational community, compromising their health or their security, disturbing the continuation of instructional activities or the educational role of the instructors, in short, [that] would disturb proper order in the establishment or the normal functioning of public service."[8]

This Solomonic judgment attempted to balance the principles of laïcité and freedom of religion and conscience. Yet instead of articulating some clear guidelines, the court left the proper interpretation of the meaning of these signs to the judgment of the school authorities. The decisive factors in curtailing the students' freedom of religion was not the individual students' beliefs about what a religious scarf (or for that matter yarmulke) meant to them, but how the school authorities interpreted the scarf's meaning, and whether or not it could be seen as a means of provocation, confrontation, or remonstration. It is not difficult to see why this judgment encouraged both sides to the conflict to pursue their goals further and led to additional repression through the promulgation on September 10, 1994, of the Bayrou Guidelines, issued by Minister of Education François Bayrou. Lamenting the ambiguities of the judgment of the court for conveying an impression of "weaknesses" vis-à-vis Islamicist movements, the minister declared that students had the right to wear discrete religious symbols, but that the veil was not among them (*Le Monde*, September 12, 1994, 10).

The Bayrou declaration further hardened the fronts of various political actors: intellectuals, teachers' unions, various Islamic organizations, antiimmigrant groups, and the like. The French population was already highly polarized on the issues of Islam, immigration, and national security. In the summer of 1994, a bomb planted by Muslim fundamentalist groups exploded in the metro in Paris; thus it seemed that France, despite herself, was sucked into the vortex of violence coming from fundamentalist Islamic groups, and that its traditions of tolerance and pluralism were misused by these groups to further their own sectarian political goals.

The evolution of SOS-Racisme's attitudes in view of these developments is quite telling. During the Creil episode in 1989, SOS-Racisme—one of the most militant antiracist groups, drawing its membership particularly from among the young—led large sections of the French left into defending laïcité and protesting the exclusion of the Muslim girls. But by 1994, the new president of the association called for a ban on all religious symbols; many had now come to see the recurrence of the wearing of the scarfs not as isolated incidents, but as a provocation on the part of an organized Islam that had to be confronted clearly and unequivocally (Brun-Rovet 2000). L'affair foulard eventually came to stand for all dilemmas of French national identity in the age of globalization and multiculturalism: how to retain French traditions of laïcité, republican equality, and democratic citizenship in view of France's integration into the European Union, on the one hand (see chap. 5 below), and the pressures of multiculturalism generated through the presence of second- and third-generation immigrants from Muslim countries on French soil, on the other hand. Would the practices and institutions of French citizenship be flexible and generous enough to encompass multicultural differences within an ideal of republican equality? Clearly, this affair is by no means over. As European integration and multiculturalist pressures continue, France, just like India and the United States, will have to discover new models of legal, pedagogical, social, and cultural institutions to deal with the dual imperatives of liberal democracies to preserve freedom of religious expression and the principles of secularism.[9]

IS MULTICULTURALISM BAD FOR WOMEN?

These three cases suggest that multicultural institutional arrangements and legal compromises very often work to the detriment of women. Either they imprison them in arcane arrangements of dependency upon their husbands and male relatives—as was the case with Shah Bano—or they render them vulnerable to oppression by withdrawing the legal protection to which they would be entitled were they not considered members of cultural minorities (as in the case of cultural defense arguments in U.S. courts) or they make women and girls objects of state regulation and punishment in order to teach the nation a lesson, as in the case of the scarf affair in France. It should thus come as no surprise that Susan Okin has raised the battle cry that "most cultures are patriarchal, then, and many (though not all) of the cultural minorities that claim group rights are more patriarchal than their surrounding cultures" (1999, 17). When such groups demand special rights, it is to be expected that these rights would function to the detriment of women and imprison them in oppressive and inegalitarian gender structures. Certainly Okin was right in raising these issues, but the tenor with which she criticized cultures for being more or less all patriarchal and, above all, the militant insensitivity she showed in her depiction of many religious practices among Orthodox Jewish and Muslim groups, raised hackles.

Responding to Okin's opening salvo in this debate, Azizah Y. Al-Hibri coined the phrase "Western patriarchal feminism." Al-Hibri argued that while the questions raised by Okin were significant, her discourse reflected "the perspective of the dominant cultural 'I,' a Western point of view burdened with immigrant problems and the human rights conflicts which they engender" (1999, 41).

Indeed, contemporary feminist discourse on these issues is strongly polarized: theorists like Okin and Martha Nussbaum who raise liberal concerns about women's equality and rights in multicultural contexts are accused of Eurocentrism, imperialism, patriarchal feminism, or simply arrogance, ignorance, and insensitivity vis-à-vis other cultures (see Okin 1999). Multicultural theorists of both genders are in turn charged with cultural relativism, moral callousness, the defense of patriarchy, and compromising women's rights in order to preserve the plurality of traditions (Wolfe 2001). The claims of moral and political autonomy contradict the pluralist preservation of multicultural traditions that seem to make no room for such autonomy. As was suggested in my considerations of Taylor and Kymlicka in the preceding chapter, autonomy and cultural pluralism appear irreconcilable. But must this indeed be so? There is little doubt that women's concerns and the status of the private sphere expose the vulnerability of multicultural arrangements and reveal the unjust moral and political compromises, achieved at the expense of women and children, upon which they often rest. But what if both positions rest upon mistaken epistemological assumptions concerning cultures, which I have criticized throughout this book? If we were to adopt the perspective of complex multicultural dialogue I am advocating, might we be able to do justice both to women's aspirations for freedom and equality and to the legitimate plurality of human cultures?

On the basis of the epistemological model of culture developed in the previous chapters, I will defend the creation and expansion of deliberative discursive multicultural spaces in liberal democracies. I will contrast this approach with a defensive liberalism that wants to uphold the private/public distinction by placing multicultural issues on the privacy side of this divide. I will also consider proposals for legal pluralism or "interlocking jurisdictional hierarchies," which have been put forth to weaken the impact of permitting cultural groups alone to define privacy and family law (Shachar 2000, 387–426). I will argue that a legal pluralist model—consistent with the following principles, already outlined in the introduction egalitarian reciprocity, voluntary self-ascription, and freedom of exit and association—can be a good complement to deliberative and discursive democratic multiculturalism.

DEMOCRATIC PRACTICES AND MULTICULTURAL SPACES

Narrativity and narrative disagreement, I have argued, are rooted in the structure of human actions, which are made of deeds and words. Humans identify what they do in that they tell a story, give an account of *what* they do; furthermore, all cultures attribute evaluations to the world around us through a series of contrasts like good and bad, just and unjust, holy and profane. Not only are actions constituted narratively, but we also possess second-order narratives that lead us to qualify and classify what we do in the light of these cultural evaluations.

The view that cultures are unified, harmonious, seamless wholes that speak with one narrative voice is, I have argued, the view of cultures from the outside. By the locution "the outside," I do not mean the standpoint of the stranger and the nonmember. The outsider is the observer, as distinguished from the actor. The outsider who is a "stranger" in the eyes of the group can also be very much an insider, in that he or she may have a full understanding of the complexities and perplexities of the culture to which he or she is denied admittance. The observer is the one who seeks to comprehend and to control, to classify and to represent the culture to the other(s). It is the epistemic interest in power, I want to suggest, that leads to the silencing of dissenting opinions and contradictory perspectives, and yields dominant master narratives of what the cultural tradition is, who is in, and who is out. This epistemic power interest can be exercised by the tribal chief as well as the enemy general, by the anthropologist in search of the truth as well as by the development worker in search of social control.

To the participants and actors, their culture presents itself as a set of competing as well as cohering accounts. In fact, when the accounts of traditions are not contested, it is because they are ossified and have already become meaningless even when they are adhered to. Cultural evaluations can be transmitted across generations only by creative and lively engagement and resignification. A story that is not well told will not be remembered.

Debates around feminism and multiculturalism get quickly polarized, because so little attention is paid to this aspect of cultures as riven by internal contestation. Although she recognizes gender as a cleavage, Okin writes as if cultures are unified structures of meaning in other respects. "Many of the world's traditions and cultures, including those practiced within formerly conquered or colonized nation-states—which certainly encompass most of the peoples of Africa, the Middle East, Latin America, and Asia—are quite distinctively patriarchal" (2000, 14). Okin maps cultures onto nation-states and onto continents. No differentiations are made between cultural traditions, peoples, territories, and political structures. The absurdity of referring to one Middle Eastern or Latin American culture, except as a caricature or simplification, does not figure in this analysis. Whose culture? Which culture? When? Where? And as practiced by whom?

Yet the standpoint of the feminist critic, in this respect, is not all that different from the standpoint of the legislator. The U.S. courts reinscribe women and children in their communities of origin by upholding, against their rights of equal protection, the rights of the defendants to their own culture. The Indian courts are obliged to accept the jurisdictional division of labor between a unified criminal code and separate private and family law for India's Muslim and Hindu communities. The French Conseil d'Etat tries to do justice to the principles of laïcité as well as the freedom of conscience and religion, but delivers the girls with the head scarves to the intensified scrutiny and authority of their school supervisors and disregards the students' own understanding of their actions.

These cases suggest that, in considering the practices of minority cultural communities and the rights of their women and children, we get stuck between the Scylla of criminalizing and policing these communities and the Charybdis of multiculturalist tolerance, and often end up indifferent to their plight. Throughout this discussion, I have been suggesting that these alternatives can be avoided, in theory as well as in practice, by modifying our understandings of culture; rejecting cultural holism, and by having more faith in the capacity of ordinary political actors to renegotiate their own narratives of identity and difference through multicultural encounters in a democratic civil society. The next two chapters will be devoted to outlining this alternative vision.

The cases discussed in this chapter illustrate what Ayelet Shachar has named "the paradox of multicultural vulnerability" (2000, 386). "Well-meaning accommodation policies by the state, aimed at leveling the playing field between minority communities and the wider society," argues Shachar, "may unwittingly allow systematic maltreatment of individuals within the accommodated minority group—an impact, in certain cases, so severe that it nullifies these individuals' rights as citizens" (386). The tension and, in many cases, the moral dilemma between accommodating difference and doing justice to all members of a minority group propels contemporary discussions of multiculturalism into a new phase. Having recognized how inevitably conflictual demands for multicultural accommodation may be within the liberal-democratic state, democratic and multicultural theorists must then address the question of *differentiated citizenship claims* in liberal-democratic societies. I want to distinguish between several normative models that have wrestled with these questions: liberal overlapping consensus; liberal egalitarianism; pluralist interlocking power hierarchies, and the deliberative democracy approach. In the next chapter, I will delineate the contrasts among them in order to highlight the strengths and weaknesses of the various approaches to multiculturalist dilemmas and to spell out my reasons for preferring the deliberative democracy model over others.

FIVE

❑   ❑   ❑   ❑

DELIBERATIVE DEMOCRACY AND MULTICULTURAL DILEMMAS

Democracy, in my view, is best understood as a model for organizing the collective and public exercise of power in the major institutions of a society on the basis of the principle that decisions affecting the well-being of a collectivity can be viewed as the outcome of a procedure of free and reasoned deliberation among individuals considered as moral and political equals. Certainly any definition of essentially contested concepts like democracy, freedom, and justice is never a mere definition. Such is the case with the above definition. My understanding of democracy privileges a deliberative model over other kinds of normative considerations. This is not to imply that economic welfare, institutional efficiency, and cultural stability would not also be relevant in judging the adequacy of a normative understanding of democracy. Economic welfare claims and collective identity needs must be satisfied for democracies to function over time. However, the normative basis of democracy as a form of organizing our collective life is neither the fulfillment of economic welfare nor the realization of a sense of collective identity alone. For just as the attainment of certain levels of economic welfare may be compatible with authoritarian political rule, so too antidemocratic regimes may be more successful than democratic ones in assuring a sense of collective identity.

The basis of legitimacy in democracy is to be traced back to the presumption that the institutions that claim obligatory power do so because their decisions represent standpoint equally in the interests of all. This presumption can be fulfilled only if such decisions are in principle open to appropriate processes of public deliberation by free and equal citizens.

DELIBERATIVE DEMOCRACY AND DISCOURSE ETHICS

In this chapter I explore whether a deliberative model of democracy, based on discourse ethics, can offer compelling answers to the challenges posed by multiculturalist demands. When compared to other contemporary positions, like those of John Rawls and Brian Barry, the strength of the deliberative model consists in its dual-track approach to politics. This dual-track approach on the one hand focuses on established institutions, like the legislature and the judiciary in liberal-democratic societies; on the other hand, the political activities and struggles of social movements, associations, and groups in civil society are brought sharply into focus through the theory of the democratic public sphere. It is in the public sphere, situated within civil society, that multicultural struggles have their place, and that political and moral learning and value transformations occur. My claim is that this emphasis on the resolution of multicultural dilemmas through processes of will- and opinion-formation in civil society is most compatible with three normative conditions: *egalitarian reciprocity, voluntary self-ascription*, and *freedom of exit and association*. I maintain that these norms expand on the principles of universal respect and egalitarian reciprocity central to discourse ethics.

The discourse model of ethics formulates the most *general principles* and *moral intuitions* behind the validity claims of a deliberative model of democracy.[1] The procedural specifics of special argumentation situations called *practical discourses*—equal opportunity for participants to introduce any topic considered relevant to the problematic norm at hand; reflexive questioning of rules for agenda setting—are not automatically transferrable to a macroinstitutional level, nor is it necessary that they be so. The procedural constraints of the discourse model can act as test standards for critically evaluating criteria of membership, rules for agenda-setting, the structuring of public discussions within and among institutions. Practical discourses are not a blueprint for institutions, but they can help evaluate prevailing institutional arrangements.

The basic premise of discourse ethics, states that "only those norms and normative institutional arrangements are valid which can be agreed to by all concerned under special argumentation situations named discourses" (see Habermas [1983] 1990; Benhabib 1992, 29ff.) I call this principle a metanorm in that more specific norms that can be deemed valid will be tested or established through procedures that can meet this criterion. This metanorm in turn presupposes the principles of *universal moral respect* and *egalitarian reciprocity*. Let me clarify that a *norm* is a rule of action, interaction, or organization, while a *principle* is a general moral and political proposition, like Do not inflict unnecessary suffering or Citizens must be treated equally. Principles permit a plurality of normative concretizations; the same principles may be instantiated through different norms and institutions. I define the principles of *universal respect* and *egalitarian reciprocity* as follows. Universal respect requires that we recognize the right of all beings capable of speech and action to be participants in the moral conversation;[2] the principle of egalitarian reciprocity, interpreted within the confines of discourse, ethics, stipulates that within discourses each should have the same right to various speech acts, to initiate new topics, and to ask for justification of the presuppositions of the conversation, and the like.[3] Within a theory of deliberative democracy, these principles can be realized through a range of legal and political arrangements as well as through noninstitutionalized practices and associations in civil society.

The relationship between the metanorm of discourse ethics, the principles of universal respect, egalitarian reciprocity, and the constitutional fundamentals of liberal democracies is not one of inference or deduction. The most general premises from which such constitutions proceed—namely, the guarantee of basic human, civil, and political rights—can be viewed as embodying and contextualizing such norms and principles in historically varying, and sociologically as well as culturally divergent, legal contexts. The general moral philosophies behind constitutional guarantees of basic human, civil, and political rights admit of various normative reconstructions: the Rawlsian theory of political liberalism, based upon a reformulated Kantian conception of the person, and the Habermasian model of deliberative democracy are only two examples of such general reconstructive moral theories. Before I spell out the implications of these normative models for multicultural conflicts and accommodations, let me develop the contrast between "the model of liberal overlapping consensus," as suggested by Rawls's work, and the deliberative democracy approach.

PUBLIC REASON AND LIBERAL OVERLAPPING CONSENSUS

The Rawlsian model of *public reason* and the deliberative model of democracy share certain fundamental premises. Both theories view the legitimation of political power and the examination of the justice of institutions to be a public process, open to all citizens. The idea that the justice of institutions be "in the public's eye," so to speak—to be open to scrutiny, examination, and reflection—is fundamental. There are three significant ways in which the Rawlsian idea of public reason differs from the model of public deliberation proposed above.

First, unlike the deliberative model which insists upon the openness of the agenda of public debate, Rawls's model restricts the exercise of public reason to deliberation about a specific subject matter. These are issues involving "constitutional essentials" and questions of basic justice. Rawls's model of public reason proceeds from a *restricted agenda*.[4]

Second, public reason in Rawls's theory is best viewed not as a *process of reasoning* among citizens, but more as a regulative principle, imposing certain standards upon how individuals, institutions, and agencies *ought to reason about public matters*. The standards for public reason are set by a *political conception of liberalism*.

Third, for Rawls the social spaces within which public reason is exercised are also restricted. The standards of public reason do not apply to personal deliberations nor "to the reasoning about them by members of associations such as churches and universities, all of which [are] a vital part of the background culture" (1993, 215). The reasoning of corporate bodies and associations is "public" with respect to its members "but nonpublic with respect to political society and to citizens generally. Nonpublic reasons comprise the many reasons of civil society and belong to what I have called the 'background culture,' in contrast to the public political culture" (220). The public sphere, for Rawls then, is not located in *civil society*, but in the *state* and *its organizations*, including first and foremost *the legal sphere* and *its institutions*.

The Rawlsian and the deliberative model diverge in three crucial respects: the deliberative model does not restrict the agenda of public conversation: in fact, it encourages discourse about the lines separating the public from the private; second, the deliberative model locates the public sphere in civil society, and is much more oriented to the ways in which political processes and the "background culture" interact; and finally, while the Rawlsian model focuses upon "final and coercive political power," the deliberative model focuses upon noncoercive and nonfinal processes of opinion formation in an unrestricted public sphere.

In order to assess the full implications of the Rawlsian model for multicultural conflicts, it should be kept in view that political liberalism proceeds from a "political" conception of the person. In this theory, individuals are viewed as autonomous creatures, in the sense that publicly—that is, from the standpoint of the major institutions of a liberal society—they are to be treated as capable of (1) forming and pursuing a sense of the good and (2) engaging in reasonable cooperation around principles of justice. As is well known, Rawls shifted from a *moral* to a *political* conception of the person in his *Political Liberalism* (1993) because he regarded the kind of moral autonomy he had advocated in *A Theory of Justice* (1971) as too controversial a premise to serve as the basis of an "overlapping consensus" in a liberal society. In such a society, different groups, associations, and organizations will pursue different conceptions of the good, some of which will clearly contradict the norm of autonomy in their practices as well as organization.

Not only Orthodox Jewish and Muslim groups in a liberal society, but the Catholic Church as well as the Amish could not pass the test of a robust criterion of moral autonomy, since autonomy means that individuals understand themselves in their rational capacities as the source of valid moral claims, and this obviously contradicts the very basis of many such associations. Relations of hierarchical subordination as well as religiously based forms of gender discrimination and differential treatment between persons could not pass the Rawlsian test. Hence, one way of understanding *overlapping consensus* in a multicultural, multifaith, and multiethnic society is to insist that, as long as different groups uphold the autonomy of persons publicly—let us say, for example, that they do not keep their spouses from voting or force them to vote in only certain ways—the fact that in their private practices, these same groups may be oppressing their women by not allowing their grown daughters to go to school, or to freely choose their partners or even their careers, would not be seen as contradicting political liberalism.

In this minimalist version of political liberalism, there would be a sharp separation between the public domain of overlapping agreement and consensus, and the private, and mainly domestic, sphere of cultural and religious differences. Since Rawls distinguishes sharply between the "background culture" and "the public political culture" of a society, a range of issues that pertain to the cultural lives of groups would then be pushed into the private sphere and precluded from public consideration. It may be argued that some model of an overlapping consensus underlies the jurisdictional division of labor between a *common* criminal code and a culturally and religiously *specific* private law as envisaged, for example, by the federal Indian constitution.

This minimalist model of political liberalism, based on an overlapping consensus, has at first blush much to recommend it. The distinction between what is of public concern to all, and must therefore be regulated in the common interest of all through an overlapping consensus, and what is of particular concern only to members of those groups whose identities are shaped by the life of the group in its specificity is certainly crucial for ensuring the vitality of pluralist traditions in the liberal-democratic state. As Rawls writes, "The political culture of a democratic society is always marked by a diversity of opposing and irreconcilable religious, philosophical, and moral doctrines. Some of these are perfectly reasonable.... How is it possible for there to exist over time a just and stable society of free and equal citizens, who remain profoundly divided by reasonable religious, philosophical, and moral doctrines?" (1993, 4).

As the many examples I have considered throughout this book suggest, however, this separation between the background culture and the public political culture, attractive as it may be, is institutionally unstable and analytically untenable. There are several reasons why: first, there are simply too many clashes and conflicts over some of the constitutional essentials to which most liberal democracies subscribe, like gender equality, bodily integrity, freedom of the person, education of children, and the practices of certain minority subcultures and groups. For example, political liberalism could not permit marriage between nonconsenting minors; nor condone the sale of young women by their families for prostitution; nor accept the infliction of irreversible bodily wounds, as is the case with female genital mutilation. Since the constitutional essentials of the liberal-democratic state, embodied in its articulation of basic human, civil, and political rights, in many cases contradict the practices of ethnic and religious minorities, clashes over the interpretation and application of these principles in the light of these practices are inevitable.

Second, different subcultures and groups will put forward competing claims for equal or for differential treatment, and these will need to be arbitrated in some fair and impartial way. For example, the Muslim girls in the school district in Creil were encouraged in their actions by the fact that Jewish students, also in this school district, could wear their yarmulkes to class and in some cases had demanded exemptions from exams on the Sabbath. What justification is there in the liberal state for treating members of one religious group differently from others? In this case, the principle of impartial and fair treatment requires equal treatment for all. In other cases, impartiality may require differential treatment: sensitivity to the needs of the handicapped means, for example, that we equip public buildings like schools, hospitals, and libraries with special access ramps and toilets. In some poor school districts, such costly building renovations can mean cutting back on music classes for talented students. Yet justice requires that those who through no fault of their own are handicapped be treated differently from those whose luck privileged them to have fully abled bodies. A minimal liberalism of an overlapping consensus does not offer guidance as to how consensus can be reestablished in the event of such clashes between constitutional essentials on the one hand and the practices of certain cultural groups on the other. In recognition of these and other dilemmas, Brian Barry has developed a more comprehensive response to multicultural questions based on the premise of *liberalism as fairness*. Barry's work shares many premises with Rawls's, but also departs from political liberalism by facing much more directly the challenges multicultural disputes pose to liberal political principles.

LIBERAL EGALITARIANISM AND MULTICULTURAL JUSTICE

Barry opens his discussion with the following observation: "Hegel said that the Owl of Minerva takes its flight at dusk, and Rawls's theory of justice provides a perfect illustration. Even in 1971, when *A Theory of Justice* was published, there were already (especially in 'new left' and feminist circles) attacks being made on the individualistic nature of liberal citizenship. . . . Since then criticisms of the liberal paradigm have grown in volume and vehemence: it is widely believed to be deeply flawed in principle" (2001, 8). Barry's work attempts to vindicate a liberal-egalitarian conception of justice in the face of multiculturalism. Along the way, a great many rhetorical flourishes are made and a number of ideological enemies slain.[5] Barry's views are important for the deliberative democracy project I defend in this book. First, like him, I reject the "tendency to assume that distinctive cultural attributes are the defining feature of all groups" (305). Group identities should not be culturalized. Second, I agree with Barry that *sometimes* "multiculturalist policies are not in general well designed to advance the values of liberty and equality" (12). Third, for Barry the most compelling reason for introducing group rights is when "a system of group-based rights for those suffering from systematic disadvantage will be a way of helping to meet the liberal egalitarian demand that people should not have fewer resources and opportunities than others when this inequality has arisen out of circumstances that they had no responsibility for bringing about" (13). Barry endorses certain kinds of affirmative action policies and accepts that to ensure equality of opportunity, certain groups need to be targeted with special redistributive measures. Besides "racialized minorities," working-class children and the disabled find his favor. On the whole, Barry defends redistribution over recognition and seems to think that multiculturalism rests either on a mistake or on ill will, or on both. And here is where I part from him. "If not culture, what is the problem and what is the solution? In many cases, there is no problem in the first place, so no solution is called for. . . . The problem is invented out of nothing by multiculturalists, who assume that equal treatment for minorities is merely an arbitrary point on a continuum between specially adverse treatment and specially favorable treatment, with neutrality having nothing in particular to commend it" (317).

So sweeping a dismissal of multicultural considerations is bad sociology. The global emergence of the politics of identity/difference, of which multiculturalism is but a subset, cannot be dismissed as if it reflected merely the inventions and faulty reasoning of elites. Even if the elites were good at inventing phony multicultural theories to justify their grab of power, we would still have to explain why their views find a hearing among large masses of the population. Since I do not subscribe to 1930s theories in which masses are putty in the hands of manipulative (and usually authoritarian) elites, we are back to the question, Why do multicultural demands have the particular resonance that they do at this time?

At various points in this book, I have suggested several reasons: (1) Reverse globalization processes, through which immigrant communities from non-Western parts of the world settle in, and are confronted with the claims of, liberal-democratic states; (2) geopolitical configurations after the end of communism in 1989 in eastern and central Europe and the emergence of nationalism as a force in formerly communist countries (see Brubaker 1996 and Benhabib 1997b); (3) The emergence of the European Union and a new rights regime (see chap. 6 below); (4) The unintended consequences of redistributive politics in capitalist democracies and the rise of protected status identities for cultural groups through such policies (see chap. 3 above); and, finally, (5) changing models of capitalist and sociocultural integration in Western liberal democracies. While agreeing with many of Barry's specific policy recommendations, I find that his dismissal of multiculturalism shows a lack of sociological appreciation for the kinds of changes our societies are facing. In Barry's as in Rawls's theory, there is a certain impatience in analyzing the relationship between liberal political principles and the background culture. This dismissive attitude toward the work of culture in liberal politics and society produces a stunted vision of democracy and of the relationship between legislative action and democratic struggle. The distinctiveness of a theory of deliberative democracy rests on its vision of the interaction between liberal commitments to basic human, civil, and political rights, due processes of law and democratic political struggles in civil society. Let me further develop the distinctive features of this model.

DELIBERATIVE DEMOCRACY
AND MULTICULTURALIST STRUGGLES

In discourse ethics, autonomy is seen as a moral as well as a political principle; this requires that we create public practices, dialogues, and spaces in civil society around controversial normative questions in which all those affected can participate. It is fundamental to autonomy that the collective practices in which we participate may be seen as the outcome of our legitimate processes of deliberation. As opposed to the privileging of legal regulation and adjudication in the political liberalism model, deliberative democracy would expand the moral/political dialogue into the civil public sphere. Deliberative democracy sees the free public sphere of civil society as the principal arena for the articulation, contestation, and resolution of normative discourses.

The deliberative democratic model is a two-track one: it accepts both legal regulation and intervention through direct and indirect state methods in multicultural disputes, and it views normative dialogue and contestation in the civil public sphere as essential for a multicultural democratic polity. There is no presumption that moral and political dialogues will produce normative consensus, yet it is assumed that even when they fail to do so and we must resort to law to redraw the boundaries of coexistence, societies in which such multicultural dialogues take place in the public sphere will articulate a civic point of view and a civic perspective of "enlarged mentality." The process of "giving good reasons in public" will not only determine the legitimacy of the norms followed; it will also enhance the civil virtues of democratic citizenship by cultivating the habits of mind of public reasoning and exchange.

Let me illustrate the way in which this deliberative model may work in some of the cases discussed above—the Shah Bano case and the scarf affair. At first glance, it may seem that discourse ethics would be almost irrelevant in the Shah Bano case, for the norms of moral autonomy and the principles of universal respect and egalitarian reciprocity are clearly contradicted by the hierarchical and inegalitarian practices of many of India's subcommunities—Hindu, Muslim, Buddhist, and others. Egalitarian deliberative models, which would seem to require an almost total transformation of such societies, can then be justly suspected of illiberalism. But discourse ethics does not present itself as a blueprint for changing institutions and practices; it is an idealized model in accordance with which we can measure the fairness and legitimacy of existing practices and aspire to reform them, *if and when* the democratic will of the participants to do so exists. Let us recall that we engage in discursive practices *when* moral and political conflicts occur and *when* everyday normative certainties have lost their governing force. Under such circumstances we enter into discursive practices with all those whose interests would be affected by the norm in question. In the Shah Bano case, the contested norms are not the amount of alimony she was accorded, but rather (1) the practices of unilateral polygamy and divorce, which asymmetrically privilege the male; (2) the expectation that a divorced woman becomes economically dependent upon her male relatives for her livelihood; and (3) the conviction that nothing can be done to enable her to achieve independence. We have to ask ourselves whether these norms could still be upheld in a situation of hypothetical discourse in which all those whose interests were affected participated freely, including, above all, Muslim woman of all ages to whom the norms apply. We would have to ask why women would freely put themselves in conditions of such subordination, vulnerability, and jeopardy. Bracketing fear of retribution, coercion, ostracism, and other punitive sanctions, which we assume would not hold in a discourse situation, the most frequent reason that women themselves give as an answer is that this is their tradition and their way of life. Yet the Shah Bano story illustrates that tradition is in transition, and that traditional mechanisms of fairness and support that may once have cared for women (and children) of the Muslim community are no longer in place: Shah Bano is angry enough at her spouse—an attorney who can manipulate the institutions of Indian courts on his behalf—and intelligent enough herself to resort to an Indian federal court in order to demand an increase in her level of alimony support. Her male kin, either because they are too poor or unwilling to support her, do not prevent her from resorting to the law. There is no mystique to tradition in this case: poverty, power, and naked self-interest combine to produce the humiliation of a woman who attempts to fight for her dignity.

As a result of this affair, the Muslim community found it necessary to reform the Marriage and Divorce Act. Women's groups, government agencies, and international development organizations participated in this process. In addition, the question of women's economic independence was put on the agenda in contemporary India. Was the Muslim community ready to be part of the national dialogue currently underway about women, rural poverty, and various forms of self-help which banks and businesses could offer, and through which the cycle of dependency in women's lives could be broken? (see Nussbaum and Glover 1995). If the leaders of the Muslim community refuse to engage in this national dialogue, how can they publicly defend their position with good reason? It will not do simply to play ostrich when it is clear that the traditional fabric of their community is unraveling at the seams, and new and more equitable ways of stitching together the torn fabric will have to be found.

Take now *l'affaire foulard*: we seem to have a paradoxical situation here in which the French state intervenes to dictate more autonomy and egalitarianism in the public sphere than the girls themselves wearing their head scarves seem to wish for. But what exactly is the meaning of the girls' actions? Is this an act of religious observance and subversion, or one of cultural defiance, or of adolescent acting-out to gain attention and prominence? Are the girls acting out of fear, out of conviction, or out of narcissism? It is not hard to imagine that their actions may involve all these elements and motives. The girls' voices are not heard in this heated debate. Although there was genuine public discourse in the French public sphere and a soul-searching on the questions of democracy and difference in a multicultural society, as Gaspard and Khosrokhavar (1995) point out, the girls' own perspectives were hardly listened to until the sociologists carried out their interviews. Even if the girls involved were not adults and, in the eyes of the law, were still under the tutelage of their families, it is reasonable to assume that at the ages of fifteen and sixteen, they could account for themselves and their actions. Had their voices been listened to and heard, it would have become clear that the meaning of wearing the scarf itself was changing from a religious act to one of cultural defiance and increasing politicization. Ironically, it was the very egalitarian norms of the French public educational system that brought these girls out of the patriarchal structures of the home and into the French public sphere and gave them the confidence and the ability to *resignify the wearing of the scarf*. Instead of penalizing and criminalizing their activities, would it not have been more plausible to ask these girls to account for their actions and doings at least to their school communities, and to encourage discourses among the youth about what it means to be a Muslim citizen in a laic French Republic? Unfortunately, the voices of those whose interests were most vitally affected by the norms prohibiting the wearing of the scarf under certain conditions were silenced.

I am not suggesting anywhere in this discussion that legal norms should originate through discursive processes. The legitimacy of the law is not at stake in this example; rather, it is the democratic legitimacy of a lawful but in my view unwise and unfair decision that is at stake. It would have been both more democratic and fairer had the school authorities not simply dictated the meaning of their act to these girls, and had the girls been given a public say in the interpretation of their own actions. Would or should this have changed the Conseil d'Etat's decision? Maybe not, but the clause that permitted the prohibition of "ostentatiously" and "demonstratively" displayed religious symbols should have been reconsidered. There is sufficient evidence in the sociological literature that in many other parts of the world Muslim women are using the veil as well as the chador to cover up the paradoxes of their own emancipation from tradition (see Gole 1996). To assume that the meaning of their actions is purely one of religious defiance of the secular state constrains these women's capacity to rewrite the meaning of their own actions and, ironically, reimprisons them within the walls of meaning from which they may have been trying to escape.

Learning processes need to take place on the part of the Muslim girls as well. The larger French society needs to learn not to stigmatize and stereotype as "backward and oppressed creatures" all those who wear what appears at first glance to be a religiously mandated piece of clothing; the girls themselves and their supporters, in the Muslim community and elsewhere, must learn to give a justification of their actions with "good reasons in the public sphere." In claiming respect and equal treatment for their religious beliefs, they have to clarify how they intend to treat the beliefs of *others* from different religions, and how, in effect, they would institutionalize the separation of religion and the state within Islamic tradition. The Muslim position is not without its contradictions. Islamic fundamentalist groups have used the loopholes of tolerance in liberal-democratic societies to further their own causes and to increase the politicization of their followers. The Islamist religious parties in Turkey, like the banned Welfare Party (Refah) and its subsequent regroupings such as the Virtue party (Fazilet), have pushed the secular constitution of the country to its utmost limits, not only by infiltrating the Ministries of Justice and the Interior, but by suggesting in open electoral processes that they intend to subvert the constitution. We cannot be naïve about such struggles, nor can we forget that at some point these issues transcend the individual exercise of freedom of conscience and religion, and become collective political contestations about the nature of the state and sovereignty, as they have, for example, in contemporary Turkey and Algeria. My Pascalian wager vis-à-vis such movements is that their democratic integration into the public sphere through electoral as well as other civic practices will force them to clarify the bigger political game at stake in their actions, whereas their marginalization and oppression will only create dangerous martyrs.

Let me emphasize the distinctivenss of the dual-track approach of the deliberative democracy model by turning once more to Brian Barry's liberal egalitarianism. At one point Barry criticizes the work of Iris Young and Nancy Fraser for propagating bad politics as well as bad sociology (2001, 276). It is unclear to me what alternative sociological model Barry has developed to contrast with Iris Young's theory of groups and Nancy Fraser's model of redistribution and recognition. Be that as it may, he is more resistant than necessary to the interdependence of politics and culture. Of particular relevance here is the difference between his approach and those like Young's, Fraser's and mine, which look at broader sociological and cultural processes and movements in evaluating multiculturalism. Barry insists that "Young and her allies have no principled objection to this politicization of culture, because, let us recall, 'no social practices or activities should be excluded as improper subjects for public discussion, expression or collective choice'" (277, quoting Young 1990, 120). I would not endorse Young's claim in its entirety: I do think that *some* practices and activities are not proper subjects for *collective action*; however, I also think that all social practices and activities *may become* proper subjects for *public discussion and expression*.

What are some pertinent examples? An intimate affair between a president and his aide is not a proper domain of *collective action*, if by collective action we mean *legislation*. But even in this domain, the actions of President Clinton were litigated against on the grounds that he perjured himself and lied to the special prosecutor. Barry and I agree that there is a fundamental right to privacy in a liberal society; but it is the laws of this very liberal society that also permit us to contest where the line between private affairs and public matters, between private liaisons and public responsibilities, is to be drawn. Culture *is* political; Barry wants to assume that there is a "baseline" of a nonpolitical culture in a liberal society, whereas feminist critical theorists claim that much of the work of democracy proceeds through the political give-and-take within an already politically suffused culture.

Even in the case of this torrid affair, which left the American public reeling from overexposure to shameless detail, a deliberative democrat searches for those moments of publicly relevant discourse that may have some redemptive value. Through the Bill Clinton and Monica Lewinsky affair we learned something about the asymmetry of power relations in the highest offices of the land. Predominantly male legislative bodies include many men who prey on younger women aides, who themselves may be neither innocent nor unwilling to extend sexual favors. Is this an insight that should result in some form of "collective action"? Maybe and maybe not. It certainly is a topic that is cultural and psychological as well as political, and it is the proper subject matter of public contention and debate. Yes, it means the politicization of culture; it means the politicization of the *culture of sexual mores* and the critique of these mores in the light of perfectly liberal norms of autonomy, fairness, and equal treatment. If we are serious about liberal egalitarianism, we cannot want to shield certain domains of culture from public debate and scrutiny, as Barry seems to want to do.

Public awareness and discussion may lead to some form of collective action; this can happen if a consensus emerges that certain forms of conduct and relationships are actionable under the norms of the liberal state. Legislation against marital rape, domestic violence, child abuse, and sexual harassment in the workplace grew in many countries as responses to the agitation and consciousness-raising activities of women's groups. There is no contradiction between the political and cultural work of social movements—groups and associations in civil society, on the one hand, and the broadening of the agenda of debate in liberal democracies on the other. Very often, it is social movements that, through their oppositional activities on behalf of women and gay people, the disabled and the abused, expand the meaning of equal rights and render what seemed merely private concerns matters of collective concern. The deliberative democratic approach focuses on this vital interaction between the formal institutions of liberal democracies like legislatures, the courts, and the bureaucracy, and the unofficial processes of civil society as articulated through the media and social movements and associations.

One of the standard objections to the dual-track approach of the deliberative democracy model is the argument that this model naïvely presupposes that engagements between different groups in civil society will generate "civil" and mutually agreeable outcomes. In fact, very often the opposite may result: particularly in highly polarized societies, in which different cultural, ethnic, and linguistic groups coexist, it may be better to minimize too many spontaneous encounters between these groups. Certainly, sufficient examples can be given from recent and distant memory in support of this objection. Nonetheless, this objection proves too much: If the hostility between different groups is too intense, the law can control the outbreak of hostilities only up to a certain point. If no true intergroup and intercultural understanding can evolve, and if the spaces for dialogue are limited, then sooner or later these intercommunal tensions will find other outlets. Indeed, as I discuss below, there are certainly instances when the actual separation of the various communities through political secession may be advisable. Between the experiences of multicultural cold war assured through legal control and those hot confrontations leading to secession lie the mostly tepid and also irritating engagements in the lives of ordinary citizens of liberal democracies. It is for them that encounters in civil society will be edifying as well as disturbing.

Among contemporary theorists of multiculturalism, some pluralists argue that certain religious and cultural differences remain irreconcilable and cannot be accommodated under a uniform constitutional rubric, as deliberative democrats and liberal egalitarians attempt to do: one must accept pluralism, they will claim, not just in civil society and its institutions, but in the official public sphere as well. Some pluralists plead for recognizing the multiplicity of jurisdictions deriving from the experience of distinct *nomos* groups (Shachar); others defend linguistic or cultural pluralization of the public sphere (Kymlicka; Parekh; Carens).

THE PLURALIST "INTERLOCKING OF POWER HIERARCHIES"

The most interesting case for reconciling women's and children's rights and multiculturalist concerns has been made by Ayelet Shachar. She is acutely aware of what she terms the "paradox of multicultural vulnerability"—namely, the unintended consequence of well-meaning state policies that aim at cultural accommodation but result in the women and children of these groups bearing a disproportionate burden (2000, 386ff.). Shachar is principally concerned with *nomoi communities* or *identity groups*. She sees religiously defined groups as "shar[ing] a comprehensive world view that extends to creating law for the community" (386 n. 8). She admits that such definitions are fraught with difficulties but nevertheless believes that these definitions can apply to other minority groups "organized primarily along ethnic, racial, tribal, or national origin lines, as long as their members share a comprehensive and distinguishable world view that extends to creating a law for the community" (386ff.).

It is a serious mistake to extend the seemingly harmless term *nomoi groups* to ethnic, national, racial, and tribal communities, and the like, insofar as they share a comprehensive worldview and aim at a law based on it. This recapitulates the mistakes of group essentialism; it makes rather strict requirement of "a shared comprehensive worldview" a distinguishing feature of groups: Why should members of the same ethnic group share a comprehensive worldview? Cannot one be Russian as well as an anarchist, a communist, or a slavophile? Can one not be black as well as a separatist, an integrationist, or an assimilationist? It is unnecessary to multiply these examples. For the purposes of the argument, then, let us assume that within the liberal-democratic state there are different nomoi groups, the most salient of which will be based on religious identity, but some of which, like the Druze in Israel, the First Nations in Canada, and the aboriginal peoples in Australia, may be formed through more or less territorially segregated and shared life-forms as well (whether as nomads, fishermen, hunters, or simply those living on a "reservation").

Shachar identifies two legal arenas significant to the group's demarcation of its membership boundaries: family and education law. In the educational arena, respect for a minority community's quest to preserve its way of life may limit children's social mobility through "a lack of exposure to more pluralist and diverse aspects of the curriculum, mandatory high school education, or participation in a learning environment that treats all persons as equal" (2000, 392). There is a rich and extensive literature on these topics both in the United States and elsewhere. I would suggest that under principles of discourse ethics, any educational system that denies the exposure of children to the most advanced form of knowledge and inquiry available to humankind is unjustifiable. The alternative moral teachings, life-forms, and religious traditions of their own communities can be made made available to these children alongside other forms of knowledge. The obligation of the liberal-democratic state is to protect not only "the social mobility" of its young, as Shachar puts it, but their equal right to develop their moral and intellectual faculties as full human beings and future citizens as well.

A number of institutional "redesigns" (see Shapiro 2001 and forthcoming) are compatible with this requirement: One may be a system of compulsory public education for all children up to a legally defined age (the French model of public schools, or the American model of compulsory education until children reach sixteen, as decided by the U.S. Supreme Court in its landmark case *Wisconsin v Yoder*). Alternatively, religious or other communally governed private elementary schools may be formed; they would not receive state subsidies, since that would jeopardize liberal state neutrality, or they would receive them only on the basis of a principle generalizable to all schools. For example, religious or parochial schools could receive government support programs for blind children or those with learning disabilities; this would not jeopardize state neutrality. Such private schools could then be asked to follow a uniform curriculum in certain obligatory subject areas, such as science, math, history, and instruction in the official language or languages of the country, province, or state in question. Thus a Muslim private school in Barcelona could be offering instruction not only in Arabic, but in Catalan as well as Castilian, since Catalan is the official language in Barcelona, but Castilian is used in all public dealings with the central Spanish government as well as in the media.

It may be possible for the liberal state to be even more lenient in defining permissible school forms and to restrain from dictating curricular requirements altogether. Instead, through the use of standardized tests and finishing exams, the public authorities can assure both that certain commonalities exist in the school curriculums and that crucial subject matters are covered at a demonstrated level of competence. New York State has its Board of Regents exams; Germany has its Habitur; Israel requires the Bagrut. Considerable variation of institutional design and redesign are permissible in these domains.

These multiple institutional arrangements should not be confused with the normative principle at issue: nomoi communities do *not* have the right to deprive their children of humankind's accumulated knowledge and civilizational achievement in order to propagate their own ways of life; they *do* have a right to transmit to their children the fundamentals of their own ways of life *alongside* other forms of knowledge shared with humankind. Of course, there will be contradictions, inconsistencies, and tensions between these teachings, but it is the mark of human intelligence to learn to deal with such contradictions and tensions. Obscurantism is not compatible with moral and political autonomy. In many cases, it may be very difficult to implement such policies and to get the various communities involved to accept them, but just because what is right is not feasible, it does not cease to be right. One of my principal objections to the pluralist position is that no clear distinction is made between the *normatively right* and the *institutionally feasible*, and that very often moral prudence and political perspicacity are confused with the claims of justice. Justice certainly entails "evenhandedness," as Joe Carens has argued in his recent book on multiculturalism (2001). But justice is not *merely* evenhandedness, for claims of justice aspire to impartiality in order to represent what "is in the best interests of all considered as equally worthy moral beings." Such claims may involve conflict. If evenhandedness is not to result in a form of moral casuistry, it must be able to justify the contextually specific nature of many decisions and policies also with respect to principles. We should not confuse what Kant would call "cleverness" (*Klugheit*) or the capacity to act with tact and strategic insight in moral and political matters with action on the basis of principle. Good politics will always require cleverness as well as strategic talent, and not only for the purpose of multicultural coexistence, but such talents cannot and should not be confused with principled argument and justification in this domain.

Ayelet Shachar's considerations do not center primarily on educational issues but around family law. She points out astutely that "traditionally, various religious (and national) communities have used marriage and divorce regulation in the same way that modern states have used citizenship law: to delineate clearly who is inside and who is outside of the collective. Family law fulfils this demarcating function by legally defining only certain kinds of marriage and sexual reproduction as legitimate, while labeling all others as illegitimate" (2000, 394). Multiculturalist accommodation in this arena, through the allocation of jurisdictional powers over marriage and divorce to the various nomoi groups, may impose a disproportionate burden upon women. Shachar's original suggestions are directed toward solving such dilemmas.

Shachar argues that a number of recent approaches to the paradox of multicultural vulnerability, like the reuniversalized citizenship option or what she names "the unavoidable costs argument" of a strong multiculturalist approach (405ff.), "require that women and other potentially at-risk group members make a choice between their rights as citizens and their group identities. Either they must accept the violation of their rights as citizens in intragroup situations as the precondition for retaining their group identities, or they must forfeit their group identities as the price of state protection of their basic rights" (405). One possible solution to such painful dilemmas is to create multiple jurisdictional hierarchies by determining which forum possesses the authority to sanction a legal union and to resolve a given legal dispute. Several institutional options are available:

Temporal Accommodation. Jurisdiction may be split between the state and the nomoi group authorities at different stages of life. Marriage may be religiously sanctioned but divorce and separation permitted only through recourse to state authorities.

The Dual-System Approach. The parties retain the option of resorting to either secular or religious authorities to grant divorce and separation. Once a party has filed for civil divorce—Shachar focuses on the case of observant Jewish women, including Hassidic women—the other party must comply by removing all religious barriers to remarriage. But while the dual system may be well suited to deal with cases of marital oppression, it does not provide an incentive for different groups to reexamine their internal discriminatory norms.

The Joint Governance Approach. Individuals are members of more than one group, and each entity controls *certain* aspects of the situation by allowing input from different sources of authority. For example, through multicultural courts, members of different groups may interact with one another by translating, interpreting, and hammering out common resolutions to various disputes on the basis of different legal traditions. Shachar further adds that "contested social arenas (such as education, family law, immigration law, criminal justice, resource development, and environmental protection) are internally divisible into submatters—multiple, yet complementary, legal concerns" (418). The joint governance model would not only establish multicultural jurisdictional authorities like courts and conflict arbitration boards, it would also permit a further subdivision of authority through the allocation of jurisdiction along submatter lines. Thus, while marriage may be sanctified by the nomoi groups, the state alone would retain the authority to determine children's allowances and to allocate family assets and other benefits. This approach has the merit of extending the benefits of full and equal citizenship to women and children of these minority groups, while acknowledging their membership in different subgroups.

If we were to apply Shachar's final proposal to the Shah Bano case, considered above, we would find that Shah Bano was correct in seeking an increase in her alimony payments through the Indian federal courts and that the system that sent her case back to the Muslim court was wrong. She should receive the same whether she is considered as a Muslim or as a full Indian citizen. Shachar concludes: "The joint governance system for dividing and sharing authority promises to establish more than one set of standards that would jointly govern or coprevail in a contested social arena. It hopes to replace the dominant all-or-nothing division of authority with a more fluid and dynamic conception of power and jurisdiction" (424).

These suggestions are among the most imaginative institutional proposals put forward to deal with the paradox of multicultural vulnerability. Shachar's recommendations on behalf of the joint governance model are of special importance from the perspective of intercultural dialogue, which I have defended in this work.

This model actively encourages cross-cultural dialogue across legal traditions of interpretation, evaluation, and judgment. The joint-governance approach—as opposed to many other multiculturalist models that shield legal traditions from interacting with one another, thus suggesting the impossibility of cross-cultural dialogue—opens new horizons for legal and political imagination.

Despite this very important contribution, however, Shachar's proposals have several institutional as well as normative shortcomings: first, procedures for institutionalizing multicultural jurisdiction may run the risk of a certain legal eclecticism, which may undermine one of the cardinal virtues of the rule of law, namely, "equality for all before the law." Of course, the multiculturalist critique is that such equality is in fact inequality, for being difference-blind does not mean equal treatment for individuals whose differences from each other seem to require precisely not unequal but differential treatment. Nonetheless, there is a distinction between exceptions made on behalf of certain groups, practices, and institutions on the basis of reasons that *all* can be expected to share, and the assumption that such reasons justifying differential treatment no longer require generalizable justification. In the latter case we may indeed fear a certain "refeudalization of the law." Without establishing very clear lines between nonnegotiable constitutional essentials and those practices, rights, and entitlements that may be governed by different nomoi groups; and without specifying the capacity of constitutional principles to trump other kinds of legal regulations, we may not be resolving the paradox of multicultural vulnerability but simply permitting its recirculation without resolution throughout the system.

Shachar's extensive definition of nomoi groups at the outset of her argument raises a real concern about the refeudalization of the law. Her proposals work best for territorially concentrated nomoi groups like the Druze in Israel, the First Nations in Canada, aboriginal peoples in Australia, and indigenous groups in central America. Even in these cases, one should not be too sanguine about the possibility of reconciling women's and children's rights and cultural autonomy concerns.

It is interesting that the group Shachar discusses most extensively—namely, the Hassidim—is not a territorially based group. Rather, the Israeli Hassidim and the Haredim (the ultra-Orthodox) owe their unique status within that society partially to the fact that Israel does not practice a separation of state and religion. In fact, there is no secular private law governing divorce and marriage in Israel, and nonbelieving and nonobservant couples have to go through the charade of Orthodox Jewish rituals of marriage and divorce. In this instance, the paradox of multicultural vulnerability does not affect Jewish religious sects but rather nonreligious and nonobservant Jews. The option of secular marriage and divorce for all faiths and groups must be a fundamental right of the autonomy of the individual in the modern state; the needs of nomoi groups must not be prioritized at the expense of violating this right of the Jewish majority.

An added danger of these very creative institutional proposals is a certain shielding of the legal process from the dynamism and unpredictability of political-cultural dialogue. As with Brian Barry's arguments considered above, in Shachar's proposals as well there is a certain privileging of the legal at the expense of the political and cultural. Multicultural accommodationism may result in a kind of multicultural cold war: there may be peace but no reconciliation; there may be bargaining but no mutual understanding; and there may be stalemates and standoffs, dictated less by respect for the positions of others than by the fear of others. It is unlikely that there will ever be politics in liberal-democratic societies that will be settled beyond such dichotomies; power is ubiquitous and will remain so. Precisely because multiculturalism, in so many of its manifestations, challenges key assumptions of liberal democracies, it needs to release its conflictual and explosive potential in the public civil sphere through the dialogue, confrontation, and give-and-take of ordinary citizens. Culture matters; cultural evaluations are deeply bound up with our interpretations of our needs, our visions of the good life, and our dreams for the future. Since these evaluations run so deep, we must, as citizens of liberal democratic polities, learn to live with what Michael Walzer has called "liberalism and the art of separation" (1984). As citizens we need to know when we reach the limits of our tolerance; nevertheless, we have to learn to live with the otherness of others whose ways of being may be deeply threatening to our own. How else can moral and political learning take place, except through such encounters in civil society? Otherwise, multiculturalism may simply become a recipe for shielding the balkanization of distinct communities and worldviews from one another. The danger in this situation is that as soon as the authoritarian structures that administer the seeming peace between the groups fall apart—historical examples would be conditions in east-central Europe and the Balkans after the fall of the Austro-Hungarian and Ottoman Empires at the end of World War I, and of Soviet communism at the end of 1989—ethnic hatreds, religious feuds, cultural vendettas, and linguistic ostracisms would rear their heads. Indeed, sometimes a cold war may be precisely what is needed to ward off ethnic hatred; but as the actual end of the historical Cold War has shown, without a civil public space of multicultural understanding and confrontation, resignification and renarration, there can be no future for a democratic polity and no habits of mind for a democratic citizenry. The law provides the framework within which the work of culture and politics goes on. The laws, as the ancients knew, are the walls of the city, but the art and passions of politics occur within those walls (see Arendt [1958] 1973), and very often politics leads to the breakdown of these barriers or at least to the assurance of their permeability (see chap. 6 below).

So there is a dialectic between constitutional essentials and the actual politics of political liberalism. Rights and other principles on which the liberal democratic state rests, such as the rule of law, the separation of powers, and judicial review, need to be periodically challenged and rearticulated in the public sphere in order to retain and enrich their original meaning. It is only through the deployment of the First Amendment right to free speech that we learn why or how burning the flag may not be protected by the First Amendment, at the same time that, the speech of corporations in the form of soft money contributions may be (see Sunstein 1995;

Butler 1997). Only when new groups claim a right that had intitially excluded them do we understand the fundamental limits of every rights claim within a constitutional tradition, as well as that claim's context-transcending validity. The democratic dialogue and also the legal hermeneutic one are enhanced through the repositioning and rearticulation of rights claims in the public spheres of liberal democracies. The law sometimes can guide this process, in that legal reform may run ahead of popular consciousness and may raise popular consciousness to the level of the constitution; the law may also lag behind popular consciousness, and may need to be prodded along to adjust itself to it. In a vibrant multicultural liberal democracy, cultural and political conflict and learning through conflict should not be stifled through legal maneuvers. The democratic citizens themselves, and not just the judges and the legislators, have to learn the art of separation by testing the limits of their seemingly overlapping consensus.

Multicultural pluralist arrangements in the legal sphere should heed the following principles.

a. Egalitarian reciprocity. Members of cultural, religious, linguistic, and other minorities must not, in virtue of their membership status, be entitled to lesser degrees of civil, political, economic, and cultural rights than members of the majority.

b. Voluntary self-ascription. An individual must not be automatically assigned to a cultural, religious, or linguistic group by virtue of his or her birth. An individual's group membership must permit the most extensive form of self-ascription and self-identification; there will be many cases when such self-identifications are contested, but the state should not simply grant the right to define and control membership to the group at the expense of the individual. It is desirable that at some point in their adult lives individuals be asked whether they accept their continuing membership in their communities of origin.

c. Freedom of exit and association. The freedom of the individual to exit the ascriptive group must be unrestricted, although exit may be accompanied through the loss of certain kinds of formal and informal privileges. Ostracism and social exclusion are the informal prices of exclusion; loss of land rights and certain welfare benefits would be formal costs. As regards the latter, the liberal-democratic state has the right to intervene and regulate the costs of exit in accordance with principles of citizens' equality.[6] These kinds of situations involve contested claims between the various parties, and there must be some procedures of adjudication as well as review for resolving them. Furthermore, the wish of individuals to remain group members, even while outmarrying, must not be rejected; accommodations must be found for intergroup marriages and the children of such marriages.

These norms expand on the principles of universal respect and egalitarian reciprocity, which are crucial to a discourse ethic. While norm *a* (egalitarian reciprocity) is a further specification of what these principles would entail under conditions of a deliberative democracy, norms *b* (voluntary self-ascription) and *c* (freedom of exit and association) expand on the concept of persons as self-interpreting and self-defining beings whose actions and deeds are constituted through culturally informed narratives. The right of voluntary self-ascription as well as the right of exit and association derive from this vision of the individual as a self-interpreting being. Rawls would define this as our capacity to be the source of self-validating claims; in Habermas's language, this would refer to our capacity for "communicative freedom"—that is, the acceptance or refusal of a communicative speech-act extended to us by others and of the validity claims entailed therein. The further concretization of these norms through institutional practices and their embodiment in social practices are subject to democratic deliberations and agreements between participants.

Not only pluralists but certain deliberative democrats as well worry that the deliberative democracy approach does not take seriously enough the presence of intractable ethnocultural conflicts in society. Most theories of deliberative democracy seem to proceed from the presupposition of a unitary polity. Can deliberative democracy accommodate deeply entrenched ethnocultural and nationalist conflicts?

DELIBERATIVE DEMOCRACY, SELF-DETERMINATION, AND MULTICULTURALISM

Jorge M. Valadez states succinctly the concerns of deliberative democrats committed also to the multiculturalist cause:

> Differences in worldview or disagreements in needs and interests between cultural groups can be so deep that the disadvantages of cultural minorities to induce social cooperation to attain their political objectives can remain very significant. When the animosity between cultural groups is very great, when disputes over limited resources make compromises very difficult, or when the cognitive and affective differences between groups are unbridgeable, for example, not even the equalization of epistemic resources and the capabilities of their effective use, equality of motivational resources, multicultural education, or reforms in forums of public deliberation, may suffice to create a deliberative milieu in which the proposals of ethnocultural minorities will receive a fair hearing. This unfortunate scenario is more likely to occur with autonomist and secessionist groups than with accommodationist groups, since the latter are typically more willing to adopt majority values and institutional practices, as well as see themselves as belonging to a common political community. (2001, 101)

Valadez expresses a number of concerns shared by other deliberative theorists like James Bohman (1996), Iris Young (2000), and Melissa Williams (1998). Let me separate these concerns into two general kinds: epistemic concerns about the cognitive and affective biases of a deliberative consensus model; and political and institutional concerns with the limits of deliberative politics.

Cognitive and Affective Biases of Deliberative Democracy

Deliberative democracy appears attractive to many because, unlike aggregative and interest-group models of democratic legitimacy, it restores a sense of democracy as a cooperative enterprise among citizens considered as free and equal moral beings.

"Collective decisions," writes Valadez, "do not result merely by aggregating the preexisting desires of citizens; rather, members of the polity attempt to influence each others' opinions by engaging in a public dialogue in which they examine and critique, in a civil and considerate manner, each other's positions while explaining reasons for their own views" (2001, 5). The emphasis of the deliberative democracy model on democratic *inclusiveness* makes it particularly attractive to the concerns of excluded minorities, whether the sources of this exclusion lie in gender, ethnic, "racial," cultural, linguistic, religious, or sexual preference grounds. Furthermore, deliberative democracy promises not only inclusion but *empowerment*, in that the insistence that democratic legitimacy can be attained only through the agreement of *all* affected assures, at the normative level at least, that norms *cannot* be adopted and institutional arrangements advocated at the cost of the most disadvantaged and disaffected.

These normative conditions of inclusion and empowerment, while making deliberative democracy attractive, also make it suspect. As with any normative model, one can always point to prevailing conditions of inequality, hierarchy, exploitation and domination, and prove that "this may be true in theory but not so in practice" (Kant [1793] 1994). The answer to this ancient conflict between norm and reality is simply to say that if all were as it ought to be in the world, there would be no need to build normative models, either; the fact that a normative model does not correspond to reality is no reason to dismiss it, for the need for normativity arises precisely because humans measure the reality they inhabit in the light of principles and promises that transcend this reality (see Benhabib 1986). The relevant question therefore is; Does a given normative model enable us to analyze and distill the rational principles of existing practices and institutions in such a fashion that we can then use these rational reconstructions as critical guidelines for measuring really existing democracies? Some deliberative democrats want to argue that the problem is not simply the lack of correspondence between the normative and the empirical, but that there may be something deeply wrong with the normative model itself.

Those who make this claim usually point to some deep-seated cognitive and affective bias, which then is supposed to silence the voices of certain kinds of participants in democratic deliberations.

The *epistemic bias* charge takes several forms: first, that the deliberative democracy model cannot really accommodate deeply divergent, perhaps even incommensurable systems of belief and worldviews; second, that the emphasis in the deliberative model upon the "public nature of reason-giving" is biased in favor of "disembodied and dispassionate norms of speech"; third, that the condition of reaching "reasoned agreement," particularly in the version given to it by Juergen Habermas, places the bar of consensus too high, a requirement both unrealistic and exclusionary.

Incommensurability. With respect to the first set of arguments, I want to recall here the claims made in chapter 2 against strong incommensurability. I want to insist that strong incommensurability is an incoherent position, for if such incommensurability of frameworks and worldviews existed, we would not be able to know it for we would not be able to state in what it consisted. More often than not, as epistemic contemporaries, we are aware that some of our beliefs may be mutually exclusive and contradictory with those held by our fellow citizens. We also may have little doubt about the lack of cognitive validity of some of their assumptions, but in the public sphere of liberal democracies, we have to accept the equal claim to moral respect of our dialogue partners who hold such beliefs. I am thinking of contested cases like evolutionism versus creationism. This controversy strains to the utmost the established canons of scientific evidence and validation, yet as epistemic contemporaries in liberal democracies, we have to learn to live with each other and cooperate on school boards as well as on library committees, and within other associations.[7]

I have been using the phrase *epistemic contemporaries* (see chap. 2 above for a further elucidation). Let me explain what I mean: Some forms of knowledge become available to us only as a result of certain historical experiences and factual discoveries. Most of the time in democratic dialogue we share an epistemic horizon;

the most difficult and intractable cases for democratic deliberation are those that involve social life-forms that coexist in the same space but do not belong within the same time horizon of experience. Such is often the case when indigenous peoples and native tribes confront their highly technological colonizers and exploiters, usurpers and imperialists. These days it is not the conquistadors, but officials of the Brazilian or Mexican governments or multinational corporations who wrench the tribes of the Amazons and the Yucatan out of their life world and catapult them a few centuries into the future within the space of a few years.

Nevertheless, most democratic debates and contentions in contemporary societies are not clashes between radical incommensurables, though there will be degrees of incompatibility, contradiction, and exclusiveness among the belief systems, even of epistemic contemporaries. The systems of belief of ordinary agents do not have the level of coherence and systematicity of scientific worldviews. Ordinary moral and political deliberators do not have Cartesian minds, and very often may not be aware of their own contradictions. For example, the beliefs of Christian Scientists about modern medicine contradict the precepts of modern science; but Christian Scientists do not altogether reject modern science and technology in that they continue to use electricity as well as cars, air conditioners as well as the modern banking system. Most democratic dialogue is not about incommensurables, but about divergent and convergent beliefs, and very often we do not know how deep these divergences are, or how great their overlap may be, until we have engaged in conversation. If, however, the intensity as well as magnitude of supposed incommensurability can itself only be established through deliberative dialogue, then what good reasons are there for dismissing such dialogue as biased and not impartial enough even before we engage in it? Even groups and individuals with deeply held divergent beliefs are motivated to engage in democratic deliberation because there is some convergence at the level of material interests and shared life-forms. Democractic deliberation between moral contemporaries whose actions and doings affect one another builds on the imperfect convergences of imperfectly held belief systems.

When multiculturalist and deliberative theorists worry about incommensurability, they assume that it is primarily social positionality or social perspectivality that causes incommensuration. Social positionality, it is said, creates a certain perspective on the world that is incompatible and asymmetrical with the viewpoint of those who have never occupied this position. When we probe further and inquire what these social positions may be, they turn out to be the usual enumeration of groups cherished by strong identity politics: gender, "race," class, ethnicity, language, sexual preference, and the like. Social positionality then falls into pure essentialism in that it is premised upon the reduction of structures of individual consciousness to delineated group identities. There seems to be little anxiety among the defenders of social positionality as to how to define these groups, and whether in fact there are such ideal-typical worldviews or a group consciousness that may be attributed to them.[8] I believe that there are no such holistic structures of consciousness and that advocates of social positionality themselves operate with the fiction of a unitary consciousness in that they reduce the contentious debates of every human group about itself and its identity to a coherent and easily delineable narrative. Ironically, cultural essentialism comes back to haunt its most vocal critics, because those who argue that human cultures are human creations also argue that individuals are imprisoned in the perspectival refractions of their social positions. Both claims—cultural essentialism as well as social perspectivism—are false.

Valadez makes an important distinction between "understanding through translation" and "understanding through familiarization." He claims that we come to understand another conceptual framework, a way of life, not through a translation of the terms of one into the terms of the other (a view he attributes to Donald Davidson as well as Richard Rorty), but through *familiarization*. "That is, we comprehend frameworks that are radically different from our own not by finding terms and claims in our framework that isomorphically correspond to the terms and claims of theirs;

rather, we gradually achieve greater and greater familiarity with the ways they use these words in their language, with the range of situations in which they use them, with the kinds of claims they make, and so forth" (2001, 91). This is a useful distinction, but must not be overdrawn. Translation involves familiarization just as much as familiarization involves some translation. When we try to understand others across time and space, we begin by translating, and if we are good enough interpreters and imaginative enough historians and linguists, ethnographers, and literary critics, we end up by familiarizing ourselves with other traditions. When we are moral contemporaries, however, and our actions and interactions have consequences for the lives of those we may not even know, then the imperative to familiarize ourselves with their ways of thinking and ways of life becomes crucial. Democratic dialogue occurs within this horizon of moral and political contemporaneity, and indeed much intercultural dialogue is such a process of familiarization. I conclude that the first objection to deliberative democracy, based on a strong thesis of incommensurability, is untenable.

The Biases in the Public Nature of Reason-Giving.   It is frequently argued that the focus on *publicity* and on *public forums* in models of deliberative democracy also creates a bias in that such institutional spaces and practices privilege a certain mode of disembedded and dispassionate form of speech (Young 1996; Williams 2000). This consequently excludes the speech of groups such as women; sexual, linguistic, and ethnic minorities; and Native American peoples whose modes of discourse may be more embedded and passionate, based on storytelling and forms of greeting. There are at least three problems with this position.

First, deliberative democracy need not proceed from a *unitary model of the public sphere*. The public sphere in the Habermasian deliberative democracy model, which Cohen and Arato (1992), Nancy Fraser (1992), and I (1992 and 1996a) have developed further, is not a unitary but a pluralistic model that acknowledges the variety of institutions, associations, and movements in civil society. Sociologically, the public sphere is viewed as the interlocking of

multiple forms of associations and organizations, through the interaction of which an anonymous public conversation results. The decentered public sphere consists of mutually overlapping networks
and associations of opinion-forming as well as decisional bodies.
Within these multiple and overlapping networks of publicity, different logics of reason giving, greeting, storytelling, and embedded
speech can flourish.

Second, I find the assumption that politically and culturally
underprivileged and marginalized groups represent "the other of
reason" to be a species of exoticism. Why are we so quick to assume
that reason corresponds to domination, while the body corresponds
to marginalization and promises some form of liberation? There are
different traditions of narrative style and reason giving and storytelling among human groups; but we would do well not to impose
metaphysical binarisms like reason versus the body, impartiality
versus embodiedness, upon such differences.

Third, the strength of the objections to the public nature of
reason giving in my view derives from the following consideration:
Publicity entails the normative requirement that for a principle, a
law, or a course of action to be deemed acceptable, it must be
judged to be so from the standpoint of all affected. Participation in
the public realm imposes the obligation to reverse perspectives and
to be ready to think and reason from the standpoint of concerned
others. This requirement of impartiality is particularly binding for
legislative and deliberative bodies that decide upon coercive rules
of action for all involved. In a series of articles, Melissa Williams
has voiced objections to this regulative principle of publicity (1998
and 2000).

Williams begins by noting that "deliberative democrats extend the liberal notion that legitimate government is based on consent by arguing that the terms of social and political cooperation
should be the outgrowth of reasoned exchange among citizens. To
sustain the claim to legitimacy, however, the processes of deliberative democracy must include all relevant social and political perspectives" (2000, 125). Williams adds that she is "not persuaded
that its defenders have adequately addressed the challenges of so-

cial difference—difference defined along the lines of gender, race, ethnicity, class, sexuality and so on—to a deliberative conception of legitimacy" (125). Williams gives a very careful defense of deliberative democracy against the criticisms of group-rights theorists by pointing out how the regulative goal of deliberative democracy would entail a reinterpretation of impartiality to include hitherto excluded and suppressed *issues, persons, and participants,* and would also *counteract the bias of privileging certain institutional structures, reasons, and outcomes alone.* (130–31) Nevertheless, Williams is skeptical that deliberative democracy can meet the challenges of group theorists adequately, and her central argument rests on the role of reasons and reason-giving in deliberative democratic processes. She writes: "Attention to the distinctive perspectives on political issues that follow the lines of social difference raises several doubts about deliberative theory's standard of 'reasonableness' and about how participants decide what counts as a reason for purposes of political deliberation. . . . The recognition of marginalized groups' reasons *as reasons for (or acceptable to) other citizens* is a highly contingent matter" (33–34, emphasis in the original). This is an important objection, which correctly represents the epistemic logic of deliberative democracy arguments and is also phenomenologically sensitive to what must go on if deliberative processes are to succeed at all.

In response I would like to distinguish between the *syntax* and the *semantics of reasons in the public sphere.*[9] The syntax of reasons would refer to certain structural features all statements that articulate public reasons would have to possess. Reasons would count as reasons because they could be defended as being in the best interest of all considered as equal moral and political beings. To claim that A is a reason for adopting policy X or law Y could then be parsed as stating that "X or Y are in the best interests of all considered equal moral and political beings. And we can justify this claim because we have established X or Y through processes of public deliberation in which all affected by these norms and policies took part as participants in a discourse." This is the *syntactical structure of public reasons in deliberative democracy models.*

The content of X and Y as well as the nature of the arguments and reasons advanced in discourses in the process of establishing such a conclusion concern the *semantics of reasons*. There is
no way to know in advance which specific group claims and perspectives may or may not count as reasons. It is conceivable that
a minority can convince the majority that it should accept its oral
narratives to serve as legitimate titles to their ancestral land. This
happened when the Supreme Court of Canada decided to accept
the oral stories of Gitxsan Indians of Kispiox, British Columbia, as
evidence to their land claims in the region (De Palma 1998). Such
oral stories were given the status of legitimate title, on the grounds
that from the standpoint of all citizens of Canada, it was fair and
just to recognize the special history and ties of the Gitxsan people
to their land. What lent legitimacy to the Canadian court's decision
was precisely their recognition of a specific group's claims to be in
the *best* interests of *all* Canadian citizens.

Certainly, Williams is right to point that majorities are not
always willing or open-minded enough to accept such grounds, let
alone recognize them as reasons. When power over resources as
well as other material interests is at stake (legitimate land use, for
example), there will be resistance on the part of majorities to recognize the rightful claims of minorities. Deliberative processes do not
obviate the need for democratic struggle through demonstrations,
sit-ins, strikes, catcalls, and blockages. Native American groups
have the right to preserve the integrity of their land by blocking the
destruction of ancestral forests, preventing strip mining, or prohibiting certain forms of hunting or the dumping of toxic materials.
Such political struggles build coalitions by gaining the sympathy
of others who come to see that the cause of the minority is just because it involves reasons that all can identify with. These would be
reasons like: It is good for all to preserve the ecologically sound use
of land, as the Indians have done for centuries and generations,
rather than to destroy the ecobalance and life-forms of human and
other living beings for the sake of profits for timber or oil compa-
nies, or fisherman and hunters. Such statements possess the semantic structure of legitimate public reasons. Indeed, as Williams ob-

serves: "When the eradication of structures of unjust inequality depends upon affirming the social meaning of a practice for marginalized groups, the justice of deliberative outcomes depends not only upon participants exhibiting the virtues of open-mindedness and mutual respect (as deliberative theory emphasizes), but also upon their possessing the virtue of empathy, and of giving marginalized-group claims the particular advantage of their empathy" (2000, 138). I have argued in other writings that Hannah Arendt's concept of the "enlarged mentality" may be a better term than "empathy" for capturing the broadening of our horizons through coming to see the perspective of others in and through political and moral struggle (see Arendt 1961, 220–21; Benhabib 1992, 89–121). I conclude that this objection, though very substantial, does not vitiate the project of deliberative democracy.

The Unattainable Goal of Consensus through Deliberation. Since its earliest formulations in works like *Legitimation Crisis* (1975), Habermas's version of deliberative democracy and his discourse theory of legitimacy have been open to the charge that the criterion for consensus among participants is far too strong. It is illusory to expect that the "force of the better argument" will always prevail and for the same reasons. Although Habermas's work has undergone considerable modifications since these early formulations (see Bohman 1996), we still encounter claims of the sort in his most recent work as well: "Whereas parties can agree to a negotiated compromise for different reasons, the consensus brought about through argument must rest on *identical reasons* that are able to convince parties in the same way" (Habermas 1996a, 344).

Such statements dismay sympathetic commentators like Bohman (1996) and Valadez (2001), each of whom is more convinced of the philosophical validity of the strong incommensurability thesis than I am. They acknowledge, however, that there are also other strands of argumentation in Habermas's work that may be more compatible with a more pluralist approach to consensus-formation. Habermas contends, for example, that we cannot know in advance which reasons are to count as public and which would be nonpublic. Since public reason is not restricted, as it is in Rawls's framework, to formulating or disputing constitutional essentials alone, the democratic give-and-take of ordinary citizens broadens our understanding of what may count as public reasons. Against Bohman and Valadez, I would like to point out that even though the semantic content of these reasons may change, their syntactical structure—that they are in the best interest of all considered as free and equal moral beings—would remain. I believe that Habermas is right on insisting on this distinction, and that even if we accept the *plurality of public reasons*, we need not *compromise on the normative syntax of public justification*.

Habermas's claim "that consensus brought about through argument must rest on *identical reasons* that are able to convince the parties in the same way" (1996a 344) needs to be carefully parsed. Habermas is concerned that the validity of normative judgments should not be reduced to agent-specific or agent-relative reasons. He argues that such justifications may yield compromises but not moral agreement. This is certainly true with respect to certain kinds of claims. Not only can we plausibly argue that moral claims, as opposed to prudential and utilitarian ones, cannot be merely agent-specific (I accept this law because it is good for me and my kin), but we can also argue that certain kinds of political principles cannot be justified merely on agent-specific grounds either. For example, suppose China and the United States are trying to reach some consensus on the content of basic human rights. The United States cannot say, "We accept human rights because, from our point of view, they are the best way to spread our way of life throughout the world"; the Chinese delegation could then argue that,"We accept a minimum list of human rights because, from our point of view, they permit us to gain international credibility and access to international markets." Very often this is exactly how delegations in international negotiations think and this is precisely why they accept certain normative arrangements on *strategic grounds*. If, however, we believe that human rights constitute the moral foundation for democracies everywhere, then we must be ready to argue for their validity on the basis of reasons we think can be justified from the standpoint of all human beings. Interpreted thus, Habermas's claim that consensually attained moral norms must convince each and every one for the same reason does not seem too implausible.

Nevertheless, political discourse and moral discourse are not identical. Political discourse is a mixed mode in which universalizable justice claims, agent- and group-relative strategic reasons, and culturally circumscribed ethical considerations, which are relative to "we communities," mix and intermingle. There is always a tension in democratic discourse between these various strands of normative reasoning and argumentation. I will argue in the next chapter that the tension between universal rights claims and the sovereignty demands of concrete human communities is constitutive of the experience of the modern nation-states within which liberal democracies are housed.

Not only are there tensions in political discourse among the constituent elements of normative and strategic reasoning, but claims and arguments may change their normative status through democratic deliberation in that *ethical considerations* may become *universalizable justice* concerns. A most interesting example of such a shift is provided by the changing international consensus on women's rights. Whereas the status of women and of children until quite recently was considered the backbone of the ethical specificity of distinct human communities, and was expected to come under the legal jurisdiction of the authorities of these communities alone, emergent international discourse on women's rights has created a transnational discursive network among women's rights activists, community representatives, legislators, and international workers. The discourse on women's and children's rights has shifted its status from a "we-specific" ethical claim to a justice-oriented universalist claim (Jaggar 1999, 320ff). Shachar's proposals for interlocking jurisdictional hierarchies are similarly motivated by the recognition that women's and children's rights are universal justice claims, which must be somehow accommodated within the framework of the cultural and legal particularities of distinct human groups. While Habermas's requirement that agreement reached through consensus should convince *all* on the *same* grounds is too

strong a condition for judging the outcomes of democratic deliberations, which present mostly mixed modes of moral, strategic, and
ethically specific forms of reasoning, this requirement is still useful
for understanding how the logic of universalizing justice claims differs from the logic of strategic as well as ethically specific claims.
Discourses are moral *and* political learning processes.

Bohman suggests that we view public deliberations as entailing "moral compromises." The requirements of morality and
those of compromise need not be mutually exclusive, as Habermas
sometimes suggests that they are. Public deliberation, as Valadez
points out in agreement with Bohman, "is first and foremost a social cooperative activity that aims at resolving concrete problematic
situations" (Valadez 2001, 63). Bohman defines moral compromise
as a situation in which "the parties do not modify the framework
to achieve unanimity, although they may when conflicts are not so
deep. Rather, they modify their conflicting interpretations of the
framework so that each can recognize the other's moral values and
standards as part of it" (1996, 91). Moral compromise is a form of
moral learning, and I agree with Bohman and Valadez that such
processes are crucial for deliberative democratic activities, which
indeed are not merely about arguments but about finding mutually
acceptable ways of cooperating and continuing to exist with one
another. Yet while recognizing the empirical logic of democratic deliberation and will-formation processes, we need not forfeit the regulative principle that the logic of public justification requires impartiality, through which the best interests of all considered as equal
moral and political beings are taken into account. I conclude then
that the critique in question—that a deliberative democracy framework based on discourse ethics contains too many epistemic and
affective biases to make it function fairly within intercultural and
cross-cultural contexts—is overstated, and that such concerns can
be accommmodated without forfeiting the essential premises of
the model.

In addition to their charge of epistemic and affective bias,
critics argue also that models of deliberative democracy proceed
from a unitary political framework and can do justice neither to

pluralist cultural power-sharing arrangements nor to secessionist cultural and nationalist demands. The next chapter will address such concerns through a case study of the problems of inclusion rather than of secession. My argument is that when we examine contemporary and evolving practices of citizenship, we see better both the moral costs and the political contradictions of secession within the modern nation-state system.

SIX

❑   ❑   ❑   ❑

WHO ARE "WE"?

Dilemmas of Citizenship in Contemporary Europe

The principles of discourse ethics require that "all those affected by the consequences of the adoption of a norm" have an
equal say in its validation if democratic legitimacy is to be attained.
For discourse ethics, territorial boundaries and state borders are not
coterminous with those of the moral community. Discursive communities can emerge *whenever* and *wherever* human beings can affect one another's actions and well-being, interests or identity. The
boundaries of the moral community and those of the political community do not overlap, and I would argue that they must be kept
distinct—for what we owe each other as human beings cannot be
reduced to what we owe each other as citizens of the same polity
or as members of a historically defined cultural "we" community
with shared memories and experiences. Our identities as modern
subjects involve all these various dimensions—moral beings, citizens, and members of an ethical community. Throughout this book,
I have explored tensions that may arise between these multiple
commitments of modern individuals.

MULTICULTURAL INSTITUTIONALISM AND
DELIBERATIVE DEMOCRACY

Critics of deliberative democracy who charge that it presupposes a
culturally unitary polity (Valadez 2001) do not heed this necessary
tension between the universalist claims of discourse ethics, which

transcend national and ethical boundaries, and the special obligations to one another created by membership in a polity. Rather, their concern is to show that even within the boundaries of a universalistically oriented deliberative democracy model, certain groups will not find their demands met, and will opt for secession in extreme cases or demand some form of power sharing in others.

Since the principle that the voice of all those affected by a norm, a legislation, a policy be included in the democratic discourse leading to its adoption is fundamental to deliberative democracy, this model is open to a variety of institutional arrangements that can assure the inclusion of such voices. Such arrangements can range from power sharing in legislative as well as judicial organs between diverse cultural groups to multilingual and multicultural media organs, including newspapers, radio, and television. Language differences ought to be no bar to democratic participation.

Special power sharing arrangements can also involve proportional representation as well as local and regional assemblies, and the devolution of power from the center to the periphery. If our principle is to be as inclusive as possible of the voices of all those affected, it would follow that many decisions need to be made at the local and regional levels by those whose interests are most significantly influenced. Throughout these diverse institutional arrangements, however, the normative principles formulated in chapter 5 need to be heeded.

Egalitarian reciprocity.　Members of cultural, religious, linguistic, and other minorities must not, by virtue of their membership status, be entitled to lesser degrees of civil, political, economic, and cultural rights than are members of the majority.

Voluntary self-ascription.　An individual must not be automatically assigned to a cultural, religious, or linguistic group by virtue of his or her birth. An individual's group membership must permit the most extensive form of self-ascription and self-identification; the state should not simply grant the right to define and control membership to the group at the expense of the individual. In multicultural societies in which the state recognizes the right of cultural and religious groups to exercise self-governance and autonomous jurisdiction in certain domains (cf. the cases of Canada, Israel, and India, as discussed in chaps. 3 and 4), it is desirable that at some point in their adult lives individuals be asked whether they accept their continuing membership in their communities of origin.

Freedom of exit and association. The freedom of the individual to exit the ascriptive group must be unrestricted, although exit may be accompanied by the loss of certain formal and informal privileges. Ostracism and social exclusion are the informal prices of exclusion; loss of land rights and certain welfare benefits would be formal costs. With regards to the latter, the liberal-democratic state has the right to intervene and regulate the costs of exit in accordance with principles of citizens' equality.

In concrete institutional terms, these normative principles suggest that if procedures of proportional representation are adopted to assure the inclusiveness of excluded minorities, such groups and associations should respect the conditions stipulated above. Proportional representation methods should not imprison individuals in their ascriptive communities that do not permit them, for example, to vote for candidates of other groups and parties. Members of minority communities should be free to establish coalitions and associations with other groups, including members of the majority who share their views. Cross-cultural and intercultural political associations, delegations, and regional assemblies should be furthered. I do not favor proportional representation methods based on culturally, ethnically, and religiously defined identities; I do, however, favor efforts to widen the democratic inclusion of underrepresented minorities by encouraging them to vote, to organize themselves, and, to establish unions and associations as well as political parties. Overall, institutional arrangements should balance the individual autonomy demands of participants, viewed as self-defining cultural beings, and the collective autonomy claims of groups who want to exercise their rights of self-determination.

Admittedly, there will be cases when such measures of democratic inclusion will not be accepted by the majority or will not suffice to meet the demands of the minority for self-determination. In such cases, we will need to distinguish between oppressive majorities and irridentist minorities and, through an examination of the history, economy, as well as the culture of the conflict, determine whether secession is morally justified. I see no reasons to argue against secession on the basis of a deliberative or discourse model. Individual and collective self-determination rights may require the establishment of new political entities.

I do see a danger, however, in the efforts by some multiculturalists and liberal nationalists to romantically obscure the moral and political costs of ever-new nation-state creations. The Russian dolls phenomenon has been noted by writers on this topic (Tamir 1993). Every new polity, if it takes the from of a nation-state—and since in most cases secessionist movements occur precisely because minority groups want to establish their own state in which their culture is hegemonic—entails moral and political costs. Every nationalist minority movement has its own "others." Every polity creates its own rules of inclusion and exclusion. Some of the dilemmas of contemporary liberal democracies can be observed most clearly through an examination of contemporary transformations in the rules and practices governing citizenship—that is, political membership. Ironically, irridentist and secessionist cultural movements are emerging in a world increasingly governed by the unstoppable movement of peoples across state boundaries and the inevitable mingling of cultures. I do not believe that cultures are pure or that they ought to be purified, or that state boundaries should coincide with those of dominant cultural communities; in this chapter, I want to juxtapose to the romance of cultural self-determination a case study about the transformations of the institutions of citizenship in the heart of the oldest nation-states on the globe, namely, those of Europe. The constitutive tension between human rights and self-determination claims is fundamental to liberal democracies if they are to remain liberal democracies and not fall for the romance of national or cultural purity.

HUMAN RIGHTS AND SELF-DETERMINATION IN A GLOBAL WORLD

With globalization and fragmentation proceeding apace, human rights and sovereignty claims today come into increasing conflict with each other (Heiberg 1994). On the one hand, a worldwide consciousness about universal principles of human rights is growing; on the other hand, particularistic identities of nationality, ethnicity, religion, race, and language, by virtue of which one is said to belong to a sovereign people, are asserted with increasing ferocity. Globalization, far from creating a "cosmopolitical order," a condition of perpetual peace among peoples governed by the principles of a republican constitution (Kant [1795] 1957), has brought to a head conflicts between human rights and the claim to self-determination by sovereign collectivities. Because sovereignty means the right of a collectivity to define itself by asserting power over a bounded territory, declarations of sovereignty more often than not create distinctions between "us" and "them," those who belong to the sovereign people and those who do not. Historically there rarely is a convergence between the identity of those over whom power is asserted because they are residents of a bounded territory and the identity of the sovereign people in the name of whom such power is exercised. In this context, Hannah Arendt's astute observations, although formulated in a different context and with respect to the difficulties of protecting human rights in the interwar period in Europe, are more perspicacious than ever. "From the beginning the paradox involved in the declaration of inalienable human rights was that it reckoned with an 'abstract' human being who seemed to exist nowhere. . . . The whole question of human rights, therefore, was quickly and inextricably blended with the question of national emancipation; only the emancipated sovereignty of the people, of one's own people, seemed to be able to insure them" ([1951] 1979, 291).

The citizenship and naturalization claims of foreigners, denizens, and residents within the borders of a polity, as well as the laws, norms, and rules governing such procedures, are pivotal social practices through which the normative perplexities of human rights and sovereignty can be most acutely observed. Sovereignty entails the right of a people to control its borders as well as define the procedures for admitting "aliens" into its territory and society; yet in a liberal-democratic polity, such sovereignty claims must always be constrained by human rights, which individuals are entitled to, not by virtue of being citizens or members of a polity, but insofar as they are simply human beings. Universal human rights transcend the rights of citizens and extend to all persons considered as moral beings. What kinds of immigration, naturalization, and citizenship practices, then, would be compatible with the commitments of liberal democracies to human rights? Can claims to sovereign self-determination be reconciled with the just and fair treatment of aliens and others in our midst?

In contemporary debates about these issues two approaches dominate: the radical universalist argument for open borders and the civic-republican perspective of "thick conceptions of citizenship." Radical universalists argue that from a moral point of view, national borders are arbitrary and that the only morally consistent universalist position would be one of open borders. Joseph Carens, for example, uses the device of the Rawlsian "veil of ignorance" to think through principles of justice from the standpoint of the refugee, the immigrant, the asylum seeker (Carens 1995, 229ff.; see Carens 2000 for modifications of these early arguments). Are the borders within which we happen to be born, and the documents to which we are entitled, any less arbitrary from a moral point of view than other characteristics like skin color, gender, and the genetic makeup with which we are endowed? Carens's answer is no. From a moral point of view, the borders that circumscribe our birth and the papers to which we are entitled are arbitrary, since their distribution does not follow any clear criteria of moral desert, achievement, and compensation. Therefore, claims Carens, liberal democracies should practice policies that are as compatible as possible with the vision of a world without borders.

Opposed to Carens's radical universalism are a range of communitarian and civic-republican positions, articulating more or less "thick" conceptions of citizenship, community, and belonging (see Galston 1991; Sandel 1996; Kessler 1998). These theories of citizenship, while not precluding or prohibiting immigration, articulate stricter criteria of incorporation and citizenship of foreigners than the theories of the universalists. Only those immigrants who come closest to the model of the republican citizen envisaged by these theories will be welcome; others will be spurned (Honig 1998, 2001). Of course, given how contested such thick conceptions of citizenship inevitably are, communitarian theories can easily lend themselves to the justification of illiberal immigration policies and the restriction of the rights of immigrants and aliens.

I would like to defend a position that will steer a middle course between the radical universalism of open-borders politics on the one hand and sociologically antiquated conceptions of thick republican citizenship on the other. Instead, stressing the constitutive tension between universalistic human rights claims and democratic sovereignty principles, I will analyze the contemporary practices of political incorporation into liberal democracies. Current developments in citizenship and incorporation practices within the member states of the European Union in particular are my primary concern. There are a number of compelling historical as well as philosophical reasons for choosing European citizenship and incorporation practices as the focal point for these concerns at the present time.

Insofar as they are liberal democracies, member states of the European Union cannot form a "fortress Europe." No liberal democracy can close its borders to refugees or asylum seekers, migrants or foreign workers. The porousness of borders is a necessary, while not sufficient, condition of liberal democracies. By the same token, no sovereign liberal democracy can lose its right to define immigration and incorporation policies.

I will distinguish conditions of *entry* into a country, like the permission to visit, work, study, and buy property, from conditions of *temporary residency,* and both in turn from *permanent residency* and *civil incorporation,* the final stage of which is *political membership.* These are different stages of political incorporation, very often collapsed into one another in theoretical discussions, but analytically distinguishable. At each of these stages the rights and claims of foreigners, residents, and aliens will be regulated by sovereign polities; but these regulations can be subject to scrutiny, debate, and contestation as well as to protest by those to whom they apply, their advocates, and national and international human rights groups. There is no step of this process that can be shielded from scrutiny by interested parties. A particular people's democratic sovereignty in immigration and incorporation policy is not an unlimited right. A people's right to self-assertion must be examined and evaluated in light of its commitment to universal human rights. Developments of citizenship and immigration practices within contemporary Europe reflect some of the deepest perplexities faced by all nation-states in the era of globalization.

DILEMMAS OF CITIZENSHIP IN THE EUROPEAN UNION

Since 1989 and the fall of authoritarian communism, the worldwide trend toward material global integration and ethnic and cultural fragmentation have coincided with another set of epochal developments on the continent: the end of the Cold War, the unification of Germany, and the emergence of the European Union as a political entity with a European Parliament, a European Council of Ministers, a European Court of Justice, and, since January 1999, a European currency—the Euro. But what is Europe? (Benhabib 1997b; 1999b).

For some Europe is not a continent, a mere geographical designator, but an ideal, the birthplace of Western philosophy and the Enlightenment, of democratic revolutions and human rights. For others Europe is a fig leaf behind which big finance capital and, in particular, the German Bundesbank, hides in order to dismantle the social-welfare states of the Union. Since the Maastricht Treaty and the requirement that national governments cut their annual budget deficits to 3-percent, member states have forced their own populations to accept fiscal stability over full employment, and to place the shared confidence that international financial markets show in their national economies over the quality of life of these countries. Europe has ceased to be an ideal; for some it has long become an illusion. Tony Judt gives voice to the Euro-pessimist position with the following words: "We shall wake up one day to find out that far from solving the problems of our continent, the myth of 'Europe' has become an impediment to our recognizing them. We shall discover that it has become little more than the politically correct way to paper over local difficulties, as though the mere invocation of the promise of Europe could substitute for solving problems and crises that really affect the place" (1996, 140).

Whether as ideal or as illusion, "Europe" is being invoked today to define a new set of boundaries. Contemporary Europe is facing the danger that its moral and political boundaries will be redefined via geographical borders. Geography once again will be used to cover the tracks of complex processes of political and moral inclusion and exclusion. Where are the borders of Europe, and within Europe itself, after 1989? How can these borders be justified as boundaries? Whether as an ideal or illusion, whom does Europe include and whom does it exclude? After the Cold War, who are Europe's "others"?

While foreigners made up 1.1 percent of the population in Germany in 1950, in 1992–93 this number rose to 8.6 percent, according to statistics provided by the Council of Europe. During the same period the foreign population of France increased from 4.2 percent to 6.6 percent; of Belgium, from 4.1 percent to 9.1 percent (in 1994, the foreign population of Belgium stood at 10.7 percent); of the Netherlands, from 1.0 percent to 5.1 percent; and of Luxembourg from 9.8 percent to 29.1 percent (in 1994 this figure was 34 percent). On the whole, the foreign population of Europe increased from 1.3 percent in 1950 to 4.9 percent in 1992–93.[1]

The year 1993 marks a turning point in immigration trends in European countries. After the increase in immigration flows during the 1980s and the beginning of the 1990s, a reduction in the number of immigrant entries occurred. The decline in the number of asylum claims during this period was offset by the predominance of flows linked to family reunion and the need for highly skilled workers (SOPEMI 1998, 15).

Reflecting these trends, and despite leveling at 8.6 percent of the total population in 1993, the foreign population of Germany increased to 8.9 percent in 1996. France has remained steady at about 6.3 percent and Belgium at about 9.1 percent. Among the European Union countries, only Austria, Germany, and Luxembourg have foreign populations higher than the 2.5 to 6 percent range characteristic of Ireland, the United Kingdom, Denmark, Sweden, and the Netherlands (as well as Norway, which is not an EU member). In Luxembourg, the foreign population increased from 31.8 percent in 1993 to 34.1 percent in 1996; during this same period, Austria's foreign population went from 8.6 percent to 9.0 percent in 1996 (SOPEMI 1998, 224).

These figures are not broken down according to geographical regions and countries of origin. Foreigners from former East European countries are included in these figures, along with guestworkers from Turkey and refugees from the former Yugoslav countries.[2] A more precise breakdown shows that ethnic Turks and ethnic Kurds are the largest group of foreigners, not only in Germany, but in Western Europe in general. In 1993, they numbered 2.7 million. Of that number, 2.1 million live in Germany and, as of 1999, make up 2.8 percent of the population.[3] The second largest group of foreigners are those from the former Yugoslav states, many of whom enjoy either full or temporary refugee status: 1.8 million Croats, Serbians, Bosnian Muslims, and Kosovo Albanians.[4]

This picture is also complicated by the increasing intercountry migration of EU residents. Already in 1993, Italians working outside their home country numbered 1.5 million; they are followed by the Portuguese, of whom about 900,000 work and live outside Portugal. Spaniards, who are members of the European

Union, and Algerians, who are not, each number around 600,000. As of the 1990 census, France counted 614,200 Algeria–born individuals, and 572,200 Moroccans among its population.

After the fall of communism in eastern and central Europe, immigration from the former East Bloc countries to the EU has continued. In 1998, 66,300 Poles entered Germany; about 10,400, France; and about 14,000, the Netherlands. In 1998, there were 20,500 Russian citizens resident in Finland; Greece is host to about 5,000 Russians, 3,000 Bulgarians, and approximately 2,700 Albanians.

Against the juridical and political background of European unification, these developments are bringing about a two-tiered status of foreignness throughout Europe. Different rights and privileges are accorded to different categories of foreigners within the fifteen member states.

1. The Treaty of Maastricht makes provisions for a "Union citizenship."[5] Nationals of all countries who are members of the European Union are also citizens of the European Union. What does being a citizen of the Union mean? What privileges and responsibilities, what rights and duties does this entitle one to? Is citizenship of the Union merely a status category, let us say, just as membership in the Roman Empire was? Does membership in the Union amount to more than a passport that allows one to pass through the right doors at border crossings?[6]

Clearly, Union membership is intended to be more than that. Not just a passive status, it is also intended to designate an active civic identity. Members of the EU states can settle in any country in the Union, take up jobs in these countries, and vote, as well as stand for office, in local elections and in elections for the European Parliament of Europe. As European monetary and economic integration progresses, Union members and observers are debating whether or not Union citizenship should also entail an equivalent package of social rights and benefits, like unemployment compensation, health care, and old-age pensions, which citizens of EU states can enjoy wherever they go.[7]

2. The obverse side of membership in the Union is a sharper delineation of the conditions of nonmembers. The agreements of Schengen and Dublin intended to reconcile diverse practices of granting asylum and refugee status throughout member states. (Neuman 1993). [8] Referred to as "legal harmonization," these agreements have made the granting of refugee and asylum status in the Union increasingly difficult. An individual who seeks refugee and asylum status in a member country is not permitted to apply in another country of the Union until the first application is resolved. Although it is left unsaid, the presumption is that once such an application has been denied in one member country, it is unlikely to succeed in another. The decision of the European Council of Ministers to erect a Union-wide office to deal with refugee and asylum issues, while creating legal and bureaucratic homogenization and standardization, by the same token intends to make Europe's borders less and less porous by disallowing individuals in need of multiple venues of aid and rescue.

3. As Union citizenship progresses, discrepancies in each member country are arising between those who are foreigners and third-country nationals, and those who are foreign nationals but EU members. A two-tiered status of foreignness is thus evolving: on the one hand there are third-country national foreign residents of European countries, some of whom have been born and raised in these countries and who know of no other homeland; on the other hand are those who may be near-total strangers to the language, customs, and history of their host country but who enjoy special status and privilege by virtue of being nationals of states which are EU members (Klusmeyer 1993). Members of the fifteen EU countries who are residents in countries different from those of their nationality can vote as well as run for and hold office in municipality elections and in elections for the European Parliament. These rights are as a rule not granted to third-country nationals, though, as I shall argue below, some EU countries like Denmark, Sweden, Finland, and the Netherlands permit foreigners who have fulfilled certain residency requirements to vote in local and, even some cases, regional elections.

Partially in response to the growing pressures created by this situation, Germany on May 7, 1999, reformed its 1913 citizenship law. The German parliament accepted by a two-thirds majority that the principle of *jus sanguinis* be supplemented by *jus soli* in the acquisition of German citizenship (see Benhabib 1999a). After January 1, 2000, children born to foreign parents who have resided in the country for eight years acquire German citizenship without forfeiting other passports they hold. When they reach the age of twenty-three, they must decide for one citizenship or another. In addition to the *jus soli* regulation, the new law expedites the acquisition of German citizenship by foreigners by reducing the residency-to-citizenship transition period from fifteen to eight years. The decision of the German parliament is, of course, to be welcome, but we can understand the significance of this new law only when we place it within a larger conceptual and institutional context.

Since the Treaty of Amsterdam, signed on May 1, 1997, EU member countries have grown aware of the necessity to harmonize the citizenship and naturalization laws of distinct member countries, and to reduce discrepancies in the juridical and political status of EU citizens and third country nationals. According to the Treaty of Amsterdam, naturalization, immigration, refugee, and asylum policies within the EU are placed in the Third Pillar. The First Pillar refers to EU-wide law and regulations; the Second Pillar concerns common security and cooperation measures, particularly those pertaining to criminality and drug traffic; the Third Pillar is defined as "intergovernmental law," and is subject to discretionary agreement and cooperation as well as to the conventions of international public law. In these areas a unanimous decision procedure will hold till the year 2004 (see Jong 2000, 21–25). In other words, although EU member countries retain sovereign discretion over their immigration and asylum policies, "the Treaty of Amsterdam firmly embeds immigration and asylum policies within an EC framework" (Jong 2000, 25).

The resolutions of the European Council, reached in Tampere, Finland, during October 15–16, 1999, reiterate the commitment to European integration based on respect for human rights, democratic institutions, and the rule of law. The Council emphasizes, however, that these principles cannot be seen as the exclusive preserve of the Union's own citizens: "It would be in contradiction with Europe's traditions to deny such freedoms to those whose circumstances led them justifiably to seek access to our territory. This in turn requires the Union to develop common policies on asylum and immigration, while taking into account the need for a consistent control of external borders to stop illegal immigration and to combat those who organize it and commit related international crimes" (van Krieken 2000, 305).

Despite these wishes and guidelines for a coherent immigration and asylum policy at the intergovernmental level of EU institutions, legal and institutional conditions for immigrants and asylees vary widely among member countries. Neither the public nor politicians are clear about how these issues relate to the foundations and well-being of liberal democracies; potentially, immigration and asylum issues remain time bombs in the hands of demagogues and right-wing politicians, ready to explode upon very short notice. Not only politically, but theoretically as well, the incorporation and acceptance of immigrants, aliens, and foreigners into liberal democracies touch upon fundamental normative and philosophical problems concerning the modern nation-state system.

Dilemmas of citizenship in contemporary Europe thus have implications for debates about citizenship in contemporary political philosophy. In discussions throughout the 1980s and 1990s, and particularly under the influence of the so-called liberal-communitarian debate, the concept and practice of citizenship was analyzed largely from a normative perspective (Galston 1991; Macedo 1990; Kymlicka and Norman 1995). Usually one aspect—the privileges of political membership—was in the foreground.[9] This normative discussion, primarily about the duties of democratic citizenship and democratic theory, was carried out in a sociological vacuum. Political philosophers paid little attention to citizenship as a sociological category and as a social practice that inserts us into a complex network of privileges and duties, entitlements and obligations. Political philosophy and the political sociology of citizenship went their separate ways. But the privileges of political membership are only one aspect of citizenship; collective identity and the entitlement to social rights and benefits are others. We need to disaggregate the theory and practice of citizenship into these various dimensions and broaden our focus to include conditions of citizenship in sociologically complex, decentered, welfare-state democracies. Through the unprecedented movement of peoples and goods, capital and information, microbes and communication across borders, individuals no longer enter their societies at birth and exit them at death, as John Rawls counterfactually assumed (see 1993, 41; Kleger 1995).

To underscore how constitutive the movements of peoples back and forth across borders have become in the contemporary world, Rainer Bauboeck has observed:

> On the one hand, immigrants who settle in a destination country for good may still keep the citizenship of the sending society and travel there regularly so that the sending country rightly regards them as having retained strong ties to their origins. . . . Temporary migrants, on the other hand, often find it difficult to return and to reintegrate. Some migrants become permanent residents in destination countries without being accepted as immigrants and without regarding themselves as such; others develop patterns of frequent movement between different countries in none of which they establish themselves permanently. . . . Contemporary migration research should go beyond these narrow national views and conceive of migration as a genuinely transnational phenomenon, not only at the moment of border crossings but also with regard to the resulting social affiliations. International migration transnationalizes both sending and receiving societies by extending relevant forms of membership beyond the boundaries of territories and of citizenship. (1998, 26; see also Cohen 1999)[10]

CITIZENSHIP AS SOCIAL PRACTICE

Sociologically, the practice and institution of "citizenship" can be disaggregated into three components: collective identity, privileges of political membership, and social rights and claims.

Collective Identity. Citizenship implies membership in a political entity that has been formed historically, that has certain linguistic, cultural, ethnic, and religious commonalties, and that can be distinguished from similar political entities. The precise form of such an entity varies historically, whether it is a multinational empire or a national republic, a commonwealth, or a federation. Viewed analytically, though, the concepts of citizenship (in the sense of membership in a political community) and national identity (in the sense of membership in a particular linguistic, ethnic, religious, and cultural group) are to be distinguished from each other. Political communities are not composed of nationally and ethnically homogeneous groups. Historically this was just as true in the multinational and multiethnic Hapsburg and Ottoman Empires as it is today in the United States, the United Kingdom, Canada, Australia, and New Zealand.

Privileges of Membership. The oldest meaning of citizenship is that of the privileges and burdens of self-governance. For the ancient Greeks the *politos* is the member of the *polis*, the one who can be called to military service as well as jury duty, who must pay taxes and serve in the Ecclesia in his capacity as member of his Demei at least one month of the year. The link between the city and the citizen is retained in the etymology of *civitas* and *citoyenne* on the one hand and *Buergher* and *Burgh* on the other.

Citizenship confers upon its holders the right of political participation, the right to hold certain offices and perform certain tasks, and the right to deliberate and decide upon certain questions. Aristotle writes in the *Politics:* "The state is a compound made of citizens; and this compels us to consider who should properly be called a citizen and what a citizen really is. The nature of citizenship, like that of the state, is a question which is often disputed: there is no general agreement on a single definition: the man who is a citizen in a democracy is often not one in an oligarchy" (1941, 1274b–75a). In making the identity of the citizen dependent upon the type of political regime, Aristotle is emphasizing the contingent nature of this concept. It is not nature but the city and its conventions, the nomoi, that create the citizen. Yet we see precisely in Aristotle's work how this insight into the socially constituted aspect of citizenship goes hand in hand with an exclusionary vision of the psychosexual attributes of citizenship. Even if regime types determine who is a citizen, only some, in Aristotle's view, are "by nature fit" to exercise the virtues of citizenship; others are not. Slaves, women, and non-Greeks are not only excluded from the statutory privileges of citizenship, but their exclusion is viewed as rational insofar as these individuals are deemed not to possess the virtues of mind, body, and character essential to citizenship. This tension between the social constitution of the citizen and the psychosexual "natural substance" that the citizen ought to possess accompanies struggles over the meaning of citizenship down to our own days. Struggles over whether women should have the vote, whether nonwhite and colonial peoples are capable of self-rule, or whether a gay person can hold certain kinds of public office are illustrations of the tension between the social and the naturalistic dimensions of citizenship.

Social Rights and Benefits. The view that citizenship can be understood as a status that entitles one to the possession of a certain bundle of entitlements and benefits as well as obligations derives from T. H. Marshall (1950). Marshall's catalog of civil, political, and social rights is based upon the cumulative logic of struggles for the expansion of democracy in the nineteenth and the early part of the twentieth centuries. *Civil rights* arise with the birth of the absolutist state; in their earliest and most basic form they entail the rights to the protection of life, liberty, and property, the right to freedom of conscience, and certain associational rights, like those of contract and marriage.

Political rights in the narrow sense refers to the rights of self-determination, to hold and run for office, to enjoy freedom of speech and opinion, and to establish political and nonpolitical associations, including a free press and free institutions of science and culture.

Social rights are last in Marshall's catalog, because they have been achieved historically through the struggles of the workers', women's and other social movements of the last two centuries. Social rights involve the right to form trade unions as well as other professional and trade associations, health care rights, unemployment compensation, old-age pensions, child care, housing and educational subsidies, and the like. These social rights vary widely from one country to another and depend thoroughly upon the social class compromises prevalent in any given welfare-state democracy.

Were we to try to apply Marshall's catalog to the condition of foreigners in the European Union, we would note an interesting reversal. In all European countries, foreigners who are third country nationals possess full protection of their civil rights under the law as well the enjoyment of most social rights. Noncitizens of EU states enjoy the same protection in the eyes of the law as citizens: their earnings and property are equally protected, and they enjoy freedom of conscience and religion.

Under the provisions of the social-welfare democracies of European states, most foreign residents are entitled to health care benefits, unemployment compensation, old-age pensions, child care, some housing and educational subsidies, as well as certain social welfare benefits, like minimum income compensation. These social benefits are not conferred automatically. They depend on the individual's length of residence in the host country, her residency status—whether permanent or temporary—and, most commonly, on her particular wage or service contract. Despite variations among member states, foreigners in most EU countries benefit from some of these social rights, but their enjoyment of political membership is either blocked or made extremely difficult.

This sociological analysis of citizenship and incorporation regimes suggests a particular methodological perspective: the collective identity of foreigners results from the complex interaction between various factors, namely, the social and cultural attributes of immigrant groups, which originate in their home country; and the juridical, political, social as well as cultural norms and practices of the host country. This then suggests the question, Why are certain rights granted to foreigners and others withheld? Why are certain identity-marking characteristics privileged in certain contexts and not in others? Note the difference between Germany and the Netherlands in their practices of defining the collective and individual status of foreigners. Countries single out certain criteria as constitutive of foreign identity. But how do these criteria compare to the history and self-understanding of a particular country? The treatment of the "others" reveals who we are, because in Julia Kristeva's words, "Nous sommes étrangers à nous même" (we are strangers to ourselves) (1991).

POLITICAL PARTICIPATION RIGHTS IN EUROPE TODAY

The highest privilege of citizenship is the possession of political rights—rights to vote, run for, and hold office—in the narrow sense. It is also through the entitlement to and the exercise of these rights that one's status as a citizen, as a member of the body politic, will be established. The lines which divide members from strangers, citizens from foreigners, the "we" from the "they" are drawn most sharply around these privileges.

Political theory on these issues lags far behind actual developments. None of the following host countries of the European Union grants foreigners the right to participate in national elections: Denmark, the Netherlands, Sweden, Belgium, France, Austria, Germany, and United Kingdom.[11] Yet in Denmark as well as Sweden, foreigners can participate and run in local and regional elections. Norway, Finland, and the Netherlands grant these rights at the local but not regional level. In Switzerland, which is not a member of the European Union, the cantons of Neufchâtel and Jura grant foreigners these rights as well. Similar attempts in Berlin, Hamburg, and Schleswig-Hollstein to grant local election rights to foreigners who have resided in Germany for more than five years, were declared "unconstitutional" by the German Constitutional Court (Weiler 1995). The Maastricht Treaty, which established Union citizenship for the citizens of the twelve member countries, rendered this decision moot (cf. BVerG, 8.1. 1997). What, then, is the link between the status of active citizenship and "national membership"?

The acquisition of citizenship rights proceeds in most countries of the world along three categories: the principles of territory, origin, or consent. The principle of territoriality known as *jus soli* means that a political community has sovereign claims over a territory: persons who live in this territory are considered either to fall under the dominion or authority of this sovereign or are themselves viewed as part of the sovereign. The first case corresponds to pre-democratic understandings of sovereignty, and defines citizens as subjects, as was the case with the absolutist regimes of Europe. Historically the Ottoman Empire as well as the Hapsburg monarchy and the German Kaiser regime followed this pattern. These old regimes always granted certain protected groups special citizenship rights and privileges—as was the case, for example, for the *Reichsjuden*, the Jews of the Empire—during the period of the Hapsburg Dual Monarchy.

The territorial principle of citizenship can also have a democratic variant. The principles of citizenship, introduced by the American and the French Revolutions, follow the democratic understanding of *jus soli*: each child born on the territory of a democratic sovereign is potentially a member of this sovereign and therefore has claims to citizenship (Brubaker 1992, 45).

The second principle according to which citizenship is granted is that of ethnic origin or belonging, *jus sanguinis*. If one considers France and the United States prime examples of countries that base citizenship on *jus soli*, Germany could until recently, be seen as paradigm example of jus sanguinis.[12] The principle of jus sanguinis means that citizenship is attained by virtue of belonging to a people or ethnic group. How is belonging to a people or ethnic group to be established? Biological lineage is the simplest and clearest criterion for defining this. The German citizenship law of July 23, 1913—*das Reichs- and Staatsbuergerschaftgesetz*, which formed the basis of Germany's citizenship law until January 1, 2000—stated that citizenship was to be inherited (Klusmeyer 1993). This law was formulated for the specific political purpose of making it impossible for the large numbers of Jews and Poles who then resided in the Kaiserreich to acquire German citizenship (Wertheimer 1987). Only a century earlier, however, the Prussian Edict of Emancipation of 1812 had granted Jews in Prussia the status of citizenship without taking into account criteria of ethnic belonging (Huber 1961). During the Weimar Republic, the German Social Democrats, much like today's coalition government, had sought to reintroduce *jus soli* into German citizenship legislation.

The third practice through which citizenship is granted is "naturalization" or "nationalization." For countries like the United States, Canada, Australia, and New Zealand, which view themselves as "countries of immigration," this procedure is as important as the acquisition of citizenship rights through birth right or descent. Increasingly, European Union countries which had not hitherto viewed themselves as such immigration societies, are also recognizing the significance of naturalization prosedures and reexamining their old practices.

Naturalization usually involves fulfilling certain years of residency in the country where citizenship is sought. Other requirements may include some proof of language competence, a demonstration of "civic knowlwdge," as is the case in the United States, employment and proof that one will not be a "financial burden on the system," and some certification of good character or conduct, usually satisfied either through searches of police records or by personal letters of affidavit from citizens. Most countries grant naturalization requests on the basis of family bonds—from a spouse, a parent, or a sibling—priority over other types.

It is important to emphasize that the procedures and decisions of naturalization policy have rarely been subject to strict scrutiny either for their constitutionality or for human rights violations. The institutional aspect of citizenship has usually been shrouded in mists of bureaucratic logic, or has subject to the vacillating will of democratic majorities.

CITIZENSHIP AND POLITICAL THEORY

I have examined dilemmas of citizenship in contemporary Europe from the standpoint of normative political philosophy. I also have suggested that these political developments should lead us to rethink our normative categories; we need to bring them more into contact with the new sociological and institutional realities of citizenship in the contemporary world.

A central thesis of my argument is that theories of citizenship have often relied upon obsolete and misleading premises. The first among them is the fiction of a "closed society." Political philosophers have often assumed a closed society with nonporous borders. In Rawls's crystal-clear formulation:

> The first is that we have assumed that a democratic society, like any political society, is to be viewed as a complete and closed social system. It is complete in that it is self-sufficient and has a place for all the main purposes of human life. It is also closed, in that entry into it is only by birth and exit from it is only by death. . . . For the moment we leave aside entirely relations with other societies and postpone all questions of justice between peoples until a conception of justice for a well-ordered society is on hand. Thus, we are not seen as joining society at the age of reason, as we might join an association, but as being born into a society where we will lead a complete life. (1993, 41)

In light of global developments in industry, finance, communication, tourism, and the arms industry it is implausible today to proceed from the counterfactual Rawlsian assumption that "a democratic society can be viewed as a complete and a closed social system." A theory of political justice must necessarily include a theory of international justice. Not only the current level of development of a global civil society, but more significantly, the fact that in democratic societies the right of exit remains a fundamental right of the citizen makes this fiction obsolete.

Furthermore, to be a foreigner does not mean to be beyond the pale of the law. It means to have a specific kind of legal and political identity that includes certain rights and obligations while precluding others. In many European host countries we see today the softening of those legal restrictions that previously made it impossible for foreigners to participate in elections and run for office. The restrictions which barred foreigners from political membership rest, in the final analysis, upon assumptions of who the citizens themselves are and of what the virtues of citizenship consist.

In this respect, the principles of neither *jus sanguinis* nor *jus soli* are consistent and plausible enough to justify the theory and practice of democratic citizenship. There is a hiatus between the self-understanding of democracies and the way they confer citizenship. While democracy is a form of life which rests upon active consent and participation, citizenship is distributed according to passive criteria of belonging, like birth upon a piece of land and socialization in that country or membership in an ethnic group.

A further assumption that has been greatly misleading in these debates is that of *state-centeredness*. Locke was right in insisting that consent was expressed through citizens' participation in the numerous activities of civil society (see [1690] 1980). Our contemporary societies are even more complex, fragmented, and contradictory than those in Locke's time. In such societies human conduct and interactions assume many and diverse forms. We are just as fully members of a family, of a neighborhood, of a religious community, or of a social movement as we are members of a state. While the modern nation-state remains a possible structural expression of democratic self-determination, the complexity of our social lives integrates us into associations that lie above and below the level of the nation-state. These associations mediate the manner in which we relate to the state. If we stop viewing the state as the privileged apex of collective identity, but instead, along with Rawls, view it "as a union of unions," then citizenship should also be understood as a form of collective identity mediated in and through the institutions of civil society.[13] In the European context this means foreigners' claims to citizenship in a political entity should be established not through hierarchical decisions from above alone, but through individuals' exercise of certain skills and the fulfillment of certain conditions. Civil citizenship should lead to political citizenship (Janoski 1998).

But what reasonable conditions need to be fulfilled in order for someone to transition from one status of alienage to another?[14] Length and nature of residency in a particular country are undoubtedly top among such criteria. Others are minimal knowledge of the language of the host country as well as certain "civil knowledge" about the laws and governmental forms of that country. Criteria such as these can be formulated and applied reasonably.

Increasingly, it is what one does and less who one is, in terms of ascribed identities of race, ethnicity, and religion, that should determine membership and citizenship claims. Applied to the case of contemporary Europe, this means very concretely: If an Italian or a Portuguese national can take up residence in Paris, Hamburg, or London and run for office as well as vote in local elections in those countries after about six months, what is the justification for denying similar rights to a Turkish or Croatian national, to a Pakistani or to an Algerian who has resided in a country, has participated in the economy and civil society, has been a member of a trade union or a religious group, a school board or a neighborhood association? The liberal-democratic state is a "union of unions"; while the virtues and abilities that make an individual a good neighbor, a reliable coworker, an honest member of the business community may not be immediately transferable to the virtues and abilities required by political citizenship, it is just not the case that there is an ontological divide between them. We must inquire about those social practices through which the transition from civil to political citizenship can be encouraged and the qualities of mind of an "enlarged mentality" can be cultivated (Benhabib 1992). Such an enlarged mentality allows us to exercise civic imagination in taking the standpoint of the other(s) into account in order to woo their agreement on controversial and divisive norms that affect our lives and interactions. Such an enlarged mentality, which I see as a sine qua non for the *practice*, not the *acquisition*, of democratic citizenship, presupposes the virtues of membership and association, an individual's ability to negotiate conflicting perspectives and loyalties, and the ability to distance oneself from one's most deeply held commitments in order to consider them from the hypothetical standpoint of a universalistic morality (Benhabib 1994). The democratic public sphere in which these virtues are cultivated is not opposed to global civil society, but is an aspect of it.

IMMIGRATION AND EMIGRATION: ARE THEY SYMMETRICAL?

Let me return to the central philosophical problem concerning the principles of liberal-democratic membership. Are there any justifiable conditions under which a liberal-democratic polity can close its borders to outsiders seeking admission? My short answer is, No, there are none. There are some justifiable restrictions on the quality and quantity of new immigration which nation-states can allow, but never a justification from closing borders completely. Furthermore, many of these plausibly justifiable restrictions, like limiting the entry of individuals and groups identified as posing a military, security or immunological threat to a country, themselves often permit serious contestation. Think of how the claim that certain individuals pose a "national security threat"[15] can and has been misused throughout history to prevent political dissidents from entering countries and has led to the creation of categories of "unwanted" aliens. The virtues of liberal democracies do not consist in their capacities to close their borders but in their capacities to hear the claims of those who, for whatever reasons, knock at our doors. Hearing these claims does not mean automatically granting them or recognizing them, but it does mean that the moral claim of the one who is seeking admission imposes a reciprocal duty upon us to examine, individually and singly, each case of those seeking membership in our midst.

There is, in other words, a fundamental human right to exit as well as to seek admission into a political community, a right grounded in the recognition of the individual as an autonomous person entitled to the exercise of rights. The fundamental right to human liberty entails the fundamental right to entry and exit. This fundamental right creates a set of reciprocal obligations and duties upon states—for example, to refrain from preventing the exit of those who want to leave or from completely blocking off those who want to enter. Any restrictions to be placed upon the rights of exit and entry must be made compatible with, as well as limited by, this fundamental human right.

This fundamental right of exit and entry is a moral claim and not a legal right, which would or could be defended by established authority with legal, coercive powers.[16] This right articulates a moral claim because the recognition of the human liberty to express allegiance to the political order knowingly and willingly entails the right to exit when such allegiance is not forthcoming. Citizens are not prisoners of their respective states. Only a polity that violated other fundamental human liberties would also be one that limited the freedom of its citizens to exit.

In one of the few contemporary discussions of these issues, Michael Walzer argues that "the fact that individuals can rightly leave their own country, however, doesn't generate a right to enter another (any other). Immigration and emigration are morally asymmetrical" (1983, 40). But the asymmetry of these rights cannot be maintained, for two reasons. The first ground is a pragmatic consideration that is also morally relevant. In a world where the surface of the earth is already divided into nation-states, or at least into political units that exercise sovereignty over their territory, the individual's right to exit effectively means that one lands upon someone else's territory. There is literally nowhere to go in today's world; at every stretch of the passage one would be crossing into the sovereign territory of some or other political entity. If this is so, then to acknowledge a human right to exit means at least to acknowledge a human right to entry. This *right to entry* must be distinguished from the *claim to membership*, but at this stage only the human right to entry is under consideration.

The second reason why this asymmetry breaks down is that the fundamental human right to exit is meaningful only if one can reverse moral perspectives and consider that for some to be able to go means, for others, that not only will strangers come, but also that we are all potentially strangers in other lands. If we argue that we have a right to leave, then we are also saying that others have to recognize us as potential strangers who may want to enter their country. But if we want this claim recognized for ourselves, then we also must recognize it for others. It is only the mutual recognition of the reciprocal obligations generated by this right that give it meaning as a moral claim. There is a fundamental human right to exit only if there is also a fundamental human right to admittance, though not necessarily to membership.

What is the distinction between *admittance* and *membership*?[17] All organized political communities have the right to control criteria of membership and procedures of inclusion and exclusion. Criteria to be fulfilled, qualifications to be met, and procedures to be followed are usually stipulated by all liberal democracies in granting access to membership and, eventually, citizenship. Admittance does not create an automatic entitlement to membership; it does entail one's moral right to know how and why one can or cannot be a member, whether one will or will not be granted refugee status, permanent residency, and so forth. In articulating these conditions, a liberal-democratic polity must treat the foreigner and the stranger in accordance with internationally recognized norms of human respect and dignity, according to transparent regulations for which identifiable governmental authorities can be held accountable. Furthermore, nonmembers and their advocates must have the right to litigate and contest decisions concerning immigration, asylum, and refugee status (cf. Walzer 1983, 60). The prerogative of democratic sovereigns to define criteria of political inclusion is not an unconditional right. Democratic sovereignty and human rights considerations must mutually limit and control each other.

Liberal democracies are always under a burden of proof, when policing their borders, to prove that the ways in which they do so do not violate fundamental human rights. A democratic state may wish to examine the marriage certificates of citizens and noncitizens for their veracity, but a democratic state that subjects women to gynecological exams in order to test whether the marriage was consummated, as Margaret Thatcher's England did, is violating a fundamental human right of equal treatment and respect of bodily integrity.

Democratic states that are anxious to maintain certain standards of living among their population are free to regulate their labor markets; they may punish employers who hire illegal aliens who lack proper documentation, pay them low wages, and furnish unjust conditions; they may allow employers to recruit workers from certain foreign countries who possess certain skills. But a democratic state that admits such individuals must specify the conditions that would allow them to stay; the opportunities that would allow them to change their status of admission once within certain borders; and the rights and benefits to which admission entitles them. A liberal democracy cannot push entire categories of peoples away, as Germany attempted to do in the early 1990s with the argument that immigrants and asylum seekers negatively affected the domestic standard of living. Besides the dubious causal economic connections established in such assertions, there is also the more fundamental problem of the violation of human rights, be it those of asylum seekers under internationally recognized conventions or the rights of foreign residents to claim political membership, with which I have dealt in this chapter. It is important to acknowledge that a state's economic interests can never alone serve as moral trumps in immigration and asylum policies, and that liberal democracies must seek to balance their economic well-being—if, in fact, immigration is affecting domestic markets adversely—with a commitment to and respect for fundamental human rights.[18]

SOVEREIGNTY, HUMAN RIGHTS AND THE NATION-STATE

In his 1923 work *The Crisis of Parliamentary Democracy,* Carl Schmitt wrote:

Every actual democracy rests on the principle that not only are equals equal but unequals will not be treated equally. Democracy requires, therefore, first homogeneity and second—if the need arises—elimination or eradication of heterogeneity. . . . Equality is only interesting and valuable politically so long as it has substance, and for that reason the possibility and the risk of inequality . . . [that] every adult person, simply as a person, should eo ipso be politically equal to every other person, this is a liberal, not a democratic idea" ([1923] 1985, 9–11)

Schmitt thus drives a wedge between liberal and democratic conceptions of equality. While he understands liberalism to advocate universal moral equality, he views democracy as stipulating only the equality of all as members of a sovereign people. This argument neglects the specificity of modern, as opposed to ancient, projects of democracy.

For moderns, the moral equality of individuals qua human beings and their equality as citizens are imbricated in each other. The modern social contract of the nation-state bases its legitimacy on the principle that the consociates of the nation are entitled to equal treatment as rights-bearing persons precisely because they are human beings; citizenship rights rest on this more fundamental moral equality, which individuals enjoy as persons. "The Rights of Man" and "The Rights of the Citizen" are coeval for the moderns.

To be sure, there are conflicts and tensions in these formulations: every national social contract circumscribes the circle of its citizens, thus creating distinctions between those who are signatories of the social contract and those to whom the contract applies but who have no standing as signatories. Modern liberal democracies, established in the wake of the American and French Revolutions, proclaim at one and the same time that the consociates of the sovereign body are to treat one another as rights-bearing individuals by virtue of their status as human beings, not just as consociates. At the same time, these very proclamations, articulated in the name of universal truths of nature, reason, or God, also define and delimit boundaries, create exclusions within the sovereign people as well as without. There are "mere auxiliaries to the Republic," as Kant called women, children, and propertyless servants within ([1797] 1996, 92), and there are foreigners and strangers without. This constitutive tension does not arise, as Schmitt assumes, because liberalism and democracy contradict each other. Rather, there is a constitutive dilemma in the attempt of modern nation-states to justify their legitimacy through recourse to universalist moral principles of human rights, which then get particularistically circumscribed. The tension between the universalistic scope of the principles that legitimize the social contract of the modern nation and the claim of this nation to define itself as a closed community plays itself out in the history of the reforms and revolutions of the last two centuries.

When Hannah Arendt wrote that "the right to have rights" was a fundamental claim as well as an insoluble political problem, she did not mean that aliens, foreigners, and residents did not possess any rights ([1951] 1979, 226). In certain circumstances, as with Jews in Germany, with Greek and Armenian nationals in the period of the founding of the republic of Turkey, and with German refugees in Vichy, France, entire groups of peoples were "denaturalized," or "denationalized," and lost the protection of a sovereign legal body. For Arendt, neither theoretical nor institutional solutions to this problem were at hand. Theoretically, she ought to have explored further the constitutive tension between national sovereignty and human rights claims; institutionally, several arrangements have emerged since the end of World War II that express the learning process of the nations of this world in dealing with the horrors of the past century: the limiting and testing of parliamentary majorities through constitutional courts, particularly in the domain of human rights issues; the 1951 Convention relating to the Status for Refugees; the creation of the United Nations High Commissioner for Refugees (UNHCR); the institution of the International Court; and, more recently, of an International Criminal Court through the treaty of Rome. While procedures of constitutional review (which are becoming more prevalent in European political practice through the development of the European Court of Justice) can help protect the fundamental human and civil rights of ethnic, religious, linguistic, sexual, and other minorities, the UN conventions remain nonenforceable humanitarian guidelines. To this day, the authority of the International Court of Justice in the Hague is contested. Even the International Criminal Court will deal first and foremost to deal with "crimes against humanity." There are still no global courts of justice with the jurisdiction to punish sovereign states for the way they treat refugees, foreigners, and aliens. Nor is there a global law-enforcement agency that would carry out such injunctions. In this domain, voluntary obligations on the part of nation-states, self-incurred through the signing of treaties, remain the norm.

Yet the treatment of aliens, foreigners, and others in our midst is a crucial test case for the moral conscience as well as political reflexivity of liberal democracies. Defining the identity of the sovereign nation is itself a process of fluid, open, and contentious public debate: the lines separating "we" and "you," "us" and "them," more often than not rest on unexamined prejudices, ancient battles, historical injustices, and sheer administrative fiat. The beginnings of every modern nation-state carry the traces of some violence and injustice; thus far Carl Schmitt is right. Yet modern liberal democracies are self-limiting collectivities that at one and the same time constitute the nation as sovereign while proclaiming that sovereignty derives its legitimacy from the nation's adherence to fundamental human rights principles. "We, the people," is an inherently conflictual formula, containing in its very articulation the constitutive dilemmas of universal respect for human rights and particularistic sovereignty claims (Ackerman 1991). The rights of foreigners and aliens, whether they be refugees or guestworkers, asylum seekers or adventurers, indicate that threshold, that boundary, at the site of which the identity of "we, the people," is defined and renegotiated, bounded and unraveled, circumscribed or rendered fluid.

SEVEN

❑   ❑   ❑   ❑

CONCLUSION

What Lies Beyond the Nation-State?

This book began with a consideration of the "strange multiplicity" of our times (Tully 1995): namely, the coexistence of different identity movements, some of which seek to assert the recognition of differences within the boundaries of existing liberal democracies; others of which seek to transform these polities toward multi- or pluricultural formations; and still others of which want to redefine existing boundaries altogether and establish new nation-states.

Completing the circle of the argument, chapter 6 analyzed transformations in citizenship within the member countries of the European Union. Distinguishing the institution of citizenship into three constituent elements—collective identity, political membership, and the right to social entitlements and benefits—I suggested that we are currently witnessing a "disaggregation effect," as a consequence of which these three dimensions of citizenship are being pulled apart. Increasingly, nationality and political membership are being torn asunder. In many European states, it is no longer necessary to be a national of a polity in order to participate in local and regional voting; likewise, one can be entitled to social rights and benefits without having voting rights or without being a national of a specific country—this is the condition of many of Europe's guestworkers. Due to the rapid development of administrative, political, and juridical mechanisms at the level of the European Union, these changes are most clearly discernible at present in the European context, but similar transformations are also evident elsewhere in the world.

Countries such as Mexico and the Dominican Republic permit their large diasporic populations to retain certain citizenship rights at home, such as voting in local and national elections and, in the case of the Dominican Republic and Colombia, even running for and holding office. In order to keep alive the ties of its large emigrant population to the home country, India has recently changed its passport and property holding regulations. Throughout Southeast Asia and Latin America, "flexible citizenship" is emerging as the norm for the twenty-first century (Ong 1999). The strange multiplicities of our times and the disaggregation or flexibility of citizenship are closely linked; together they herald deep transformations in the modern nation-state system.

The modern nation-state in the West, in the course of its development from the sixteenth to the nineteenth centuries, struggled to attain four goals: territorial dominion; administrative control; consolidation of collective cultural identity; and the achievement of political legitimacy through increased democratic participation. There is widespread consensus that these four functions of the state are all undergoing profound transformations. The modern nation-state system, characterized by the "inner world" of territorially bounded politics and the "outer world" of foreign military and diplomatic relations—in short, the "state-centric" system of the nineteenth and early-twentieth centuries—is, if not at an end, at a minimum undergoing a deep reconfiguration (Rosenau 1997, 4ff.). Arguing that these contemporary developments present a qualitatively altered stage in the development of the world political system, David Held and his colleagues have introduced the phrase the "deterritorialization of politics, rule, and governance" to capture these changes (Held et al. 1999, 32).

Globalization brings with it the embedding of the administrative-material functions of the state in an increasingly volatile context that far exceeds its capacities to influence decisions and outcomes. The nation-state is, on the one hand, too small to deal with the economic, ecological, immunological, and informational problems created by a more interdependent environment; on the other hand, it is too large to contain the aspirations of identity-driven social and regionalist movements. Under these conditions, *territoriality* is fast becoming an anachronistic delimitation of material functions and cultural identities. As a global economy undermines the power of nation-states to define redistributive policies and to achieve economic justice at home, alternative sources of cultural hegemony are provided by the inter- and transnationalization of culture, the movement of peoples across porous state borders, and the rise of global media. *Democratic legitimacy* now has to be attained in nation-states where the "we" of "we, the people," is increasingly frayed and amorphous. The crises of redistributionist politics affect solidarity across social classes, while the rise of multiculturalist and identity-driven movements fragment the "we" and render its boundaries fluid and porous. Who are "we"? Along with the weakening of democratic sources of legitimacy through the decline of the redistributive role of the state, collective cultural identities grow increasingly volatile and fragmented.

The changing character of the nation-state has implications for citizenship. Citizenship in the modern world has meant membership in a bounded political community that was either a nation-state, a multinational state, or a federation of states. The political regime of territorially bounded sovereignty, exercised through formal-rational administrative procedures and dependent upon the democratic will-formation of a more or less culturally homogeneous group of people, can function only by defining, circumscribing, and controlling citizenship. The citizen is the individual who has membership rights to reside within a territory, who is subject to the state's administrative jurisdiction, and who is also, ideally, a member of the democratic sovereign in the name of whom laws are issued and administration is exercised. Following Max Weber, we may say that this unity of *residency, administrative subjection, democratic participation,* and *cultural membership* constituted the "ideal typical" model of citizenship in the modern nation-state of the West (see Weber [1956] 1978, 901–26). The influence of this model, whether or not it adequately corresponds to local conditions, extends far beyond the West: modernizing nations in Africa, the Middle East, Latin America, and Asia, which entered the process of state-formation at later points than had their West European counterparts, copied this model wherever they came into existence as well.

Despite the hold of this model upon our political and institutional imagination—and nowhere is this more evident than in practices governing naturalization, immigration, asylum, and refugee rights—we have entered a world in which liberal democracies will have to come to grips with the end of unitary citizenship. Multicultural movements are an expression of these transformations, as well as players in shaping the future. Multiculturalist demands are antithetical to the Weberian model in every respect: they plead for the *pluralization* of cultural identities; they demand the *decentering* of administrative uniformity and the creation of *multiple* legal and jurisdictional hierarchies; they ask for the *devolution* of democratic power to regions or groups; and they welcome the *weakening* of the bond between continuing territorial residency and citizenship responsibilities.

Without a doubt, a central factor driving all these changes is the new global stage of the world economy. With the tremendous expansion of the means of transportation and communication worldwide, more and more peoples of the world are traveling and coming into contact with one another. The migrants of the twenty-first century, unlike their ancestors in the last two centuries, are not obligated to lose their ties to their home countries— either legally, politically, or economically. With the liberalization of citizenship concepts in the receiving countries through the rise of multiculturalism, immigrants are entering societies in which pressures to "naturalize" and to "become like the natives" have weakened considerably. Immigrants need not change their names as they once did upon reaching Ellis Island in New York, nor do their children even need to learn the official language of the receiving country: in many cases they can disappear into the ethnic economic enclaves of most metropolitan centers. Such economic enclaves, which feed the large service sectors of big urban centers—hotels, restaurants, hospitals, sanitation, and the like—also provide environments in which the cultures of countries of origin can be perpetuated, diffused, and sometimes transformed beyond recognition. As long as big capitalist liberal democracies like the United States and those of Europe continue to need cheap labor from the rest of the world, "reverse globalization," whereby the periphery migrates to the center, will continue, and with it, the weakening of residency, cultural identity, and citizenship claims.

The main trajectory of globalization, however, is still from the center to the periphery, rather than vice versa. This is a process in which transnational and global corporations are networking the world through markets in commodities and securities, stocks and microchips, television networks and satellite dishes. Even within the European Union, the movement of capital and services across nation-state boundaries far exceeds that of individuals. Undoubtedly, the emergence of a common market of 370 million consumers, expected to increase to over 650 million with the EU expansion eastward to include the countries of eastern and central Europe by 2007, is enticing to European capitalists, no matter what the occasional conflict of national interests between them may be. What then is the alternative to the contemporary waning nation-state system? A *res publica mundialis* or a *global.com*? A world republic or unbridled capitalist expansion that undermines nation-states as well as the democratic controls that stand in its path?

We are facing the genuine risk that the worldwide movement of peoples and commodities, news and information will create a permanent flow of individuals without commitments, industries without liabilities, news without a public conscience, and the dissemination of information without a sense of boundaries and discretion. In this "global.com civilization," persons will shrink into e-mail addresses in space, and their political and cultural lives will proliferate extensively into the electronic universe, while their temporal attachments will be short-lived, shifting and superficial. Democratic citizenship, internet utopias of global democracy notwithstanding, is incompatible with these trends. Democratic citizenship requires commitment; commitment requires accountability and a deepening of attachments.

Yet globalization also heralds other developments more compatible with democratic citizenship: the emergence of a world-wide discourse of human rights; the growth of transnational networks of solidarity across cultures and religions around issues like the environment, global warming, women's and children's rights; the rise of NGOs working to combat AIDS, to ameliorate the predicament of prisoners of conscience (Amnesty International), and to bring medical relief to millions around the world (Médecins sans Frontières); the spread of a global youth culture; the emergence of transnational structures of governance, like the EU—these are all indicators of new modalities of political and ethical action and co-ordination in a new world. They suggest that democratic citizenship can also be exercised across national boundaries and in transnational contexts. The most urgent question facing future democratic theory and practice will be whether, in view of the obsolescence of the unitary model of citizenship, we can still preserve such aspects of democratic agency.

In view of our contemporary condition, Kant's concept of "cosmopolitan citizenship" has been frequently invoked as a possible alternative (see Nussbaum 1997; Bohman and Bachmann 1997). But Kant viewed cosmopolitanism as an ethical attitude, not as a form of political organization; the ethical interest in the world that the world citizen must show was possible only against the background of the citizen's attachments to a specific republic. Kant envisaged a world in which all members of the human race would become participants in a civil order and enter into a condition of "lawful association" with one another. Kant's cosmopolitan citizens still need their individual republics to be citizens at all. This is why he is so careful to distinguish a "world government" from a "world federation." A world government, he argues, would be a "soulless despotism," whereas a world federation would still permit the exercise of citizenship within bounded communities (Kant [1795] 1914, 453; [1795] 1957, 112; see Benhabib 2001b).

The *res publica mundialis* cannot be a single world republic; only a federation of individual republics is compatible with the republican idea of freedom If we go to the root of the word *republic* and recall that it derives from the Latin *res publica*, meaning "the common thing" or "that which is shared by all," our contemporary question is: After the waning of unitary models of citizenship, what form will bounded communities and democratic citizenship assume to enable the exercise of democratic deliberation and experimentation as well as the recognition of diversity? A global civilization that is to be shared by world citizens will need to be nourished by local attachments; rich cultural debate; contestations about the identity of the "we"; and a sense of democratic experimentation with institutional design and redesign. As long as future collectivities reconstitute themselves through the democratic resignification of their cultural legacies in which all those affected can participate, new territorial boundaries and national frontiers can be drawn, and new institutions of power sharing, representation, and governance can be reimagined. This is the future challenge of synthesizing democratic equality and cultural diversity.

Throughout this book I have suggested that institutional experimentation and redesign is quite compatible with a philosophically adequate understanding of cultures and cultural identity. Such an understanding would emphasize that cultures are formed through complex dialogues and interactions with other cultures; that the boundaries of cultures are fluid, porous, and contested. Cultural identities in complex, pluralist democratic societies should seek public recognition of their specificity in ways that do not deny their fluidity. However, a great deal of contemporary debate on these issues has been bogged down by false epistemological assumptions. Once these assumptions are rejected, new modalities of pluralist cultural coexistence can be reimagined.

I see two challenges to this vision of cultural plurality and democratic contestation: cultural differences that are rooted in ways of life attached to the land and fundamentalist movements that abhor hybridity and deny cultural complexity. In this book I have not addressed the unique life situations and cultural heritages of the world's indigenous peoples. From the tribes of the Amazon to the Saami of Norway, from Australian Aborigines to the First Nations of the Canadian Federation, there are peoples whose cultural identity is rooted in ways of life attached to a particular region, territory, or hunting and fishing domain. These peoples are seeking not to preserve their languages, customs, and culture alone but to retain the integrity of ways of life greatly at odds with modernity. So far, many nation-states have exploited, conquered, policed, or subjugated these minorities. While being greatly skeptical about the chances for survival of many of these cultural groups, I think that from the standpoint of deliberative democracy, we need to create institutions through which members of these communities can negotiate and debate the future of their own conditions of existence. I follow Kymlicka and Valadez in advocating certain land, language, and representation rights for indigenous populations (Kymlicka 2001; Valadez 2001). As I have suggested in chapter 4, the self-determination rights of many of these groups may clash with gender equality norms of the majority culture. If self-determination is viewed not simply as the right to be left alone in governing one's affairs but is also understood as the right to participate in the larger community, then the negotiation of these ways of life to accommodate more egalitarian gender norms becomes possible.

The dilemmas of the coexistence of aboriginal groups within the larger society pale in comparison with the rise of fundamentalist movements in the contemporary world. Clearly, fundamentalism is a deep reaction not only against globalization, but against the increasing hybridization of cultures, peoples, languages, and religions that inevitably accompanies globalization. Contemporary fundamentalist movements are felt within every major religious tradition, and are not confined to Islam alone. Some fundamentalisms can coexist with the pluralist ethos of contemporary democracies by finding methods of accommodation and compromise: the splitting of the private spheres of family and religious observance from politics and the economy is one of the most common strategies of accommodation (cf. chap. 4 above). Many Christian, Jewish, Muslim, as well as other groups are capable of such accommodation.

It is the rejectionist fundamentalists who find it most difficult to live in a globalized world of uncertainty, hybridity, fluidity, and contestation. Unable to make the daily compromises that the practice of any firmly held religious belief in the contemporary world would require, these groups declare war on global civilization or consume themselves in acts of apocalyptic fervor; often they do both. Such searches for "purity"—be it the racial purity dreams of the Nazis in the previous century or the "true Islam" dreams of the twenty-first century—are doomed to failure, but not before they cause a great deal of mischief and human suffering, instability and fear. Whether these movements will unravel under the weight of their own contradictions, through internal defection, disillusionment, and betrayals, or whether they will have to be defeated by force cannot be foreseen. Yet it is clear that the greatest challenge for contemporary democracies will be to retain their dearly won civil liberties, political freedoms, and representative deliberative institutions, while defusing the fundamentalists' dream of purity and of a world without moral ambivalence and compromise. The negotiation of complex cultural dialogues in a global civilization is now our lot.

NOTES

❑   ❑   ❑   ❑

CHAPTER ONE

A portion of this chapter previously appeared as "The Intellectual Challenge of Multiculturalism," in *Cultureworks*, ed. Marjorie Garber (New York: Routledge). It is reproduced here by permission of Routledge, Inc., part of the Taylor & Francis Group.

1. "If intellectual powers in various manifestations are the advantage of the Europeans, then *they can live up to this advantage in no other way but through reason and goodness* (both of which, fundamentally, are only one). If they act impotently, in furious passion, out of cold greed, in meanly exalted pride, then *they* are the animals, the *demons* opposing their fellow humans. . . . *So, let no one augur the decline and death of our entire species because of the graying of Europe!* What harm would it be to our species if a degenerate part of it were to perish?" (Herder [1797] 1997, 46–47, my emphasis). Note here how the critique of "civilization" is also a critique of Europe and a defense of alternative models of culture and civilization.

2. Samuel Huntington's much-acclaimed *The Clash of Civilizations and the Remaking of World Order* (1996) exhibits such confusions concerning *culture* and *civilization* most vividly. Huntington spends considerable time drawing distinctions between culture, civilization, and race, and concludes: "A civilization is the broadest cultural entity" (43). But he also adds that "Civilizations have no clear-cut boundaries and no precise beginnings and endings. People can and do redefine their identities and, as a result, the composition and shape of civilizations change over time. The cultures of peoples interact and overlap. . . . Civilizations are nonetheless meaningful entities, and while the lines between them are seldom sharp, they are real" (43). Despite these socially constructivist premises, he goes on to defend an essentialist view in the rest of the book in

that he seeks a system of clear individuation of civilizations that can then serve as an explanation for global conflict and international realignments. "Peoples and countries with similar cultures are coming together. Peoples and countries with different cultures are coming apart" (125). There are two major difficulties in this explanatory model: First, if one cannot clearly individuate the explanans, how can one use it at all? According to Huntington, it is uncertain whether there are five, six, or eight civilizations in the contemporary world (Sinic, Japanese, Hindu, Islamic, and Western, with, arguably, Orthodox Russian civilization, Latin American, and perhaps African to be included in the list). But how can these unclearly delineated entities then serve as explanations for the primary source of conflict? We seem to have a claim of the kind, Identity conflict is caused by civilizational differences. But this is tautological, since identities in turn are defined by the civilizations and cultures to which one belongs. The concept of cultural/civilizational identity is an explanans as well as an explanandum.

Second, Huntington vacillates between "objectivist demarcations" of culture and civilization and "subjective identifications," or between third- and first-person narratives concerning cultural identities. Thus, in addition to common objective elements of language, history, religion, customs, and institutions, Huntington observes that "the civilization to which he belongs is the broadest level of *identification* with which he strongly *identifies*" (43, emphases mine). We are not told what would count as independent evidence for such manifestations of identification in cases of conflict and struggle. The danger here is that the social scientist will impose an artificial coherence and unity upon cultural struggles, which are fought precisely around discrepancies that frequently arise between objective and subjective criteria of cultural identification, and around the legitimacy of subjective accounts themselves.

Of course culture matters (see Harrison and Huntington 2000). Yet much contemporary social science, like advocacy of identity politics itself, has retreated into nineteenth-century banalities that all too quickly create seamless analogies between cultures, nations, territories, value attitudes, worldviews, and institutional patterns. Contemporary anthropology is to some extent an exception to this rule. There are also stellar and clearheaded applications of the concept of culture to social-scientific explanations, like those in Orlando Patterson's work. Patterson notes the oddities and contradictory attitudes that prevail toward culture in the academy as well as in public discourse (2000, 202–3). While politically the preservation and defense of cultural identities is generally considered to be a good thing, there is also widespread resistance to the use of culture as an explanatory variable in the social sciences, for fear that such usage would "essentialize" cultural differences among human groups. Patterson claims that while we welcome cultural essentialism politically, in the social sciences we repudiate it as an explanatory variable. He argues for a responsible use of culture-based variables in the explanation of human behavior (202). I agree. Although in this book I focus on the use of culture in normative theory, I think that social-scientific approaches to culture and normative discussions mutually influence each other, so that a careful examination of one field may have consequences for another.

3. Cf. Amelie Rorty's astute observation. "The distinction between 'culture' and economic or sociopolitical structures is a theory-bound distinction, one which once marked differences between academic disciplines—between anthropology, sociology, and economics—rather than differences in the practices or texts they analyze. . . . On the one hand, culture cannot be understood in abstraction from the dynamics of political organization. On the other hand, economic exchange, judicial processes, medical procedures, or patterns of kinship and friendship cannot be understood independently of their cultural significance" (A. Rorty 1994, 155). Let me also add that I will be using the terms *narrative* and *narrativity* throughout this work in their meaning in ordinary English usage, as a more or less coherent telling or accounting. There is no philosophical commitment on my part either to strong views of agency or emplotment or sequentiality that the use of terms like *narrative* suggests in literary criticism. I have explored conceptions of selfhood and styles of narrative recounting in Benhabib 1999e, 335–61.

4. Culture is a notoriously difficult concept to define, for it is "theory-laden," like many other foundational concepts in social analysis—individual, structure, etc. Note, for example, the definition of culture in the *Encyclopaedia Britannica*: "When words are considered in their relationship to the human organism—that is, as acts—they become behaviour. But when they are considered in terms of their relationship to one another—producing lexicon, grammar, syntax, and so forth—they become language, the subject matter not of psychology but of the science of linguistics. **Culture**, therefore, is the name given to a class of things and events dependent upon symboling (i.e., articulate speech) that are considered in a kind of extra-human context" in *Encyclopaedia Britannica Online*. http://www.eb.com:180/bol/culture, s. v. "culture." This definition is itself linguistically biased, since "symboling" is not exclusively linguistic. Also unclear is what the authors may mean by "a kind of extra-human context." What is helpful in this definition is the emphasis on the perspective of the social inquirer. The same social reality can become the subject matter of many different forms of social inquiry, i.e., anthropology, sociology, linguistics, etc. I follow here Max Weber, who noted that it is the knowledge- and value-interests of the student of human affairs that render the "infinite space-time sequence" into an object of scientific and theoretical inquiry, and nothing intrinsic to the object of study itself. Cf. Max Weber [1917] 1949, 1–50.

5. Ernest Gellner's striking book on nationalism is a very fine example of the strengths as well as limits of his quasi-Marxist functionalist approach. Ac-

cording to Gellner, "The cultural shreds and patches used by nationalism are often arbitrary historical inventions. Any old shred and patch would have served as well. But in no way does it follow that the principle of nationalism itself, as opposed to the avatars it happens to pick up for its incarnations, is itself in the least contingent and accidental"(1983, 56). It is not obvious that "the cultural shreds and patches, used by nationalism are . . . arbitrary historical inventions" (56). There has to be an "elective affinity" between the narratives, works of art, music, and painting through which the nation is narrated, and the past history as well as anticipated and projected future of this group of people.

6. These issues came before the U.S. Supreme Court in a 1990 case known as *Employment Division, Department of Human Resources of Oregon v. Smith.* The case involved two members of the Native American Church who were also employees in a private drug rehabilitation clinic. They applied for unemployment benefits after they had been fired for using peyote in a religious ceremony. The Employment Division denied their claim on the grounds that they were fired for misconduct at work, but the state Supreme Court held that using peyote as part of a religious ceremony could not constitute misconduct. In the back-and-forth between the Oregon court and the U.S. Supreme Court, the precedent established in *Sherbert (Sherbert v. Verner,* 374 U.S. 398; 83 S.Ct. 1790; 9163 U.S.Lexis 976), that "undue burdens" could not be imposed upon an individual for following his or her religious beliefs and practices without demonstration of a "compelling state interest," was overturned. In the majority opinion written by Justice Antonin Scalia, the Court appealed to the importance of enforceable general laws—which did not intend to discriminate against any religion in particular—for maintaining order and stability in a diverse nation. (*Employment Division, Department of Human Resources of Oregon v. Smith,* 494 U.S. 872, 110 S. Ct. 1595 [1990]. These cases well illustrate the difficulties associated with differentiating between kinds of religious practices in the liberal state by applying the principles of toleration. I am grateful to Annie Stilz for bringing this case to my attention through her paper, "Free Exercise Revisionism and the First Amendment," submitted to my course Government 2064, "Nations, States, and Citizens," Harvard University, fall 2000.

7. Discourse ethics has been charged by many critics with exhibiting a rationalist bias, in that it appears to restrict the domain of moral discourse only to those who can linguistically represent themselves in the discursive context. But clearly we have moral obligations toward all beings whose interests and well-being we can affect through our actions, whether or not they are capable of linguistic competence. This is certainly true; yet we should not ignore that the content of these obligations is itself subject to discursive debate among parties, some of whom act as *advocates* in the name of those who cannot adequately represent themselves. The whales do not speak to us, even though we can com-

municate with certain species of dolphins. But the argument about preserving some species by protecting their habitats from commercial fishing and touristic use, etc, is an argument made by various human advocacy groups like Greenpeace, the Sierra Club, Japanese, Canadian, and Russian fishermen, and their respective governments. And of course, children and the differently abled exhibit moral agency along a certain developmental spectrum. At a certain point, the child is perfectly capable of linguistic and moral agency, even if he or she is still in a condition of tutelage and dependence. The morality of child raising very much depends on treating the child with the knowledge that he or she will become your equal. We should also not forget that children are moral and legal persons, protected by the state, even against the institutions of their own family, when need be. Moral and legal personality can precede full agency.

The differently abled persons are always part of our community of discourse, although, depending on the severity of their disablement, they may be more or less capable of moral and legal agency. But they possess moral and legal personality. The emergence of the movement for the disabled in almost all democratic societies in the last three decades indicates how norms in this domain as well—from such mundane measures as creating ramps and special toilets for the differently abled, to programs for the full hiring and integration into the labor force of differently abled citizens—are subject to discursive validation.

Let me put the point as follows: Although our moral obligations exceed the community of those who can only be represented as full discursive and linguistic agents, the norms of our interaction with these beings are themselves subject to discursive argumentation as well as debate. Moral obligations do not come into existence only through discourses; communicative ethics fully acknowledges the embeddedness of morality in the ethical, political, and cultural context of our everyday life-world. Once these norms become problematic, however—as does child abuse in a dysfunctional family, for example—a moral discourse is needed, and of course, many times much more than discourse is required in order to restore the content as well as validity of the ruptured moral fabric of everyday interactions.

8. Offe analyzes the dynamic relationship between the three i's and the three r's: interest-based, ideology-based, and identity-based conflicts and their resolutions through the redistribution of rights, resources, and recognition. He suggests how conflicts of one kind can be moved up "one level" if resolutions around certain issues leave actors unsatisfied with existing distributional and symbolic arrangements. Thus unresolved redistribution conflicts can take the form of ideological ones, and both in turn can result in identity conflicts. Offe's approach is welcome because it suggests that we need not be stuck in dichotomous thinking around "redistribution" or "recognition" or in considerations

as to whether all identity groups are cultural groups—clearly they are not; the disabled are not a cultural group—or whether cultural groups can be reduced to socioeconomic cleavages, i.e, to class. Such discussions about the "whatness" of groups should be replaced by considerations of their "whoness"—i.e., their self-presentation in the public political sphere as actors. See Offe 1998, 119–23. See the exchange between Nancy Fraser and Iris Young, which largely centers around such typologies. Fraser 1997a: 189–297; Young 1997,147–60; Fraser 1997c, 126–29.

9. Recent controversy over a proposal to reform bilingual education programs in New York City public schools suggests that self-ascription and self-identification should be taken more seriously in determining whether minority children should receive education in their own languages. Immigrant ethnic groups show large variation with respect to their desire to continue to educate children in their native tongues. Although most Latin and Central American parents would like their children to receive some kind of Spanish language instruction in the schools, not all of them approve of the present, highly ascriptive system; and a great many immigrants from the former Soviet Union and its Republics—like the Ukraine, Georgia, Adzerbaijan—have little interest in their children continuing these languages at all. While some Indian immigrants who speak Urdu are happy to retain it as their language at home, they generally support English language proficiency in public spaces (Mireya Navarro, "Consensus Is Lacking on Bilingual Education," *New York Times*, February 24, 2001). I support the creation of flexible multicultural policies for pluricultural societies, which not only support individuals' options in naming their own cultural identities but also broaden children's imagination by confronting them with the variety and plurality of human tongues and ways of being.

CHAPTER TWO

This chapter has previously appeared as " 'Nous' et 'les Autres': The Politics of Complex Cultural Dialogue in a Global Civilization," in *Multicultural Questions*, ed. Christian Joppke and Steven Lukes, 44–63 (Oxford: Oxford University Press, 1999). It has been revised and expanded for inclusion in this volume. It is reproduced here with permission of Oxford University Press.

1. See brief entry "Medieval Philosophy," in Spade 1994, 82ff; Fakhry 1983, 55–77.

2. Galileo Galilei, *Dialogue of the Two New Sciences* (1638), in Adler 1990, 125–260.

3. It may seem that there is no difference between positions 3 and 4, insofar as any defense of a legal system based upon the recognition of universal

human rights would involve a moral view of the human person as a being entitled to such rights. I agree; in that sense, legal universalism without moral universalism is an incoherent position. Nonetheless, there are attempts in contemporary philosophy to give a weaker—more political and pragmatic and less moral—justification of legal universalism. The question is whether this is a defensible philosophical option. My own view is that position 4 inevitably slides into position 3, which then leads to some form of 2.

4. In *The Postmodern Condition* Lyotard is more explicit about the link between claims of conceptual incommensurability and issues raised by the encounters of cultures. He concludes that the epistemologically enlightened postmodernist, as opposed to the imperialistically oriented Eurocentric scientist, does not seek legitimation, but instead assumes the attitude of the curator of a conceptual museum and "gaze(s) in wonderment at the variety of discursive species, just as we do at the diversity of plant or animal species" (1984, 26–27).

5. It is inconsistent of Richard Rorty, after his admission that there is no essential asymmetry between intercultural and intracultural disputes, to continue to assert that "the pragmatist, dominated by the desire for solidarity, can only be criticized for taking his own community too seriously. He can only be criticized for ethnocentrism, not for relativism. To be ethnocentric is to divide the human race into the people to whom one must justify one's beliefs and others. The first group—one's ethnos—comprises those who share enough of one's beliefs to make conversation possible" (1985, 13).This manner of putting the issue is misleading. The word *ethnos* has referred since Aristotle to those who share a certain *ethike*, a certain way of life and a certain set of values. In our days, this word designates linguistic and cultural descent. Thus, in the United States we speak of Italian Americans, Jewish Americans, Chinese Americans, African-Americans, and others as constituting "ethnic" groups. Certainly, it would be a moral and political calamity if what Rorty meant was that Italian Americans needed to justify their views and beliefs only to other Italian Americans. This kind of justification of solidarity would be only a philosophical whitewash for all sorts of ethnic and cultural prejudice and racism. Rorty does not mean this. Why then does he continue to write and speak in ways that on the one hand echo older forms of hermetic and pre-Davidsonian cultural relativism and on the other hand, reject radical cultural relativism and incommensurability? A distinction between the general idea of a community of conversation and a culturally specific ethnic community would help sort out some of these contradictions.

6. Greek thought distinguished between *fusis* and *nomos*—between what is "by, according to, or from nature" and what is due to human convention and custom. Things by nature were and should be everywhere the same, whereas the *nomoi*—the laws—reflected great range and variation across human communities. Thus there could be no human community without a regime of prop-

erty, but whether property should be held in common by members of the Demei, owned jointly but worked upon individually, or both owned and worked upon privately was dependent upon specific nomoi. Both Greek historians like Herodotus and philosophers like Aristotle are deeply aware of cultural variation and the challenges this poses to finding the "best by nature" in human affairs.

7. The verses from Paul Celan's famous poem "Todesfuge" (Deathfugue) ([1952] 2000, 31) are:

> Black milk of daybreak we drink you at night
> we drink you at morning and midday we drink you at evening
> we drink and drink
> A man lives in the house he plays with his vipers he writes
> he writes when it grows dark to Deutschland your golden hair
> Margareta
> Your ashen hair Shulamith we shovel a grave in the air
> where you won't lie too cramped.

8. I find quite compelling Alasdair MacIntyre's claim that such a transcultural conversation may force us to revise forms of theory and practice embodied within our own tradition and that this is a demand of rationality. "Rationality, understood within some particular tradition with its own conceptual scheme and problematic, as it always has been and will be, nonetheless requires qua rationality a recognition that the rational inadequacies of that tradition from its own point of view . . . may at any time prove to be such that perhaps only the resources provided by some quite alien tradition . . . will enable us to identify and to understand the limitations of our own tradition; and this provision may require that we transfer our allegiance to that hitherto alien tradition" (1987, 408). My only disagreement with this formulation would be that traditions, like cultures, are not unities with clearly definable borders but hybrid conversations and argumentations, so that when we "transfer allegiances," we are less choosing a new allegiance or partisanship than positioning ourselves in an "in-between space" of narration, where we can hear and impersonate many and divergent conflicting voices and stories. MacIntyre has defended this view of traditions as "conversations in crisis" in other works, including "Epistemological Crises, Dramatic Narrative, and the Philosophy of Science" (1977, 433–72).

9. In *Ethics and the Limits of Philosophy*, Bernard Williams introduces a distinction between "real" and "notional" confrontations between cultures, which sheds some light on the interdependence of understanding and evaluation. According to Williams, "a real confrontation between two divergent outlooks occurs at a given time, if there is a group of people for whom each of the outlooks is a real option. A notional confrontation, by contrast, occurs when some people know about two divergent outlooks, but at least one of these outlooks does

not present a real option. The idea of a 'real option' is largely, but not entirely, a social notion" (1985, 161). Williams calls relativism seen in this way the "relativism of distance" (162).

10. I add this distinction between "moral contemporaries" and "moral partners" to stress the fact that contemporary conditions have created a de facto contemporaneity, but that this de facto contemporaneity has not yet evolved into mutual moral obligations. While it has become increasingly difficult to justify nonintervention and indifference in the face of the plight of others, there is also widespread "compassion fatigue" (Moeller 1999), as the peoples of the world who are made aware of the miseries and sufferings of others experience a kind of sensory overload and retreat into indifference.

11. It is difficult to assess how much Locke really believed in these claims or how much he was simply blinded by cultural otherness and retreated from it defensively to his own preconceptions. What does not stand in question is how deeply he was involved politically in the colonization of the Americas. As Tully notes: "Locke had extensive knowledge of and interest in European contact with aboriginal peoples. A large number of books in his library are accounts of European exploration, colonization, and of aboriginal peoples, especially Amerindians and their ways. As secretary to Lord Shaftesbury, secretary of the Lord Proprietors of Carolina (1668–71), secretary to the Council of Trade and Plantations (1673–74), and member of the Board of Trade (1696–1700), Locke was one of the six or eight men who closely invigilated and helped to shape the old colonial system during the Restoration" (1993, 140). Part of the fascination with and respect for other cultures in contemporary liberal political thought derives from a desire to undo the historical wrong done to aboriginal peoples in the Americas and elsewhere in the world during the process of Western imperialist expansion. These concerns are very clear in Tully's subsequent work (1995).

CHAPTER THREE

In the spring of 2000 I had the honor of teaching at the Department of Philosophy of the University of Amsterdam as Baruch de Spinoza Professor. Some of the themes discussed in this section formed the topic of a graduate seminar, "Multiculturalism, Feminism, and Human Rights." Many observations I make here are drawn from individual communications and conversations with my students. I would like to thank them all for their enthusiastic readiness to "lay their identities on the line," but in particular Lulu Helder, Laila al Harak, Claus Pirschner, Suzanne Kroeger, and Irene Rosenthal for acting as my willing informants.

1. It is surprising that little attention has been paid to this conflation. I am wholly in agreement with Maeve Cooke's excellent critique of Taylor in this respect. Cooke writes: "Furthermore, in its initial formulation the politics of difference—like the politics of equal dignity—does not presuppose distinctiveness: it leaves open the question whether the identity formed, and life lived, by each individual is unique; nor does it imply that uniqueness is normatively significant. To this extent, in its initial formulation, the politics of difference is not connected with the ideal of authenticity. For this ideal attributes moral value to individual distinctiveness: it emphasizes each individual's capacity to live a life and form an identity that is distinct form every other and that is, by virtue of its very distinctiveness, worthy of recognition" (1997, 261).

There are difficulties in rendering the ideal of authenticity coherent in moral philosophy. And Cooke analyzes some of these difficulties very well. The principal philosophical difficulty is this: How can the ideal of authenticity be given moral content without falling into some form of romanticized essentialism, which ascribes to each individual a unique selfhood, over and against which her actions and conduct can be judged to be authentic or inauthentic? But then where do these criteria of judgment themselves derive from? Are there intersubjectively binding criteria for judging what counts as an "authentic life"? And how successfully can they be differentiated from moral criteria of autonomy? For a formulation of such criteria of what counts as an authentic life, see Ferrara 1994.

2. "The Constitution Act, Part 1: Canadian Charter of Rights and Freedoms" (Salhamy 1986, 156).

3. The Canadian Charter of Rights and Freedoms is itself an ambiguous document, which not only leaves these issues unresolved, but possibly contributes to their exacerbation by proclaiming in section 25 that "the guarantee in this Charter of certain rights and freedoms shall not be construed so as to abrogate or derogate from any aboriginal treaty, or other rights or freedoms that pertain to the aboriginal peoples of Canada including a) any rights or freedoms that have been organized by the Royal Proclamation of October 7, 1763" (cf. Salhamy 1986, 160). This article can be and has been construed to mean that determining of tribal citizenship is a privilege of the aboriginal peoples of Canada. Thus any contradictions that may exist between women's claims to equality and the rights and freedoms of the aboriginal peoples are built right into this document. As Lilianne E. Krosenbrick- Gelissen observes, the women of the First Nations of Canada, through their dual identity as women and as members of First Nations, have been placed in the most precarious position of balancing gender and ethnic rights. The Native Women's Association of Canada has tried to retain citizenship status for women in First Nations while de-

manding the full recognition by the Tribal Councils and Elders of the equal civil and political status of women (Krosenbrink-Gelissen 1993, 207–24).

4. Barry argues that "in neither case is something's being part of the culture itself a reason for doing anything" (2001, 258). From whose perspective is this so? For members of a cultural community, patterns of interpretation of actions, patterns of evaluation of the good, the bad and the ugly, as well as the many reciprocal expectations of their cultural world can very well constitute "reasons" for action. From the standpoint of the observer or the theorist, such reasons may seem spurious and unjustifiable or simply wrong. But this judgment should not be conflated with the way in which aspects of culture function as reasons for members of a culture. I think Barry confuses the *subjective interpretation of reasons for one's actions* with the *objective assessment of the validity of such reasons to serve as justifications for actions*. Since I agree with Barry that intercultural evaluation and understanding is possible, I also agree that cultural reasons are not always equivalent to normatively defensible justifications, but we should distinguish *agent-relative reasons* from *intersubjectively valid justifications*.

5. A very interesting typology of groups, which is far more dynamic than the model used by Kymlicka, has recently been developed by Valadez (2001). Valadez distinguishes three kinds of groups: accommodationist cultural groups who seek self-determination within the institutional structures of the majority society; cultural groups who strive for self-determination through autonomous governance within the boundaries of the state; and cultural groups seeking secession and either independent statehood or irredentist integration (122ff.). In sifting through such group claims, Valadez combines arguments from cultural preservation with arguments for democratic self-determination rights and rectificatory justice. He points out interesting tensions between these various kinds of claims; but the group typology he introduces is extremely helpful and superior to Kymlicka's in that it focuses on these groups as political actors, rather than stressing the genealogical and territorial features of their formation. Such a focus on groups as political actors with political demands in the public spheres of liberal democracies—regardless of how they may have emerged as groups—permits a political assessment of their claims from the standpoint of both justice and deliberative democracy. For further discussion of Valadez see chapter 5 below.

6. Let me illustrate this point again with reference to the case of Catalonia. A large number of Andalusians reside in this province. They are largely working class in origin and came to Catalonia early in the twentieth century to work in the various industrial sectors. When the Catalonian government adopted Catalan as the official language of instruction in its schools, in the 1980s, it effectively blocked the access of those ethnic Spaniards who did not master Catalan to higher-status and better-paying jobs in the bureaucracy and civil

service. Indeed, every language policy creates its exclusions, and there are always losers and winners. But it does matter to know, for example, whether specific language policies target specific minority ethnic groups, and are designed to exclude them from certain positions. We may decide in many such cases that these language policies are so unfair from the standpoint of justice and the equal consideration of the interests of all that they are not worthy of our support. Considerations about how children of the linguistic minority are treated in schools—whether they are given some special language instruction, whether members of ethnic groups who are not competent in the official language are given chances to complete some instruction and some competency exams in this language, and the like—are all important in our assessments. Liberal justice does not require that we give every nationalist striving or movement a carte blanche. We have to evaluate carefully the mix of culturalist aspirations and egalitarian claims. My criticisms of Kymlicka's framework parallel in many respects Joseph Carens's, and like Carens I am very concerned about the relatively limited cultural rights of immigrants in Kymlicka's theory. I shall have more to say about this in chapter 6. See Carens 2000, 73ff.

7. I would like to thank Tamar Szabo Gendler for extremely important comments on an earlier version of this chapter, delivered as a lecture at Syracuse University in December 1998. Gendler argues that Kymlicka's distinction between national minority cultures and immigrant cultures, rests in the final analysis, upon "all and only those cases where we might reasonably expect the group in question to maintain a sufficiently rich set of cultural institutions to allow it to support the autonomy which serves as the justification for group rights in the first place" (1998). But this is not convincing. Gendler thinks that Kymlicka prioritizes autonomy over cultural rights; I do not think he does, or at least the juggling of priorities between "external protections" and "internal freedoms" suggested above quickly dissipates, and Kymlicka accepts noninterference in illiberal cultures. See note 9 below. Empirically as well, the evidence is that antiintegrationist groups that meet Kymlicka's description of societal culture, are also more likely to be less nurturing of autonomy claims. Autonomy must always include exit rights; and for many national minorities, this is extremely problematic. While the policing of marriage, divorce, and inheritance rights, about which I shall say more below, may contribute to "a sufficiently rich set of cultural institutions," such are not always compatible with moral autonomy.

8. In an incisive critique of Kymlicka, Sandra Badin has written: "If it is *not* the case that all cultures provide their members with a range of meaningful options from which they can choose their conceptions of the good, if, in other words, it is true—as it undoubtedly is—that some cultures *do not* provide their members with a range of meaningful options or do not distribute the range of

options equitably among all their members, or do not allow (some of) their members to revise their conceptions once chosen, then what are we to make of the relationship between membership in *one's own* societal culture and the realization of individual freedom? Certainly, it is not the easy, straightforward and uncomplicated relationship that Kymlicka seems to think it is" (1999, emphasis in the original).

9. See Kymlicka's astonishing concession: "In cases where the national minority is illiberal, this means that the majority will be unable to prevent the violation of individual rights within the minority community. Liberals in the majority group have to learn to live with this, just as they must live with illiberal laws in other countries" (1995, 168). Surely the analogy between a national minority living in a polity whose citizens still consider themselves as belonging to the same entity in some sense and the attitude toward "illiberal laws" in other countries cannot be valid. The virtues of forbearance in the first case are required in order to right some historical injustice, and in order to establish intragroup justice; but precisely the exercise of these virtues may also dictate the opposite of moral indifference toward these cultural communities. They may involve active engagement, dialogue, and mutual transformation between members of different cultural groups. Furthermore, whether or not liberals should simply accept "illiberal laws" in other countries is also a matter of measure. Kymlicka himself admits that "gross and systematic violations of human rights, such as slavery or genocide or mass torture and expulsions" (169), may require intervention. But between the two extremes of moral forbearance on the one hand and forceful intervention on the other, there is political cooperation occurring at the level of sub- and transnational human-rights groups and activities, international organizations, and agencies. Most politics of human rights, including women's rights, which will be discussed in the next chapter, take place at this level of organization, cooperation, and agitation. Is it merely a coincidence then that Kymlicka's liberal principles are repeatedly compromised for the sake of the preservation of national minority cultures? I have tried to suggest in this chapter that there are deep flaws in his concept of culture that lead to these slips and concessions to illiberal practices.

10. Fraser has emphasized that this dualistic model does not imply that most social movements do not incorporate dimensions of struggles for recognition as well as redistribution. There has been considerable debate about this issue. See Fraser, 1997a. "On Iris Young's *Justice and the Politics of Difference,*" Fraser 1997b; Young's critique of Fraser's dual systems theory, in Young 1997; and see Fraser's rejoinder (1997c).

11. Some compelling studies of this process of identity reconstitution through questioning of gender, racial, and ethnic boundaries are Kerber 1997; Scott 1988 and 1997; Ryan 1992 and 1997; Landes 1988; Gilroy 1995 and 2000; Malcomson 2000; and Patterson 1999.

12. See *www.census.gov/population/cen2000/phc-t1/tab02.pdf.*

13. "OMB [Office of Management and Budget] officials are also at considerable pains to emphasize that (as cited earlier) "we don't classify individuals around here.' Though literally true, this claim is misleading. While OMB has never told individual Americans what their racial or ethnic identity is, the agency has not, until quite recently, permitted individuals to claim multiple or overlapping identities" (Skerry 2000, 71). Nancy Fraser has suggested to me that it may be interesting to tabulate identity categories in the census along two axes: which groups individuals consider *themselves* to belong to, and which groups *others* consider them to be members of. Discrepancies among such replies could then permit an assessment of the realities of group discrimination as felt and experienced even by individuals who do not consider themselves to be members of some particular group.

14. Peter Skerry writes: "Hence the political environment in which OMB [Office of Management and Budget] and Census Bureau operate is an arcane realm dominated by activists and insiders who know every twist and turn in the corridors of administrative power. Needless to say, this political environment is one that leaves the mass of ordinary Americans very much on the outside. The experts and professionals at OMB and the bureau find themselves in the uncomfortable position of having to make critical decisions about racial and ethnic statistics without the support, or knowledge, of a broad segment of the public" (2000, 79).

15. This discussion has started in the wake of the 2000 census, which for the first time permitted people to identify themselves as belonging to "more than one race," and left the determination of such belonging to individual discretion. Thus, it was possible for a person who was white and Asian American to consider herself "white," "Asian-American," or of "two or more races." Nevertheless, the indiscriminate mixture of cultural categories with skin color—as in the case of all African American peoples, whether they are American-born or born in the West Indies—or the marginalization of culture through racial color coding—as in the case of the Hispanics and Latino groups, who were still asked to identify themselves as white or black—is both sloppy from a social-scientific point of view and insulting to the individuals involved.

The census 2000 website contains the following disclaimer: "The concept of race used by the Census Bureau reflects self-identification by people according to the race or races with which they most closely identify. These categories are socio-political constructs and should not be interpreted as being scientific or anthropological in nature. Furthermore, the race categories include both racial and national-origin groups" (www.census.gov/prod/cen2000/doc/ ProfilesTD.pdf, 5–2). Given these disclaimers and doubts, we have to ask whether we cannot do better than to recirculate obsolete pseudoscientific race concepts in our public life. At least the 2000 census has initiated this discussion. For some astute commentaries, which dissect the paradoxes of American attachment to classificatory schemes on the one hand and the freedom for self-identification on the other, see Russell Thornton, *New York Times*, March 23, 2001; and Steven A. Holmes, *NY Times*, June 3, 2001.

16. Paul Scheffer, *"Het multiculturele Drama"* (The multicultural drama) in *NRC Handelsblad*, January 29, 2000. Thanks to Irene Rosenthal for translating parts of this article and debate for me from the Dutch and for her paper discussing these issues, which was submitted to the course mentioned in the at the beginning of this chapter.

CHAPTER FOUR

1. I distinguish three principal meanings of the *private sphere*. First and foremost, in the liberal state privacy refers to the individual's right to determine and choose the dictates of his or her moral and religious conscience. A second set of privacy rights pertains to economic liberties, such as the freedoms of contract, commodity exchange, and wage labor. Third, privacy refers to the "intimate sphere," that is, the domain of the household, of meeting the daily needs of life, of sexuality and reproduction, of care for the young, the sick and the elderly. See Benhabib 1992, 107–9. These three meanings are not only frequently conflated; more significantly, legislators as well as individual citizens in the liberal state use one set of privacy rights to legitimize practices in other domains. In the multicultural conflicts considered in this chapter, privacy rights in the first sense (that is, the liberties of religion and conscience), have been used to protect and legitimize practices in the third sphere (that is, the domain of the household). When this occurs, the clash of rights and claims implicit between the liberty of conscience of the male subjects on the one hand and the equal treatment of their women and children on the other more often than not gets obscured.

2. de Beauvoir 1949, 306ff.; and Ortner, "Is Male to Female as Nature Is to Culture?" (1974).

3. I would like to caution against the imprecise usage of the term *immigrant* in this otherwise excellent article: we are not told the legal status of the defendants. Is the Chinese husband a permanent resident or a recent U.S. citizen? What about the Japanese mother? We know the young Hmong woman was a U.S. citizen, either born in this country or who acquired citizenship through the refugee status of her family, who most likely were among the boat people fleeing Laos and Cambodia during the last phases of the Vietnam War. Referring to all these individuals as "immigrants" may suggest an all too easy link

between immigration and criminality; and in the last case, it is deeply troubling that the judge in question negates the citizen status of the young Hmong to judge her in accordance with the practices of her natal community.

4. Jeremy Waldron clarifies very helpfully what it might mean to use "culture" as a defense strategy in criminal cases: (1) A person is charged with murder and the charge is

> "reduced," on account of a "cultural defense." (2a) A charge of murder is reduced to manslaughter because some essential element of murder is lacking. Or (2b) A charge of murder is reduced because of provocation, and a cultural element is invoked in characterizing the "reasonableness" of the defendant's response to provocation. Or (2c) the presence of some other particular element—like "reasonable explanation or excuse"—leads us to reduce a charge from first- to second-degree. Or (2d) we accept a complete or partial excuse of insanity or duress or diminished responsibility, accepting cultural elements as part of the case that is made for the existence of the excusing condition. Or (2e) a cultural factor, or some heading under which a cultural element might be taken into account, is mentioned in sentencing guidelines. Or (2f) if the sentencing guidelines are not rigid, cultural considerations are taken into account as a mitigating factor by the judge (2001, 12).

5. Practices relating to inheritance by spouses, children, and relatives, as well as to the status of jointly or individually owned property before, during, or after a marriage, clearly show the intermingling of the three senses of privacy discussed in n. 1. Should these practices be covered by religious law, as Orthodox Muslim and Jewish communities may demand? Should they be covered by the law of the land, whatever that may be? Or should some kind of multiple jurisdiction be worked out? And how are these various arrangements to be made compatible with the requirements of capitalist economies that the sale and exchange of goods and services proceed unimpeded? Multicultural legal arrangements, no less than other social and cultural practices, have to face the iron logic of capitalist commodity exchange. Often, women in Third World countries seem forced to substitute one set of oppressive arrangements, that is, multicultural arrangements in accordance with religious law, for the sake of another, that is, the oppression by ruthless global firms and employers. See Benhabib and M. Chen, "Cultural Complexity, Moral Interdependence and the Global Dialogical Community," in Nussbaum and Glover 1995, 235–55.

6. Upendra Baxi, "Text of Observations Made at a Public Meeting on the Muslim Women (Protection of Rights) Bill," *Hindustania Andolan* (Bombay 1986), cited in Das 1994, 127.

7. My discussion of these incidents relies primarily upon two sources: *Le Foulard et la République*, by Francoise Gaspard and Farhad Khosrokhavar (1995), and an excellent seminar paper by Marianne Brun-Rovet, "A Perspective on the Multiculturalism Debate: 'L'affaire foulard' and Laicité in France, 1989–1999" (2000).

8. The original decision is from the *Avis du Conseil d'Etat du 27 Novembre 1989*. Excerpts from the decision can be found at *http://www.unc.edu/ depts/europe/conferences/Veil2000/Annexes.pdf*. More information on l'affaire foulard can be found at *http://www.conseil-etat.fr/cedata/juris/jurisprudence/92/ ensei92.htm*.

9. The French scarf affair is being followed very closely in Turkey, a secular, multiparty democracy, the majority of whose population is Muslim. Throughout the 1980s Turkey confronted its own version of l'affaire foulard. As the Islamist parties, and in particular the Welfare Party, increased their power in parliament and in society at large, unprecedented numbers of Turkish Islamist women began attending institutions of higher learning, and they insisted on wearing the scarf to cover their heads. Their argument was that Islamic law forbade them to show their uncovered hair to men unrelated to them and in public. The scarf was seen as a symbol of female modesty and purity. From the standpoint of the Turkish state authorities, however, the scarf was seen as a challenge to the secularist and "laic" principles, which Mustafa Kemal Ataturk, the founder of the modern republic of Turkey in 1923, had adopted, following French republican principles. The wearing of the scarf by large numbers of young women was perceived as a direct threat to the separation of state and religion, and to the state guidance of the Muslim religion, practiced carefully by institutions like the Directorate General of Religious Affairs.

As Yesim Arat presents it, "In 1981, the Council of Ministers approved a statute, which required female employees in public institutions and students in schools tied to the Ministry of National Education to dress without headscarves. Following this decision, in 1982, the Council of Higher Education banned the use of headscarves in the universities. Islamist groups and women with headscarves protested the decision. Under increasing pressure from the Islamists, in 1984, the Council of Higher Education allowed women to cover their hair with a turban, a scarf tied at the back and covering only the hair" (2002 forthcoming, 8). After a series of interventions, including from the president of the Republic, who banned the turban in 1987, the Turkish Constitutional Court decided in 1989 that the use of the turban in the universities was unconstitutional and banned it. As in the French case, the students and Islamist organizations representing them appealed. Article 24 of the 1982 Turkish Constitution, guarantees freedom of religious expression, and Article 10 prohibits discrimination due to religious belief and differences in language, ethnicity, and gender; the Council of State and the Constitutional Court both claimed that "rather than an innocent custom, it (the headscarf) has become a symbol of a world view opposed to the fundamental principles of the Republic" (cited in Arat 2002, 11; based on a circular distributed within the universities in 1998 and called "Statutes and Legal Judgments Concerning Dress Codes in Institutions of Higher Education").

CHAPTER FIVE

Parts of this chapter have previously appeared as "The Embattled Public Sphere: Hannah Arendt, Juergen Habermas, and Beyond," *Theoria: South African Journal of Philosophy* (December 1997). They appear here with permission of the editors.

1. Models of deliberative democracy have been widely discussed in recent years, and there are a number of related but subtly competing models circulating in the literature. The most prominent among them are: Cohen 1989; Dryzek 1990; Fishkin 1991; Gutmann and Thompson 1996; Habermas 1996a. I discuss the conceptual as well as sociological differences among some of these models in Benhabib 1996a.

2. I have explained above that we have moral obligations toward beings who are not capable of speech and action or who are so only in a very limited sense. See chap. 1 above. Moral obligations to others cannot be measured by others' capacity to become members in communities of discourse. We have obligations to all beings, including nonhumans, whose well-being can be affected through our actions. The extent as well as content of these obligations require discursive specification.

3. In *Situating the Self: Gender, Community, and Postmodernism in Contemporary Ethics* (1992), I distinguished between "formal" and "complementary" norms of reciprocity. I define *formal reciprocity* as achieved primarily through public and institutional norms, which usually take the form of "If I have a right to X, then you have the duty not to hinder me from enjoying X and conversely" (159). I define *complementary reciprocity* as follows: "Each is entitled to expect and to assume from the other forms of behavior through which the other feels recognized and confirmed as a concrete, individual being with specific needs, talents and capacities" (159). Such norms are usually, though not exclusively, private ones, pertaining to the domains of friendship, love, and care, as well as to other civic associations like religious and professional ones, community and neighborhood organizations, and the like.

4. In an earlier version of this chapter, "Toward a Deliberative Model of Democratic Legitimacy" (in Benhabib 1996a, 74ff, 91 n. 25), I outlined why this critique of Rawls should not be taken to suggest that there are any restrictions in his theory on First Amendment freedom of speech and association. It is the normative model of what counts as public reason that I am criticizing; I am not suggesting that Rawls restricts our freedom of expression.

5. Throughout *Culture and Equality* (2001), Barry attacks "new left" positions, claiming that defenders of group identities are "anti-universalistic

in their thrust" (5); that their theories "fit in nicely with the essentialism of the Counter-Enlightenment" (11), that multicultural politics produces "Commissioners of Political Correctness" (328), etc. Yet the wide array of authors he considers—some, like Iris Young, are sympathetic to multiculturalism and are on the left; others, like Todd Gitlin, do not share her sympathies, but would also consider themselves on the left—suggests that there is just as little consensus on these issues on the left as there is among authors like Will Kymlicka, Joseph Carens, and Melissa Williams, who describe themselves as "liberals" and "deliberative democrats." The unnecessary polarization created by Barry's rhetorical flourishes detracts from the merits of his arguments.

6. I have in mind the much-discussed case of *Santa Clara Pueblo v. Martinez*. This ruling upheld a Santa Clara ordinance granting member status to the children of men who married outside of the tribe while excluding the children of women who did so. The children of Julia Martinez, a Pueblo woman who married a Navajo man, were prevented from gaining title to her Pueblo-administered public housing (*Santa Clara Pueblo v. Martinez* 98 US 1670 [1978]).

7. Consider Walter Lippmann's passionate attempts to distinguish democracy from "simple majority rule," and to refute the claim that democratic majorities can determine the truths of science, philosophy, and ethics:

> When the majority exercises the force to destroy public schools, the minority may have to yield for a time to this force but there is no reason why they should accept the result. For the votes of a majority have no intrinsic bearing on the conduct of a school. They are external facts to be taken into consideration like the weather or the hazard of fire. Guidance for a school can come ultimately only from educators, and the question of what shall be taught as biology can be determined only by biologists. The votes of a majority do not settle anything here and they are entitled to no respect whatever. They may be right or they may be wrong; there is nothing in the majority principle which will make them either right or wrong (Lippmann [1947] 1965, 13–14).

8. Iris Young, for example, writes, "Each social perspective has an account not only of its own life and history but of every other position that affects its experience. Thus listeners can learn about how their own position, actions and values appear to others from the stories they tell. Narrative thus exhibits the situated knowledge available to the collective from each perspective, and the combination of narratives from different perspectives produces the collective social wisdom not available from any one position" (1996, 132).

Young inherits the concept of a "social perspective" from phenomenology and in particular the later Sartre of the *Critique of Dialectical Reason* ([1960] 1982). Usually phenomenological analysis moves at the level of a transcendental or quasi-transcendental explication of the conditions of our life-world, and seeks to render visible those assumptions about ourselves, others, and our worlds that we must always already have made in order for our worlds to be put together in terms we would recognize as constituting "our world." Be it in the work of Husserl, Heidegger, the later Wittgenstein, or Sartre, there is always a problem of *mediating* the level of phenomenological analysis with the empirical constituencies of any given historical life-world. Phenomenology is not empirical sociology. Wittgenstein's language games do not overlap with the empirical attributes of ethnocultural language groups any more than Heidegger's "Das Man" refers simply to the masses in industrial democracies. Iris Young's work, although it borrows from phenomenology, is free of such anxieties about how to mediate the empirical and the transcendental. She reifies "social positions" in that she translates transcendental terms of analyses into empirical social groups; furthermore, these social groups bear an uncanny resemblance to constituencies of identity politics of recent decades in Western capitalist democracies, like women, "racial" and ethnic minorities, gays and lesbians, the handicapped, Jews, Gypsies, and the like. There is no compelling reason why a phenomenological life-group would overlap or be identical to social groups mobilized as social movements. On the difficulties and subtleties of constructing social groups, see Schutz 1982, 164–203. As I have argued above (chap. 1) , this confusion of levels in Young's work is also characteristic of her critique of deliberative democracy and her attempt to substitute "communicative" for deliberative democracy. See Benhabib 1996a and 1999c for further exchanges with Iris Young.

9. Michael Rabinder James distinguishes between *formal* and *substantive* criteria in the justification of norms. "These, then, are the *formal* criteria for the justification of a norm: legitimate norms must be consensually justified by all affected parties through a rational, moral discourse conducted under fair conditions. However, the substantive content of norms is not specified within Habermas's theory and hence can vary according to culture. . . . The formal conditions under which a norm was created, not the specific content of the norm itself, is what Habermas's theory evaluates. And it is these conditions of fair, rational, normative consensus that provide the universalistic form for culturally diverse substantive norms" (1999, 65). This is quite an apt formulation; I would also like to add that formal conditions constrain processes of norm creation in such ways that certain material norms could simply not pass the muster of rational discourses. The formal features of the process do constrain some, though not all, aspects of the material outcome.

CHAPTER SIX

I would like to thank Juergen Habermas, Daniel Bell, Richard Tuck, Caroline Emcke, Glyn Morgan, Sanford Levinson, Andrea SanGiovanni, Sayres Rudy, and Arash Abizadeh for their comments on earlier drafts of this chapter. Comments and questions raised by Riva Kastoryano, Yasemin Soysal, Yael Tamir, James Tully, and Ulf Hedetoft during the "Reimagining Belonging" conference organized by the Center for International Studies of Aalborg University, Denmark, in May 1998, greatly influenced the final form of these reflections.

An earlier version of this chapter has appeared in German as: Benhabib, *Demokratische Gleichheit und kulturelle Vielfalt*, in *The 1997 Horkheimer Lectures*, chap. 3 (Frankfurt: Fischer Verlag, 1999); an English translation was published as Benhabib, "Citizens, Residents, and Aliens in a Changing World: Political Membership in the Global Era," *Social Research* 66, no. 3 (Fall 1999): 709–44. The following chapter is a revised and expanded version of both pieces and is reprinted here with the permission of the editors of *Social Research*. In addition to updating demographic figures, the current article also incorporates developments in immigration and asylum issues occurring within the EU as a result of the Treaty of Amsterdam (1997) and the Tampere Council Resolutions (October 1999).

1. Cited by Rainer Muenz, "Migrants, Aliens, Citizens: European Migration and Its Consequences" (conference paper presented at the European Forum, 1995–96 Citizenship Project, European University Institute, Florence, April 1996), p. 14). Recent publications do not indicate great variations in these figures. Figures from 1999 still set the percentage of foreigners in Germany at 8.9, and their number at roughly 7.3 million.

After the passage of the new "asylum laws" in Germany, first on June 26, 1992, and then on July 27, 1993, Germany is much more effectively controlling its borders and the number of foreigners allowed into the country; however since 1996, and largely as a result of the civil wars between the member states of the former Yugoslav federation, inflows of asylum seekers into Germany increased in numbers to 100,440 in 1986; the 1996 figure is much lower than the 438,200 who applied for asylum in 1992, but still higher than the 57,400 asylum seekers in 1987.

2. Next to foreign workers, asylum applicants, and refugees, the third significant category of "outsiders" in Germany are the "ethnic Germans." They are not native-born Germans but Germans who since the thirteenth century settled in various central European, Baltic, and formerly Soviet territories. After World War II millions of this group, referred to as the *Vertriebene* (expellees) and *Aussiedler* (outsettlers), were expelled from the Soviet Union and other central and eastern European countries. A 1953 statute defines the *Aus-*

siedler as *Volkszugeroehige* (belonging to the people), and Article 116 (1) of the Basic Law of Germany allows them the right to resettle in Germany. In the last twenty years some 1.9 million expellees from Poland, Romania, and the former Soviet Union have entered Germany. See Kanstroom 1993, 165–67. As of 2001, 3.2 million *Aussiedler* live in German and make up 3.9 percent of the population. See Muenz 2001, 1. For an overview of the changing composition of immigrant groups in various European countries, see Messina 1996, 130–54.

3. The persecution of the Kurdish population, in the northern and southeastern regions of the country in particular, and the continuing conflict between the Kurdish Communist Party (known in German as the PKK) and the Turkish government have given rise to a new group of asylum seekers—ethnic Kurds who are officially Turkish citizens but persecuted by a country friendly to Germany and aspiring future membership in the European Union. In 1995, 25,000 Turkish citizens are reported to have sought asylum in Germany; they were preceded by 33,000 citizens of the states of the former Yugoslavia. The recent capture of the fugitive leader of the PKK, Abdullah Ocalan, has led to confrontations in all major European cities between Kurdish sympathizers and local and international government authorities. In Berlin, confrontations occurred when Kurdish guerillas attacked Turkish businesses and community centers. These disturbances and the civil war–like conditions created in major German cities were undoubtedly a major factor in the rejection by large parts of the German public of the new "dual citizenship" legislation, proposed by the SPD-Green Coalition.

4. As of 1998, for example, there were 719,500 former Yugoslavs resident in Germany (Serbs, Montenegrins, and Kosovo Albanians), as well as 283,000 Croatians and 190,100 citizens of Bosnia Herzegovina (SOPEMI 2000, 339). By the year 2000, the number of Bosnians living in Germany, including war refugees living under temporary protection, increased to 281,000 (Muenz 2001, 8). Among the EU countries most affected by the breakup wars of the former Yugoslavia, and the resulting inflow of migrants, refugees, and asylees, are the Netherlands, where as of 1998 citizens of former Yugoslavia numbered 47,5000; Sweden, where the corresponding figure is 70,900; and Italy, in which 40,800 former citizens of Yugoslavia as well as 91,500 Albanians have settled. Since 1996, Sweden has also given refuge to about 48,000 Bosnia-Herzegovinians.

5. See Article 8 of Section C, Part 2. "1. Citizenship of the Union is hereby established. Every Person holding the Nationality of a Member State shall be a citizen of the Union." Facsimile reproduction on file with the author.

6. The institution of citizenship for individuals who do not have a common language, a common public sphere, and effective channels of participation is giving rise to a number of very important and compelling contemporary debates in political theory and jurisprudence. Some see European citizenship as a fig leaf to cover the considerable divestment of the democratic powers of

sovereign peoples to an anonymous "Eurocracy" sitting in Brussels and Stras-
bourg, and still more others warn of the growing "democratic deficit" in the
Union. Citizenship without participation looms on the horizon, they argue. See
Preuss 1995, 267–81; Balibar 1996, 355–76; and Percy B. Lehning, "European
Citizenship: A Mirage?" (paper delivered at the Tenth International Confer-
ence of Europeanists, Chicago, March 14–16, 1996); Lehning and Weale 1997.

7. "Fuer ein Europa der politischen und sozialen Grundrechte" (Report of
the "Committee of the Wise") under the directorship of Maria de Lourdes Pintasilgo (Brussels: Publications of the European Commission, October 1995–
February 1996). Other members of this Committee of the Wise are: Eduardo
Garcia de Enterria, Hartmut Kaelble, Louka Katseli, Frederic Pascal, Bengt
Westerberg, and Shirley Williams. Jytte Klausen pleads for a strong differentiation between citizenship rights and redistributive policies in "Social Rights
Advocacy and State Building: T. H. Marshall in the Hands of Social Reformers"
(1995, 244–67). While in the European Union context the trend is toward the
integration of such rights and redistributive benefits through Union-wide "social rights," for third-country nationals the curtailment of social rights and benefits, which they have hitherto enjoyed, looms in the offing. Klaus sees an inevitable trade-off between the continuance of protective welfare communities,
globalization, and the development of less exclusionary absorption and immigration politics (266). The danger in the current context, though, is that the
political voicelessness of third-country nationals in the EU will make it all the
more likely that their social rights will be curtailed, without a corresponding
liberalization trade-off in naturalization and immigration policies. See also De
Swaan 1997, 561–75. For a helpful overview of the current state of policy and
jurisprudential reasoning in the Union, see Shaw 1997.

8. See Gerald L. Neuman, "Buffer Zones against Refugees: Dublin,
Schengen, and the Germany Asylum Amendment" (1993, 503–26). The Dublin
Convention and the Second Schengen agreement were signed in June 1990.
Schengen included initially Belgium, the Netherlands, Luxembourg, France,
and Germany. Italy joined the group in December 1990; Portugal and Spain,
in June 1991; Sweden, Finland, and Austria, subsequently. Both agreements
contain rules for determining a "responsible state" that agrees to process an
applicant for asylum from a non-EU country. The Schengen Convention attempts to abolish border controls along the common frontiers of the parties
and to compensate for the relaxation of borders by more vigilant migration
and law enforcement policies at airports. There is also the establishment of a
Schengen Information System, which creates an electronic database to facili-
tate control of criminals and terrorists. See Neuman 1993, 506–7; and Kanast-
room 1993, 198ff.

9. A few notable exceptions to this widespread neglect of citizenship issues
have been Barbalet 1988; Shklar 1991; and Schuck and Smith 1985. Undoubt-

edly, conditions of globalization the world over are leading to a renewal of interest in citizenship in political theory as well. See Spinner 1994.

10. Although this chapter focuses on Europe in general, and Germany in particular, with the introduction of NAFTA similar developments are taking place in the North American continent. So far, the fact that United States and Canada define themselves as "countries of immigration" has created a situation normatively different from that of most European Union Countries, which do not consider themselves immigrant societies. The passage of Proposition 187 in California and the ensuing battle against the curtailment of the social benefits to nonlegal resident aliens; the shameful treatment of Haitian refugees; recent administrative irregularities at the INS concerning adequate background checks of prospective citizens; and so forth, are all events pointing to the growing salience of these issues for the United States. Normatively, the theory and practice of acceptance into the political commonwealth through incorporation into civil society is most clearly practiced in Canada and the United States. The practices of immigration and naturalization in these countries present a clear alternative to the models prevailing on the European continent at the present time.

11. The United Kingdom does permit voting rights to those who hold Commonwealth citizenship, for example, citizens of Canada.

12. In a recent paper, "Access to Citizenship: A Comparison of Twenty-five Nationality Laws," Patrick Weil has argued that "starting with different legal traditions and different historical patterns of immigration, emigration and minorities, convergence occurs; they converge through different paths and political agendas because, in the context of stabilization of borders and incorporation of democratic values, many of these countries faced problems of immigration. The *jus soli* states became slightly more restrictive and the jus sanguinis ones moved towards *jus soli.*"(2000, 3–4, on file with the author) Weil expresses the same hopes and reaches the same conclusions as do the authors of the *Asylum Acquis Handbook* (Van Krieken 2000), all of whom similarly urge EU-wide convergence and harmonization. I personally see a bumpier road ahead and anticipate that there will be backlashes, coming both from the left and the right of the spectrum, against an all-too-speedy liberalization of citizenship and asylum regulations. Particularly, when the EU expands to twenty-one countries in 2003 (when the Czech Republic, Cyprus, Poland, Hungary, Slovenia, and Estonia become members) and to twenty-seven in 2007 (with the inclusion of Romania, Bulgaria, Lithuania, Latvia, the Slovak Republic and Malta), different historical and constitutional traditions regarding the treatment of minorities and foreigners will have to mix and mingle with one another in a very short span of time. Just consider, for example, the issues that will arise concerning the Roma and Sinti and other Gypsy populations of Europe, whose migratory patterns of movement cut across Spain, the Czech Re-

public, Slovakia, Hungary, and Romania. The EU will be faced with the citizenship claims of one of Europe's oldest deterritorialized peoples, and thus will have to reconsider the strong linkage between nationality and citizenship that still forms the normative basis of citizenship of the Union; according to the policy, only citizens of member EU states can be citizens of the EU, and others cannot.

The fact that EU expansion plans at this stage do not include Turkey and the former republics of Yugoslavia (with the exception of Slovenia), and the fact that populations drawn from these countries still form the largest group of third-country nationals in the EU only suggests that EU expansion will exacerbate rather than ameliorate existing discrepancies.

13. Craig Calhoun has pointed out to me that in the modern nation-state, citizenship status is an unmediated relationship between the state and the individual, in that citizenship is not normatively dependent upon membership upon some secondary mediating body, like a church or a corporation. This is, of course, legally and constitutionally true, in that citizenship in the modern state is an individual right and not a privilege of a corporate body, let us say, a guild, as it was in the Middle Ages. However, I am stressing that the relationship of the individual to the state is sociologically, de facto, if not de jure, mediated by civil society and its institutions. In fact, through the recognition of family unification as a basic human right, international law also acknowledges this mediated relationship to membership in the state. Furthermore, almost all liberal democracies respect the principle that the economic, scientific, artistic, technological, and medical needs of civil society offer sufficient conditions for the entry, as well as permission to work, of many foreigners. In this respect too, the nation-state accepts the mediation of civil society institutions on the road leading to political membership. I am pleading here for a recognition of this mediation process between civil society—including the family and the market—and the state.

14. From the standpoint of political philosophy, we are entering the domain of administrative detail better left to legislators and bureaucrats. As Hegel is reported to have quipped about Fichte's political theory, he did not have to be concerned about passports! Yet today the passport has become the symbolic document that represents in its pages all the perplexities and inequities of current citizenship regimes and practices. It is no less worthy of philosophical reflection than the postcard!

Also, criteria of immigration, such as length of residency and language requirements, can affect diverse sectors of the foreign population of a particular country very differently. These issues of differential impact can, in turn, enable or hinder the acquisition of citizenship rights by different groups. For example, a language proficiency proof of some sort seems to me an eminently reasonable requirement on the part of a host country in granting residency and citizenship permits to foreigners. On the other hand, this requirement will most likely disadvantage women, who usually, though not in all cases, enter the host country under family unification clauses and who do not participate in the civil society and economy of the public sphere of the host country or do so to a very limited extent. Under these circumstances, language proficiency requirements not accompanied by subsidized language instruction could be discriminatory against women and the elderly members of the foreign population.

15. In view of the events of September 11, 2001, and the legitmate security concerns of the United States as well as governments around the world in protecting their populations from future terrorist attacks, this claim may appear extreme. However, I would argue that security threats fall under the category of legitimate restrictions that can be applied to curtail immigration into a country. Nevertheless, such restrictions cannot provide governments and other agencies with unlimited discretion to violate the civil rights of immigrants, of suspected detainees, and of other categories of noncitizens. In the wake of the arrest by the Bush administration of over six hundred suspected individuals, most of whom are of Arab American descent, and not all of whom are immigrants, legitimate concerns have been raised about the violation of the civil rights of these individuals. Equally, the plan to try captured terrorists under the "unlawful combatant" category, and in front of military, rather than civilian, tribunals, has drawn great concerns and criticism. In a robust democratic culture, not even security concerns can simply override the civil rights of noncitizens.

16. This distinction was brought to my attention by Professor Juergen Habermas. However, although no authority exists to coerce nation-states to accept refugees and asylum seekers, citizens' groups of the concerned countries may themselves litigate against their own government and agencies on the grounds that these may have violated fundamental human rights, the constitution, or administrative procedures in their treatment of foreigners. In such cases, concerned citizens act against their own governmental authority as the advocates of the stranger and the foreigner. Of course this legal right to "sue" your own state authorities is not equivalent to a coercive right against them, but as recent battles over the treatment of refugees, asylum seekers, and immigrants the world over show us, there is "communicative power" that derives from such actions and that may attain coercive influence.

17. I want to thank Glyn Morgan for bringing this distinction to my attention in his comments delivered at the "Dilemmas of European Citizenship" Conference in CES, Harvard University, Cambridge, October 1997.

18. California adopted Proposition 187 through a 1994 referendum; this measure denied all state services, including medical care, to illegal immigrants. Although a federal district court judge in Los Angeles struck down Proposition 187 (the case is still under appeal), in 1996, as part of its welfare reform

agenda, Congress enacted a bill that denied certain welfare benefits, including food stamps and financial support for the aged and the disabled, to all immigrants, whether legal or illegal. The law, passed on August 22, 1996, was unusual in that it applied even to those admitted to the USA before that date; a year later a law passed that restored certain benefits to the infirm and the aged who had been previously admitted, and in June 1998 food stamps were restored to the children, the elderly, and the disabled.

In a provocative piece, Owen Fiss argues that these amendments raise "with special urgency and clarity, the question whether enactments imposing social disabilities on immigrants can be squared with the Constitution, particularly the provision that guarantees to all persons—not all citizens, but all persons— equal protection of the laws." See Fiss 1998 and the responses that follow his article.

BIBLIOGRAPHY

❑   ❑   ❑   ❑

Ackerman, Bruce. 1991. *We, the People.* Cambridge: Harvard University Press, Belknap Press.

Adler, Mortimer, ed. 1994. *Great Books of the Western World.* 5th ed. Chicago: Encyclopedia Britannica.

Adorno, Theodor, and Max Horkheimer. [1947] 1969. *Dialektik der Aufklaerung: Philosophische Fragmente.* 2d ed. Frankfurt am Main: Fischer Verlag.

Al-Hibri, Azizah Y. 1999. "Is Western Patriarchal Feminism Good for Third World/Minority Women?" In *Is Multiculturalism Bad for Women?* by Susan Moller Okin, edited by Joshua Cohen, Matthew Howard, and Martha C. Nussbaum. Princeton: Princeton University Press, 41–47.

Arat, Yesim. 2002. "Group Differentiated Rights and the Liberal Democratic State: Rethinking the Headscarf Controversy in Turkey," *New Perspectives on Turkey.*

Arendt, Hannah. [1951] 1979. *The Origins of Totalitarianism.* New York: Harcourt, Brace and Jovanovich.

———. [1958] 1973. *The Human Condition.* 8th ed. Chicago: University of Chicago Press.

———. 1961. "Crisis in Culture." In *Between Past and Future: Six Exercises in Political Thought.* New York: Meridian Books.

Aristotle. 1941. *Politics.* In *Basic Works of Aristotle.* Edited by Richard McKeon, translated by Benjamin Jowett. New York: Random House.

"Auslaenderrecht." 1997. *Die Gesetzestexte des "Deutschen Bundesrechts."* Version of September 12, 1996. Frankfurt: Suhrkamp.

Badin, Sandra. 1999. "Kymlicka's Liberal Theory of Multicultural Rights: A Critical Examination." Paper on file with author.

Balibar, Étienne. 1996. "Is European Citizenship Possible?" *Public Culture* 8 (1996): 355–76.

Barbalet, J. M. 1988. *Citizenship: Rights, Struggle, and Class Inequality.* Minneapolis: University of Minnesota Press.

Barber, Benjamin. 1995. *Jihad versus McWorld: How Globalism and Tribalism Are Reshaping the World.* New York: Tarmans Books.

Barry, Brian. 2001. *Culture and Equality.* Cambridge: Harvard University Press.

Bauboeck, Rainer. 1994. *Transnational Citizenship: Membership and Rights in International Migration.* Cornwall: Edward Elgar.

———. 1998. "The Crossing and Blurring of Boundaries in International Migration: Challenges for Social and Political Theory." In Rainer Bauboeck and John Rundell, eds, *Blurred Boundaries: Migration, Ethnicity, Citizenship.* Vienna: Ashgate Publications.

Beiner, Ronald, ed. 1995. *Theorizing Citizenship.* Albany: State University of New York Press.

Bell, Daniel. [1978] 1996. *The Cultural Contradictions of Capitalism.* New York: Basic Books.

Benhabib, Seyla. 1986. *Critique, Norm, and Utopia: A Study of the Normative Foundations of Critical Theory.* New York: Columbia University Press.

———. 1992. *Situating the Self: Gender, Community, and Postmodernism in Contemporary Ethics.* New York: Routledge; London: Polity.

———. 1994. "The Intellectual Challenge of Multiculturalism and Teaching the Canon." In *Cultureworks*, edited by Marjorie Garber. New York: Routledge.

———. 1995. "Cultural Complexity, Moral Interdependence, and the Global Dialogic Community" In *Development, Culture, and Women*, edited by Martha Nussbaum and Jonathan Glover, Oxford: Clarendon Press, 235–59.

———. 1996a. "Deliberative Rationality and Models of Democratic Legitimacy." In *Democracy and Difference: Contesting the Boundaries of the Political.* Princeton: Princeton University Press.

———. 1996b. *The Reluctant Modernism of Hannah Arendt.* Sage Publications. Thousand Oaks, Calif.: new edition, Totowa, N.J.: Rowman and Littlefield, Forthcoming 2002.

———. 1997a. "The Embattled Public Sphere: Hannah Arendt, Juergen Habermas and Beyond." *Theoria: South African Journal of Philosophy* (December 1997):1–24; rev. version reprinted in *Reasoning Practically*, edited by Edna Ullmann-Margalit, Oxford: Oxford University Press, 2000, 164–82.

———. 1997b. "Strange Multiplicities: The Politics of Identity and Difference in a Global Context." In *The Divided Self: Identity and Globalization*, edited by Ahmad I. Samatar, 27–59. St. Paul, Minn. Macalaster College, Macalaster International Publications.

———. 1998. "Democracy and Identity: In Search of the Civic Polity." *Philosophy and Social Criticism* 24, nos. 2–3: 85–100.

———. 1999a. "Germany Opens Up." *Nation* (June 21, 1999); 6.

———. 1999b. *Kulturelle Vielfalt und demokratische Gleichheit: Die Horkheimer Vorlesungen.* Frankfurt: Fischer Verlag.

———. 1999c. "The Liberal Imagination and the Four Dogmas of Multiculturalism." *Yale Journal of Criticism* 12, no. 2 (1999): 401–13.

———. 1999d. " 'Nous' et 'les Autres': The Politics of Complex Cultural Dialogue in a Global Civilization." In *Multicultural Questions*, edited by Christian Joppke and Steven Lukes. Oxford: Oxford University Press, 44–62.

———. 1999e. "Sexual Difference and Collective Identities: The New Global Constellation." *Signs: Journal of Women in Culture and Society* 24, no. 2: 335–61.

———. 2001a. *Transformations of Citizenship: Dilemmas of the Nation-States in the Global Era: The Spinoza Lectures.* Amsterdam: Van Gorcum Publishers.

———. 2001b. "Of Guests, Aliens, and Citizens: Rereading Kant's Cosmopolitan Right," In *Pluralism and the Pragmatic Turn: Transformations of Critical Theory*, edited by William Rehg and James Bohman, 361–87. Cambridge: MIT Press.

Benjamin, Jessica. 1988. *The Bonds of Love: Psychoanalysis, Feminism, and the Problem of Domination.* New York: Pantheon Books.

Bernstein, Richard. 1981. "Incommensurability and Otherness Revisited." In *The New Constellation.* London: Polity Press.

Bhabha, Homi. 1994. *The Location of Culture.* New York: Routledge Press.

Bohman, James. 1996. *Public Deliberation: Pluralism, Complexity, and Democracy.* Cambridge: MIT Press.

Bohman, James, and Mathias Lutz-Bachman. 1997. *Perpetual Peace: Essays on Kant's Cosmopolitan Ideal.* Cambridge: MIT Press.

Brubaker, Rogers. 1992. *Citizenship and Nationhood in France and Germany.* Cambridge: Harvard University Press.

———. 1996. *Nationalism Reframed. Nationhood and the National Question in the New Europe.* Cambridge: Cambridge University Press.

Brun-Rovet, Marianne. 2000. "A Perspective on the Multiculturalism Debate: 'L'affaire foulard' and *laïcité* in France, 1989–1999." Seminar paper submitted to Professor Benhabib's class "Nations, States, and Citizens," Harvard University, Department of Government. On file with the author.

Bundes Verfassungs Gericht (*German Constitutional Court*). 1997. "Unionsbuergerwahlrecht" (European Union Citizens' Voting Rights). 2BvR 2862/95. Decided on 8.1.1997. Hamberg, Germany.

Butler, Judith. 1997. *Excitable Speech: A Politics of the Performative.* New York: Routledge.

The Canadian Charter of Rights and Freedoms. 1986. In *The Origin of Rights*, edited by Roger Salhamy. Toronto. Carswell.

Carens, Joseph. 1995. "Aliens and Citizens: The Case for Open Borders." In *Theorizing Citizenship*, edited by Ronald Beiner. Albany: State University of New York Press.

———. 2000. *Culture, Citizenship, and Community. A Contextual Exploration of Justice and Evenhandedness.* Oxford: Oxford University Press.

Celan, Paul. 1983. "Todesfuge," in *Gesammelte Werke*. Frankfurt am Main: Suhrkamp Verlag.

———. 2001. *Selected Poems and Prose of Paul Celan*. Translated by John Felstiner. New York: W. W. Norton.

Cohen, Jean L. 1999. "Changing Paradigms of Citizenship and the Exclusiveness of the Demos." *International Journal of Sociology.* 14, no. 3 (September 1999): 245–68.

Cohen Jean L., and Andrew Arato. 1992. *Civil Society and Political Theory.* Cambridge: MIT Press.

Cohen, Joshua. 1989. "Deliberation and Democratic Legitimacy." In *The Good Polity,* edited by A. Hamlin and P. Petitt. London. Blackwell.

Coleman, Doriane Lambelet. 1996. "Individualizing Justice through Multiculturalism: The Liberals' Dilemma." *Columbia Law Review* 96, no. 5 (June 1996): 1093–1167.

Connolly, William. 1991. *Identity Difference—Democratic Negotiations of Political Paradox.* Ithaca: Cornell University Press.

Cooke, Maeve. 1997. "Authenticity and Autonomy: Taylor, Habermas, and the Politics of Recognition." *Political Theory* 25, no. 2:258–88.

Council of Europe Publishing. 1996. *Recent Demographic Developments in Europe.* Strasbourg.

Das, Veena. 1994. "Cultural Rights and the Definition of Community. In *The Rights of Subordinated Peoples,* edited by Oliver Mendelsohn and Upendra Baxi; 117–58. Delhi: Oxford University Press.

De Beauvoir, Simone. 1949. *Le Deuxième Sexe.* Paris: Editions Gallimard.

De la Vega, Garcilaso. [1605 and 1616–17] 1966. *Royal Commentaries on the Incas and the General History of Peru.* Ps. 1 and 2. Translated by Harold V. Livermore. Austin: University of Texas Press.

———. [1616–17] 1980. *The Florida of the Inca.* Translated and edited by John Gier Varmer and J. Johnson Varmer. Austin: University of Texas Press.

DePalma, Anthony. 1998. "Canadian Indians Win a Ruling Vindicating Their Oral History." *New York Times,* February 9, 1998.

De Swaan, Abram. 1997. "The Receding Prospects for Transnational Social Policy." *Theory and Society: Renewal and Critique in Social Theory* 26, no. 4 (August 1997): 561–75.

Derrida, Jacques.1986. "Declarations of Independence." In *New Political Science* (Summer): 6–15.

———. 1992. *The Other Heading: Reflections on Today's Europe.* Translated by Pascal-Anne Brault and Michael B. Nass. Bloomington: Indiana University Press.

Dryzek, John S. 1990. *Discursive Democracy.* Cambridge: Cambridge University Press.

Edmonston, Barry, ed. 1996. *Statistics on U.S. Immigration: An Assessment of Data Needs for Future Research,* compiled by the Committee on National Statistics and Committee on Population, the Commission on Behavioral and Social Sciences and Education, and the National Research Council. Washington, D.C.: National Academy Press.

Fanon, Frantz. 1968. *The Wretched of the Earth.* Translated by Constance Farrington. New York: Grove Press.

Ferrara, Alessandro. 1994. "Authenticity and the Project of Modernity." *European Journal of Philosophy* 2, no. 3:241–73.

Fakhry, Majid. 1983. "Philosophy and History." In *The Genius of Arab Civilization: Source of Renaissance.* Cambridge: MIT Press; and London: Eurabia Publishing.

Fichte, Johann G. [1808] 1979. *Addresses to the German Nation.* Westport, Conn.: Greenwood Publishing Group.

Fishkin, James S. 1991. *Democracy and Deliberation: New Directions for Democratic Reform.* New Haven. Yale University Press.

Fiss, Owen. 1998. "The Immigrant as Pariah." *Boston Review* 23, no. 5 (October–November 1998):4–6.

Fraser, Nancy. 1992. "Rethinking the Public Sphere: A Contribution to Actually Existing Democracy." In *Habermas and the Public Sphere,* edited by Craig Calhoun. Cambridge: MIT Press.

———. 1997a. "Culture, Political Economy, and Difference: On Iris Young's *Justice and the Politics of Difference.*" In *Justice Interruptus: Critical Reflections on the "Postsocialist" Condition,* 189–207. New York: Routledge.

———. 1997b. *Justice Interruptus: Critical Reflections on the "Postsocialist" Condition.* New York: Routledge Press.

———. 1997c. "A Rejoinder to Iris Young." *New Left Review,* no. 223 (May–June 1997): 126–29.

Fraser, Nancy. "Sexual Justice in the Age of Identity Politics: Redistribution, Recognition, and Participation." (Forthcoming).

Friedman, Jonathan. 1995. *Cultural Identity and Global Process.* London: Sage Publications.

Frug, Gerald E. 1980. *The City as Legal Concept.* Cambridge: Harvard Law Review Association.

Fukuyama, Francis. 1989. "Entering Post-History." *New Perspectives Quarterly* 6, no. 3:49–53.

———. 1992. *The End of History and the Last Man.* Toronto: Maxwell Macmillan International.

Gadamer, Hans Georg. [1960] 1975. *Truth and Method.* Translated by William Glen-Doeppel. London: Sherd and Ward.

Galston, William. 1991. *Liberal Purposes: Goods, Virtues, and Duties in the Liberal State.* Cambridge: Cambridge University Press.

Gaspard, Françoise, and Farhad, Khosrokhavar, 1995. *Le Foulard et la République.* Paris: Decouverte.

Gellner, Ernest. 1983. *Nations and Nationalism.* Ithaca: Cornell University Press.

Gendler, Tamar Szabo. 1998. "Comments on Seyla Benhabib, 'Multiculturalism and Gendered Citizenship.'" Syracuse University, December 4, 1998. On file with the author.

Gilroy, Paul. 1995. *Black Atlantic. Modernity and Double Consciousness.* Cambridge: Harvard University Press.

———. 2000. *Against Race: Imagining Political Culture beyond the Color Line.* Cambridge: Harvard University Press.

Glazer, Nathan. 1997. *We Are All Multiculturalists Now.* Cambridge: Harvard University Press.

Göle, Nilufer. 1996. *The Forbidden Modern: Civilization and Veiling.* Ann Arbor: University of Michigan Press.

Greenfeld, Liah. 1992. *Nationalism: Five Roads to Modernity.* Cambridge: Harvard University Press.

Guinier, Lani. 1998. *Lift Every Voice: Turning a Civil Rights Setback into a New Vision of Social Justice.* New York: Simon and Schuster.

———. 1999. *Reflecting All of Us: The Case for Proportional Representation,* New Democracy Forum with R. Richie, Steven Hill, edited by Micah Kleit. Boston: Beacon Press.

Gupta, Akhil and Ferguson, James. 1992. "Beyond 'Culture:' Space, Identity, and the Politics of Difference." In *Cultural Anthropology,* Vol 7. No. 1.

Gutmann, Amy and Thompson, Dennis. 1996. *Democracy and Disagreement.* Cambridge: Harvard University Press.

Habermas, Juergen. 1975. *Legitimation Crisis.* Translated by Thomas McCarthy. Boston: Beacon Press.

———. 1981. *Theorie des kommunikativen Handelns.* Frankfurt am Main: Suhrkamp. Translated by Thomas McCarthy as *The Theory of Communicative Action,* Boston: Beacon Press, 1984.

———. [1983] 1990. "Diskursethik: Notizen zu einem Begruendungsprogramm." In *Moralbewusstsein und kommunikatives Handeln.* Frankfurt am Main: Suhrkamp. Translated by Christian Lenhardt and Shierry Weber Nicholsen as "Discourse Ethics: Notes on a Program of Philosophical Justification," in *Moral Consciousness and Communicative Action*, 43–116. Cambridge: MIT Press. 1990.

———. 1996a. *Between Facts and Norms: Contributions to a Discourse Theory of Law and Democracy.* Translated by William Regh. Cambridge: MIT Press.

———. 1996b. "Citizenship and National Identity." In *Between Facts and Norms: Contributions to a Discourse Theory of Law and Democracy,* translated by William Regh, App. 2. Cambridge: MIT Press.

———. 1998. "The European Nation-State: On the Past and Future of Sovereignty and Citizenship." In Ciaran Cronin and Pablo De Greiff, eds. *The Inclusion of the Other: Studies in Political Theory.* Cambridge: MIT Press.

Havel, Václav. 1995. "A Conscience Slumbers in Us All." Commencement speech at Harvard University. June 8, 1995. CTK National News Wire.

Hegel, G.W.F. [1807] 1977. *The Phenomenology of Spirit.* Translated by A. V. Miller. Oxford: Clarendon Press.

Heiberg, Marianne, ed. 1994. *Subduing Sovereignty: Sovereignty and the Right to Intervene.* London: Pinter Publishers.

Held, David. 1999. *Global Transformations*, with Anthony McGrew, David Goldblatt, and Jonathan Perraton. Stanford, Calif.: Stanford University Press.

Herder, Gottlieb. [1797] 1997. "Whether We Need to Know the End of History in Order to Write History." In J. G. Herder, *On World History*, edited by Hans Adler and Ernest A. Menze, 44–49. London: M. E. Sharpe.

Hobbes, Thomas. [1651] 1996. *Leviathan.* Cambridge Texts in the History of Political Thought. Cambridge: Cambridge University Press.

Hobsbawm, Eric. 1990. *Nations and Nationalism since 1780: Programme, Myth, Reality.* Cambridge: Cambridge University Press.

Hollinger, David A. 1995. *Postethnic America: Beyond Multiculturalism.* New York: Basic Books.

———. 1999. "Authority, Solidarity, and the Political Economy of Identity: The Case of the United States." *Diacritics* 29, no. 4: 116–27.

Holmes. Steven A. 2001. "The Confusion over Who We Are." *New York Times, Week in Review*, 1–5. June 3, 2001.

Honneth, Axel. 1996. *The Struggle for Recognition: The Moral Grammar of Social Conflicts.* Translated by Joel Anderson. Cambridge: MIT Press.

Honig, Bonnie. 1998. "Immigrant America? How 'Foreignness' Solves Democracy's Problems," *Social Text* 3 (Fall 1998): 1–27.

———. 1999. "My Culture Made Me Do It." In *Is Multiculturalism Bad for Women?* by Susan Moller Okin, edited by Joshua Cohen, Matthew Howard, and Martha Nussbaum. Princeton: Princeton University Press.

Honig, Bonnie. 2001. *Democracy and the Foreigner.* Princeton: Princeton University Press.

Huber, Ernst, R. 1961. *Dokumente zur deutschen Verfassungsgeschichte.* Vol. 1. Stuttgart: Kohlhammer.

Huntington, Samuel. 1996. *The Clash of Civilizations and the Remaking of World Order.* New York: Simon and Schuster.

Huntington, Samuel, and Lawrence Harrison, eds. 2000. *Culture Matters: How Values Shape Human Progress.* New York: Basic Books.

Ignatieff, Michael. 1995. *Blood and Belonging: Journeys into the New Nationalism.* New York: Noonday Paperbacks.

Inglehart, Ronald. 1990. *Culture Shift in Advanced Industrial Society.* Princeton: Princeton University Press.

Jagger, Alison, 1999. "Multicultural Democracy." In *Journal of Political Philosophy* 7, no. 3: 308–29.

James, Michael Rabinder. 1999. "Tribal Sovereignty and the Intercultural Public Sphere." *Philosophy and Social Criticism* 25 (September): 57–96.

Janoski, Thomas. 1998. *Citizenship and Civil Society.* New York: Cambridge University Press.

Jong, Cornelius. 2000. "Harmonization of Asylum and Immigration Policies: The Long and Winding Road from Amsterdam via Vienna to Tampere." In Peter J. Van Krieken, ed., *The Asylum Acquis Handbook,* 21–37. The Hague: T.M.C. Asser Press.

Joppke, Christian, and Steven Lukes, eds. 1999. *Multicultural Questions.* Oxford: Oxford University Press.

Judt, Tony. 1996. *A Grand Illusion? An Essay on Europe.* New York: Hill and Wang.

Kakar, Sudhir. 1990. *Intimate Relations: Exploring Indian Sexuality.* Chicago: University of Chicago Press.

Kanstroom, Daniel. 1993. "Wer Sind Wir Wieder? Laws of Asylum, Immigration, and Citizenship in the Struggle for the Soul of the New Germany." *Yale Journal of International Law* 18:155ff.

Kant, Immanuel. [1793] 1994. "On the Common Saying: 'This May Be True in Theory, but It Does Not Apply in Practice.'" In *Kant: Political Writings,* edited by Hans Reiss, translated by H. B. Nisbet. Cambridge: Cambridge University Press.

———. [1795]. 1914. "Zum Ewigen Frieden. Ein philosophischer Entwurf." In *Immanuel Kants Werke,* edited by A. Buchenau, E. Cassirer, and B. Kellermann. Berlin: Verlag Bruno Cassirer.

———. [1795] 1957. "Perpetual Peace." Translated by Lewis White Beck. In *On History,* edited by Lewis White Beck. Indianapolis: Library of Liberal Arts.

————. [1797]. 1996. *The Metaphysics of Morals*. Translated by Mary Gregor. Cambridge: Cambridge University Press, 1996.

Kerber, Linda. 1997. *Women of the Republic: Intellect and Ideology in Revolutionary America*. Chapel Hill: University of North Carolina Press.

Kessler, Charles R. 1998. "The Promise of American Citizenship." In *Immigration and Citizenship in the 21st Century*, edited by Noah M. J. Pickus. 3–41. New York: Rowman and Littlefield.

Klausen, Jytte. 1995. "Social Rights Advocacy and State Building: T. H. Marshall in the Hands of the Reformers." *World Politics* 47 (January 1995): 244–67.

Kleger, Heinz. 1995. "Transnationale Staatsbuergerschaft oder: Laesst sich Staatsbuergerschaft entnationalisieren?" *Archiv fuer Rechts- und Sozialphilosophie* 62 (1995): 85–99.

Klusmeyer, Douglas B. 1993. "Aliens, Immigrants, and Citizens: The Politics of Inclusion in the Federal Republic of Germany." *Daedalus* 122, no. 3 (1993) (Summer Issue on "Reconstructing Nations and States"): 81–114.

Kraus, Peter. 2000. "Political Unity and Linguistic Diversity in Europe." *Archives Européennes de Sociologie* 41 no. 1: 138–63.

Krausz , Michael. 1989. *Relativism: Interpretation and Confrontation*. Notre Dame, Ind.: University of Notre Dame Press.

Kristeva, Julia. 1991. *Strangers to Ourselves*, Translated by Leon S. Roudiez. New York: Columbia University Press.

Krosenbrink-Gelissen, Lilianne. 1993. "The Canadian Constitution, the Charter, and Aboriginal Women's Right: Conflicts and Dilemmas." *international Journal of Canadian Studies/Revue internationale d'études canadiennes* 7–8. (Spring–Fall): 207–24.

Kymlicka, Will. 1995. *Multicultural Citizenship: A Liberal Theory of Minority Rights*. Oxford: Oxford University Press.

————. 1996. "Three Forms of Group-Differentiated Citizenship in Canada." In *Democracy and Difference: Contesting the Boundaries of the Political*, edited by Seyla Benhabib. Princeton: Princeton University Press.

————. 1997. *States, Nations, and Cultures: Spinoza Lectures. The University of Amsterdam*. Assen: Van Gorcum.

Kymlicka, Will and Norman, Wayne. 1995. "Return of the Citizen: A Survey of Recent Work on Citizenship Theory." In *Theorizing Citizenship*, edited by Ronald Beiner, 283–323. Albany: State University of New York Press.

————. 2000. *Citizenship in Diverse Societies*. Oxford: Oxford University Press.

————. 2001. *Politics in the Vernacular*. Oxford: Oxford University Press.

Landes, Joan. 1988. *Women and the Public Sphere in the Age of the French Revolution*. Ithaca: Cornell University Press.

Lehning, Percy, and Albert Weale, eds. 1997. *Citizenship, Democracy, and Justice in the New Europe*. London: Routledge.

Lévi-Strauss, Claude. 1969. *Elementary Structures of Kinship*. Boston: Beacon Press.

Lippmann, Walter. [1947] 1965. "Should the Majority Rule?" In *The Essential Lippmann. A Political Philosophy for Liberal Democracy*, edited by Clinton Rossiter and James Lare, 3–14. New York: Vintage Books.

Locke, John. [1690] 1980. *Second Treatise of Civil Government*. Indianapolis: Hackett Publishing.

Lyotard, Jean-François. 1984. *The Postmodern Condition: A Report on Knowledge*. Translated by Geoff Bennington and Brian Massumi. Minneapolis: University of Minnesota Press.

———. 1988. *The Différend: Phrases in Dispute*. Translated by George Van Den Abeele. Minneapolis: University of Minnesota Press.

Macedo, Stephen. 1990. *Liberal Virtues*. Oxford: Oxford University Press.

———. 1999. *Deliberative Politics: Essays on Democracy and Disagreement*. Oxford: Oxford University Press.

MacIntyre, Alasdair. 1977. "Epistemological Crises, Dramatic Narrative, and the Philosophy of Science." *Monist* 60 (1977): 433–72.

———. 1987. "Relativism, Power, and Philosophy." In *After Philosophy: End or Transformation?* Edited by Kenneth Baynes, James Bohman and Thomas McCarthy. Cambridge: MIT Press.

Malcomson, Scott. 2000. *One Drop of Blood: The American Misadventure of Race*. New York: Farrar, Straus, and Giroux.

Mansfield, John H. 1993. "The Personal Laws or a Uniform Civil Code?" In *Religion and Law in Independent India*, edited by Robert D. Baird, 139–77. Monohan.

Markell, Patchen. 1999. *Bound by Recognition: The Politics of Identity after Hegel*. Ph.D. dissertation, Harvard University, Department of Government.

Marshall, T. H. 1950. *"Citizenship and Social Class" and Other Essays*. London: Cambridge University Press.

Marx, Karl. [1857–58] 1973. *Grundrisse: Foundations of the Critique of Political Economy*. Middlesex: Penguin Books.

McCall, Leslie. 2001. *Complex Inequality: Gender, Class, and Race in the New Economy*. New York: Routledge.

McCarthy, Thomas. 1991. *Ideals and Illusions: On Reconstruction and Deconstruction in Contemporary Critical Theory*. Cambridge: MIT Press.

Mendes, Candido, and Luis E. Soares. 1996. *Cultural Pluralism, Identity, and Globalization*. Rio de Janeiro: UNESCO/ISSC/EDUCAM Publications.

Messina, Anthony. 1996. "The Not So Silent Revolution. Postwar Migration to Western Europe." *World Politics* 49 (October 1996): 130–54.

Moeller, Susan D. 1999. *Compassion Fatigue: How the Media Sell Disease, Famine, War, and Death.* New York: Routledge.

Muenz, Rainer. 1996. "Migrants, Aliens, Citizens: European Migrations and Its Consequences." Paper presented at the European Forum, 1995–96 Citizenship Project, European University Institute, Florence.

———. 2001. "Ethnos or Demos? Migration and Citizenship in Germany." Lecture delivered at the Center for European Studies. On file with the author.

Narayan, Uma. 1997. *Dislocating Cultures: Identities, Traditions, and Third World Feminism.* New York: Routledge.

Neuman, Gerald. L. 1993. "Buffer Zones against Refugees: Dublin, Schengen and the German Asylum Amendment." *Virginia Journal of International Law* 33: 503–26.

Nussbaum, Martha, and Jonathan Glover, eds. 1995. *Women, Culture, and Development: On Human Capabilities.* Oxford: Clarendon Press.

———. 1999. *Sex and Social Justice.* New York: Oxford University Press.

Nussbaum, Martha. 1997. "Kant and Cosmopolitanism." In *Perpetual Peace: Essays on Kant's Cosmopolitan Ideal,* edited by James Bohman and Matthias Lutz-Bachmann. Cambridge: MIT Press.

———. 1999. *Sex and Social Justice.* New York: Oxford University Press.

Offe, Claus. 1998. " "Homogeneity" and Constitutional Democracy: Coping with Identity Conflicts through Group Rights." *Journal of Political Philosophy* 6, no. 2 (June 1998): 113–42.

Okin, Susan Moller. 1999. "Is Multiculturalism Bad for Women?" In *Is Multiculturalism Bad for Women?* by Susan Moller Okin, edited by Joshua Cohen, Matthew Howard, and Martha C. Nussbaum. Princeton: Princeton University Press.

Olson, Emilie A. 1985. "Muslim Identity and Secularism in Contemporary Turkey: 'The Headscarf Dispute.'" *Anthropological Quarterly* 58, no. 4: 161–69.

O'Neil, Onora. 1986. *Faces of Hunger: An Essay on Poverty, Justice, and Development.* New York: George Allen and Unwin.

Ong, Aihwa. 1999. *Flexible Citizenship: The Cultural Logics of Transnationality.* Durham, NC: Duke University Press.

Ortner, Sherry B. 1974. "Is Female to Male as Nature is to Culture?" In *Women, Culture, and Society,* edited by M. Z. Rosaldo and L. Lamphere, 67–69. Stanford, Calif.: Stanford University Press.

Parekh, Bhikhu. 2000. *Rethinking Multiculturalism: Cultural Diversity and Political Theory.* Cambridge: Harvard University Press.

Parens, Joshua. 1994. "Multiculturalism and the Problem of Particularism." *American Political Science Review* 88, no. 1 (March 1994): 169–81.

Patterson, Orlando. 1999. *Rituals of Blood: Consequences of Slavery in Two American Centuries.* Washington, D.C.: Civitas/Counterpoint Press.

Patterson, Orlando. 2000. "Taking Culture Seriously: A Framework and an Afro-American Illustration." In *Culture Matters: How Values Shape Human Progress,* edited by Lawrence E. Harrison and Samuel P. Huntington, 201–19. New York: Basic Books.

Pintasilgo, Maria de Lourdes. 1995–1996. "Fuer ein Europa der politischen und sozialen Grundrechte." Report of the "Committee of the Wise." Brussels: Publications of the European Commission, October 1995-February 1996.

Plato, *The Republic.* 1968. Edited and translated by Allan Bloom. New York: Basic Books.

Polanyi, Karl. 1971. *Primitive, Archaic, and Modern Economies: Essays of Karl Polanyi.* Boston: Beacon Press.

Preuss, Ulrich. 1995. "Problems of a Concept of European Citizenship." *European Law Journal* 1, no. 3 (November 1995): 267–81.

Putnam, Hilary. 1981. *Reason, Truth, and History.* New York: Cambridge University Press.

Randal, Jonathan C. 1997. *After Such Knowledge, What Forgiveness? My Encounters with Kurdistan.* New York: Farrar, Straus and Giroux.

Rawls, John. 1977. *A Theory of Justice.* Cambridge: Harvard University Press.

———. 1993. *Political Liberalism.* New York: Columbia University Press.

———. 1999. *The Law of Peoples.* Cambridge: Harvard University Press.

Rorty, Amelie. 1994. "The Hidden Politics of Cultural Identification." *Political Theory* 22, no. 1 (February 1994): 152–66.

———. 1995. "Rights: Educational, Not Cultural." *Social Research* 62, no. 1 (Spring) 10.

Rorty, Richard. 1983. "Postmodernist Bourgeois Liberalism." *Journal of Philosophy* 80 (1983): 583–89.

———. 1984. "Habermas and Lyotard on Postmodernity." *Praxis International* 4, no. 1: 32–44.

———. 1985. "Solidarity or Objectivity." In John Rachman and Cornell West, eds., *Post-Analytic Philosophy.* New York: Columbia University Press.

———. 1986. *Contingency, Irony, and Solidarity.* Cambridge: Cambridge University Press.

Rosenau, James. 1997. *Along the Domestic-Foreign Frontier: Exploring Governance in a Turbulent World.* Cambridge: Cambridge University Press.

Rousseau, J. J. [1764] 1986. *First and Second Discourses and the Essay on the Origins of Languages.* Edited and translated by Victor Gourevitch. New York: Harper and Row.

Ryan, Mary. 1992. *Women in Public. Between Banners and Ballots*. Johns Hopkins Symposia in Comparative History. Baltimore: John Hopkins University Press.

———. 1997. *Civic Wars: Democracy and Public Life in the American City During the Nineteenth Century*. Berkeley and Los Angeles: University of California Press.

Salhamy, Roger E., ed., 1986. *The Origin of Rights*. Toronto: Carswell.

Sandel, Michael. 1996. *Democracy's Discontent: America in Search of a Public Philosophy*. Cambridge: Harvard University Press, Belknap Press.

Sartre, Jean-Paul. [1960] 1982. *Critique of Dialectical Reason: Theory of Practical Ensembles*. Translated by Alan Sheridan-Smith, edited by Jonathan Ree. London: Verso.

Scheffer, Paul. 2000. "Het multiculturele Drama." In: *NRC Handelsblad*. 1/29/2000.

Schmitt, Carl. [1923] 1985. *The Crisis of Parliamentary Democracy*. Translated by Ellen Kennedy. Cambridge: MIT Press.

Schuck, Peter and Smith, Rogers. 1985. *Citizenship without Consent. Illegal Aliens in the American Polity*. New Haven and London. Yale University Press.

Schutz, Alfred. 1982. *The Problem of Social Reality: Collected Papers*. Vol. 1. The Hague: Martinus Nijhof Publishers.

Scott, Joan. 1988. *Gender and the Politics of History*. New York: Columbia University Press.

———. 1997. *Only Paradoxes to Offer: French Feminists and the Rights of Man*. Cambridge: Harvard University Press.

Shachar, Ayelet. 2000. "The Puzzle of Interlocking Power Hierarchies: Sharing the Pieces of Jurisdictional Authority." *Harvard Civil Rights—Civil Liberties Law Review* 35, no. 2 (Summer 2000): 387–426.

Shapiro, Ian. 2001. *Democratic Justice*. ISPS Series. New Haven: Yale University Press.

Shapiro, Ian. 2002 (forthcoming). "Democratic Justice and Multicultural Recognition." In *Multiculturalism Reconsidered*, edited by David Held and Paul Kelly. London: Polity Press.

Shaw, Jo. 1997. "The Many Pasts and Futures of European Citizenship in the European Union." *European Law Review* 22.

Shklar, Judith. 1991. "American Citizenship: The Quest for Inclusion." *The Tanner Lectures on Human Values*, vol. 10, 386–439. Cambridge: Harvard University Press.

Shimon, Gideon. 1999. *Theodor Herzl: Visionary of the Jewish State*. New York: Herzl Press.

Skerry, Peter. 2000. *Counting on the Census? Race, Group, Identity, and the Evasion of Politics*. Washington, DC: Brookings Institution Press.

Sleeper, James A. 1997. *Liberal Racism*. New York: Viking Press.

SOPEMI Publications. 1998 and 2000. The OECD Continuous Reporting System for Migration, *Trends in International Migration. Annual Report*. Paris.

Soysal, Yasemin. 1994. *Limits of Citizenship: Migrants and Postnational Membership in Europe*. Chicago: University of Chicago Press.

Spade, Paul Vincent. 1994. "Medieval Philosophy." In *The Oxford History of Western Philosophy*, 82ff. Oxford: Oxford University Press.

Spatz, Melissa. 1991. "A 'Lesser' Crime: A Comparative Study of Legal Defenses for Men Who Kill Their Wives." *Columbia Journal of Contemporary and Social Problems* 24: 597–620.

Spence, Donald. 1987. "Turning Happenings into Meanings: The Central Role of the Self." Eds., Polly Young Eisendrath and James A. Hall. In *The Book of the Self: Person, Pretext, and Process*, 131–51. New York: New York University Press.

Spinner, Jeff. 1994. *The Boundaries of Citizenship: Race, Ethnicity, and Nationality in the Liberal State*. Baltimore: The Johns Hopkins University Press.

Stilz, Annie. 2000. "Free Exercise Revisionism and the First Amendment." Seminar Paper submitted to Government 2064, "Nations, States and Citizens," Harvard University, Professor Benhabib, Fall 2000. On file with the author.

Strauss, Claude-Levy. 1969. *Elementary Structures of Kinship*. Boston: Beacon Press.

Sunstein, Cass. 1995. *Democracy and the Problem of Free Speech*. New York: Free Press.

Tamir, Yael. 1993. *Liberal Nationalism*. Princeton: Princeton University Press.

Taylor, Charles. 1985. *Philosophical Papers*. Cambridge: Cambridge University Press.

———. 1989. *Sources of the Self*. Cambridge: Harvard University Press.

———. 1992. *Multiculturalism and the Politics of Recognition*. Princeton: Princeton University Press.

———. 1993. *Reconciling the Solitudes: Essays on Canadian Federalism and Nationalism*. Edited by Guy Leforest. Montreal: McGill-Queens University Press.

———. 1994. *Multiculturalism: Examining the Politics of Recognition*. Princeton: Princeton University Press.

———. 1995. *Philosophical Arguments*. Cambridge: Harvard University Press.

Thornton, Russell. 2001. "What the Census Doesn't Count." *New York Times*. March 23, 2001, Op-Ed. A:19.

Todorov, Tzvetan. 1993. *Nous et les Autres. On Human Diversity, Racism, and Exoticism in French Thought*. Translated by Catherine Porter. Cambridge: Harvard University Press.

Toynbee, Arnold. 1966, Foreword to Garcilaso de la Vega, *Royal Commentaries on the Incas and General History of Peru*, trans. Harold V. Livermore. Austin: University of Texas Press.

Tully, James. 1993. *An Approach to Political Philosophy: Locke in Contexts.* Cambridge: Cambridge University Press.

———. 1995. *Strange Multiplicity: Constitutionalism in An Age of Diversity.* Cambridge: Cambridge University Press.

Turner, Terence. 1993. "Anthroplogy and Multiculturalism: What Is Anthropology that Multiculturalists Should be Mindful of It?" *Cultural Anthropology* 8 (no. 4): 411–29.

Valadez, Jorge M. 2001. *Deliberative Democracy, Political Legitimacy, and Self-Determination in Multicultural Societies.* Boulder: Westview Press.

Van Amersfoort, Hans. 1982. *Immigrants and the Formation of Minority Groups: The Dutch Experience.* Cambridge: Cambridge University Press.

Van Krieken, Peter J., ed. 2000. *The Asylum Acquis Handbook: The Foundations for a Common European Asylum Policy.* The Hague: T. M. C. Asser Press.

Waldron, Jeremy. 2001. "Actions and Accommodations." The Kadish Lecture, University of California, Berkeley, February 23, 2001. Manuscript on file with the author.

Walzer, Michael. 1983. *Spheres of Justice: A Defense of Pluralism and Equality.* New York: Basic Books.

———. 1984. "Liberalism and the Art of Separation." *Political Theory* 12, no. 3 (August): 315–30.

Weber, Max. [1956] 1978. *Economy and Society: An Outline of Interpretive Sociology.* Edited by Guenther Roth and Claus Wittich. Translation of *Wirtschaft und Gesellschaft. Grundriss der verstehenden Soziologie.* Berkeley and Los Angeles: University of California Press.

———. [1917] 1949. "The Meaning of Ethical Neutrality in Sociology and Economics." In: *Max Weber on the Methodology of the Social Sciences*, edited and translated by Edward A. Shils and Henry A. Finch. 1–50. Glencoe, IL. : Free Press.

Weil, Patrick. 2000. "Access to Citizenship: A Comparison of Twenty-Five Nationality Laws." On file with the author.

———. 2001. "The History of French Nationality: A Lesson for Europe." *Toward a European Community: Citizenship, Immigration, and Nationality Law in the EU*, Randall Hansen and Patrick Weil, eds. Houndmills and New York: Palgrave, 52–69.

Weiler, J. H. 1995. "Does Europe Need a Constitution? Demos, Telos and the German Maastricht Decision." *European Law Journal* 1, no. 3 (November): 219–58.

Wertheimer, Jack. 1987. *Unwelcome Strangers: East European Jews in Imperial Germany.* New York: Oxford University Press.

Williams, Bernard. 1985. *Ethics and the Limits of Philosophy.* Cambridge: Harvard University Press.

Williams, Melissa. 1998. *Voice, Trust, and Memory: Marginalized Groups and the Failings of Liberal Representation.* Princeton: Princeton University Press.

———. 2000. "The Uneasy Alliance of Group Representation and Deliberative Democracy." In Will Kymlicka and Wayne Norman, eds., *Citizenship in Diverse Societies,* 124–52. Oxford: Oxford University Press.

Wolfe, Alan. 2001. "Alien Nation." *New Republic* (March 26, 2001).

Young, Iris. 1990. *Justice and the Politics of Difference.* Princeton: Princeton University Press.

———. 1996. "Communication and the Other: Beyond Deliberative Democracy." In Seyla Benhabib, ed. *Democracy and Difference: Contesting the Boundaries of the Political.* Princeton: Princeton University Press.

———. 1997. "Unruly Categories: A Critique of Nancy Fraser's Dual Systems Theory." *New Left Review,* no. 222: 147–60.

———. 2000. *Inclusion and Democracy.* Oxford: Oxford University Press.

Zolberg, Aristide R., and Long Litt Woon. 1999. "Why Islam Is Like Spanish: Cultural Incorporation in Europe and the United States," *Politics and Society* 27, no. 1 (March): 5–38.

INDEX

❏   ❏   ❏   ❏

Calhoun, Craig, 211n.13
California Proposition 187, 212n.18
Canada: First Nations kinship/marriage
regulations in, 53–54, 59, 196n.3;
Gitxsan Indians of, 141; self-defined
as country of immigration,
210n.10
Canadian Charter of Rights and Freedoms (1982), 54, 196n.3
Canadian Indian Act (1876), 54
Carens, Joseph, 125, 152–53, 198n.6
Catalonian separatist movement, 17, 63,
64, 65, 197n.6
Celan, Paul, 34, 194n.7
Chandrachud, Chief Justice, 91
Chenière, Ernest, 96
children: institutional redesign protecting
social mobility of, 125–28; liberal-democratic state obligations toward, 123–25;
paradox of multicultural vulnerability
and, 88–91, 104, 122; practices leading
to intercultural clashes and, 83–84;
rights considered in universalist context, 40–42; *Santa Clara Pueblo v. Martinez* case on, 205n.7; Western philosophical tradition regarding status of, 82–83
children's rights: globalization and discourse on, 183; shifting to justice-oriented discourse on, 144–45
Christian Scientists, 136
citizenship: collective identity component
of, 162, 169–70; comparing radical universalist and civic-republican views of,
152–54; criticism of individualistic liberal, 112–13; dilemmas of the European
Union, 154–61, 208n.6; emerging flexible, 179; enlarged mentality for practice
of, 170; European Union, 157–58; German reform (1999) of laws on, 159; *glob-
al.com* civilization, 182–83; ideal typical
model of nation-state, 180–81; implications of changing nation-state for, 180–
81; *jus sanguinis* (ethnic origin) principle of, 166–67, 168, 169; *jus soli* and territorial principles of, 166, 167, 168;

Kant's concept of cosmopolitan citizenship, 183; multiculturalism as antithetical to Weberian model of, 181; naturalization, 167; paradox of multicultural
vulnerability and, 88–91, 104, 122; political philosophy vs. sociology of, 160–61;
political theory and, 167–70; privileges
of membership component of, 162–63;
public reason model on, 108–12; social
rights/benefits component of, 163–65;
state-centeredness assumption of, 169;
as state-individual relationship,
211n.13; transition from civil to political, 169–70. *See also* consensus; gendered citizenship; political membership
civic-republican argument, 152–54
civil incorporation, 154
civilization: distinguishing between
culture and, 2, 3, 187n.2; encounters
between modern Western and other,
22–23
civil rights: authenticity and autonomy,
53–54, 57, 196n.1; as citizenship component, 163; clash of culture over, 47–48,
59–67; cultural self-expression founded
on, 26; of EU third country nationals,
164; German/Dutch incorporation of
identity and, 76–80; given to foreigners
in EU, 157–58, 159–60, 164; national minority vs. immigrant, 61; paradox of
multicultural vulnerability and, 88–91,
104, 122; philosophies behind constitutional guarantees of, 107–8. *See also*
human rights
Civil Rights Act (1964), 73
Civil Rights movement, 52, 72
Clinton, Bill, 120
"closed society" fiction, 167–68
colare (cultivating, tending to), 2
Cold War, 130, 155
Coleman, Doriane Lambelet, 86–87, 88, 90
collective actions: deliberative democracy
cognitive/affective biases and, 133–46;
public discussion leading to, 120–22

universalist vs. substitutionalist univer-
salisms and, 13–14
discrimination: restructuring socioeco-
nomic relations to eliminate, 69; self-re-
spect damaged by, 52
"DissemiNation: Time, Narrative, and the
Margins of the Modern Nation"
(Bhabha), 8–9
Dominican Republic, 179
Dublin Convention, 209n.8
Dutch corporate identity formation,
76–80
Dutch pillarization policy, 78
Dworkin, Ronald, 27
dynamic constrictions of identity,
64

Eastern European countries, 156, 157
Edmonston, Barry, 75
egalitarian reciprocity: complementary
vs. formal, 204n.4; as counterfactual
guides to action, 37; defining, 19; metanorm of discourse ethics assumption
of, 107–8; multicultural pluralism use
of, 131; required for multiculturalism in-
stitutionalism, 148; required for resolution of multicultural dilemmas, 106;
strategies for justifying, 37–39
The Elementary Structures of Kinship
(Levi-Strauss), 84
"El Inca" (Garcilaso de la Vega), 22–23
emigration rights, 171–74
Employment Division, Department of
Human Resources of Oregon v. Smith,
190n.6
empowerment condition, 134
Emre, Yunus, 24–25
enlarged mentality concept, 142, 170–71
epistemic contemporaries, 21, 135–36
equality. See moral equality
the ethical, 40
Ethics and the Limits of Philosophy (Williams), 194n.9
ethnic groups: American census recognition of, 73–74, 200n.15; denaturalization
of, 176–77; distinction between national

minorities and, 62–65; federal ethnic/ra-
cial classification standards on, 75–76;
German and Dutch identity incorporation of, 76–80; jus sanguinis principle of
citizenship and, 166–67; normative
rules for identifying, 63–64; paradox of
multicultural vulnerability and, 88–91,
104, 122; separatist movements of, 17,
21, 63; tensions between social/natural-
istic citizenship dimensions and rights
of, 163; vulnerability paradox and accommodation policies for, 104. See also
national minorities
ethnocentrism, 24–26, 28–29, 193n.5; contingent overlap between solidarity and,
32–33; universalism as being, 24–26,
28–29. See also other/otherness
European Union (EU): capital/services
movement across, 182; civil rights/priv-
ileges given to foreigners in, 157–58,
159–60, 164; dilemmas of citizenship in,
154–61, 208n.6; "fortress Europe" of,
153; future of immigration in, 210n.12;
as ideal, 154–55; immigration trends in,
155–57; increasing intercountry migration in, 156–57; "legal harmonization"
agreements in, 158; naturalization citizenship process in, 167; political participation rights and naturalizational policies in, 165–67
the evaluative, 40
evenhandedness principle of justice, 125
external protections, 59

familiarization, 137–38
family law: demarcating function fulfilled
by, 125–26; Shachar's arguments regarding, 125–29; Shah Bano case and Muslim, 91–92, 94, 115–17. See also legal
sphere
Federal Republic of Germany, 76–80 See
also Germany
feminist discourse: in context of culture,
103–4; polarized contemporary, 101
Ferguson, James, 67
First Nations (Canada), 53–54, 59, 196n.3

immigrants/immigration (*cont'd*)
of ignorance" view of justice by, 152–
53. *See also* foreign residents; freedom
of exit/association
impartiality principle: moral equality
and, 111–12; reinterpreted to include excluded issues/persons, 140
inclusion condition, 134
incommensurability issue: consensus
using deliberation and, 142–46; deliberative democracy and strong, 21–22,
135–37; Lyotard on multiculturalism
and raised, 193n.4; relating to genres of
discourse, 30–31; relativism as aspect
of, 31–33
incorporation regime, 77
India, 91, 179
Indian Code of Criminal Procedure (section 125), 91
individual choice, 66–67
individualism: premise regarding recognition of, 56–57; state of nature metaphor
for, 43–44. *See also* self
"Individualizing Justice through Multiculturalism: The Liberal's Dilemma" (Coleman), 86–87
injustice recognition vs. redistribution
paradigm, 69
institutions. *See* social institutions
interactive universalism, 13–14
internal restrictions, 59
International Criminal Court, 177
Inter-University Center (Dubrovnik), 22
Iphegenia, 89

Jospin, Lionel, 97
Judt, Tony, 155
jus sanguinis (ethnic origin) citizenship,
166–67, 168, 169
jus soli citizenship, 166, 167, 169
justice: evenhandedness principle of, 125;
Fraser on redistribution paradigm of,
68–69; multiculturalism and liberal-
egalitarian conception of, 112–14; open-
mindedness/mutual respect requirements of, 142; recognition paradigm

on, 69; theory of political, 168; "veil of
ignorance" device to view, 152–53
*Justice Interruptus: Critical Reflections on
the "Postsocialist" Condition* (Fraser),
49, 68–69

Kant, Immanuel, 13, 125, 176, 183
Khan, Mohammad Ahmad, 91, 92
Khosrokhavar, Farhad, 97, 117
kinship patterns: Canadian First Nations
marriage and, 53–54, 59, 196n.3; cul-
tural regulation of, 84–86; demarcating
function of family law on, 125–26;
Santa Clara Pueblo v. Martinez case on
Native American, 205n.7
Kristeva, Julia, 165
Kultur (culture), 2, 3
Kurdish population, 156, 208n.3
Kymlicka, Will, 48, 59–67, 68, 75, 77, 185,
198n.7, 199n.9

language: democratic participation and
differences in, 148; national minorities
shared, 64; proposed NYC bilingual education controversy and, 192n.9; Turkish nationalism expressed through, 9–
10; worldview constituted through, 55
The Law of Peoples (Rawls), 28
"legal harmonization" agreements (EU),
158
legal sphere: denationalization and, 176;
multicultural defense used in criminal,
86–91, 202n.4; multicultural pluralist arrangements in, 131–32; national minorities and illiberal laws in, 199n.9; naturalization of citizenship and, 167–68;
pluralism in, 21, 90–91; Shachar's arguments regarding family, 125–29; syntax
vs. semantics of reasons in, 140–41. *See
also* family law
legitimacy. *See* political legitimacy
Legitimation Crisis (Habermas), 142
Leviathan (Hobbes), 43
Levi-Strauss, Claude, 3, 84
Levy, David, 18
Lewinsky, Monica, 120

norms: conflict between reality and ideal, 134; consensually attained, 143–44; contested during Shah Bano case, 115–17; defining, 107; formal vs. substantive justification of, 206n.10; political liberalism, 107–8
Nussbaum, Martha, 101

Okin, Susan Moller, 86, 100, 101, 103
"one drop of blood" rule, 73, 75
open borders argument, 152–54
Oriental Jews, 17–18
other/otherness: human encounters and evaluation of, 41–42; Locke's Amerindians and the positioning of, 46; recognition through negating status of, 8; tolerance required for, 130; universalism as ethnocentric and, 24–26, 28–29, 193n.5; universal respect applied to, 14. *See also* ethnocentrism
Otto-Apel, Karl, 27, 37
Ottoman Empire, 9, 166
overlapping consensus, 109–12

paradox of multicultural vulnerability: cultural defense in US courts and, 88–91, 202n.4; described, 104, 122
Parekh, Bhikhu, 83–84
permanent residency, 154
Phenomenology of Spirit (Hegel), 50
pillarization policy (Dutch), 78
Plato, 25, 82, 83
pluralism: acceptance of as necessary, 122; bilingual education and, 192n.9; deliberative democracy compatibility with, 21; interlocking of power hierarchies through, 122–32; interpretation of culture in universalism, 36–37; legal, 21, 90–91; normatively right/institutionally feasible issue of, 125; public sphere acceptance of, 122; three principles required for multicultural, 131–32; two challenges to vision of cultural, 184–85. *See also* multiculturalism
political discourse, 144–45

political legitimacy: based on consensus, 63, 139–40; changing criteria of, 179, 180; consensus as basis of, 63, 139–40; "equal say" universalism required for, 147–48; moral equality basis of nation-state, 174–77; tracing deliberative democracy, 105–6
political liberalism: based on overlapping consensus, 110–12; culture and individual choice in, 66–67; dialectic between constitutional essentials and, 130–31; differentiated citzenship claims and, 104; human rights/self-determination tension in, 150–51; Kymlicka's reconciliation of cultural rights and, 59–67; norms and principles of, 107–8; privacy convictions of, 85–86; standards for public reason set by, 108. *See also* civil rights; democratic theory; liberal democracies
Political Liberalism (Rawls), 109
political membership: citizenship privileges of, 162–63; demonstrating worthiness of practicing, 169–70; distinction between admittance and, 172–74; European discussions regarding, 160–61; stages leading to, 154. *See also* citizenship
political participation rights: defining citizenship, 163–64; in Europe today, 165–67; three acquisition categories leading to, 166–67
political power: democracy model for organizing exercise of, 105–6; proportional representation and devolution of, 148; Rawls's public reason model on exercise of, 109–12
political theory: mistaken premises of citizenship in, 168–69; theory of global civil society and, 168
politics: deliberative model dual-track approach to, 106, 119–22; distinction between recognition and identity, 69–71; multicultural demands of contemporary, 113–14
Politics (Aristotle), 82–83, 162–63